The Bible Speaks Today

Series editors: Alec Motyer (OT)
John Stott (NT)
Derek Tidball (Bible Themes)

The Message of Holiness

Restoring God's masterpiece

The Bible Speaks Today: Bible Themes series

The Message of Holiness

Restoring God's masterpiece

Derek Tidball

*Formerly Principal
of London School of Theology*

Inter-Varsity Press

InterVarsity Press
P.O. Box 1400, Downers Grove, IL 60515-1426
Internet: www.ivpress.com
E-mail: email@ivpress.com

©*Derek Tidball 2010*
Study Guide by Ian Macnair ©Inter-Varsity Press 2010

Published in the United States of America by InterVarsity Press, Downers Grove, Illinois, with permission from Inter-Varsity Press, England.

InterVarsity Press® is the book-publishing division of InterVarsity Christian Fellowship/USA®, a movement of students and faculty active on campus at hundreds of universities, colleges and schools of nursing in the United States of America, and a member movement of the International Fellowship of Evangelical Students. For information about local and regional activities, write Public Relations Dept., InterVarsity Christian Fellowship/USA, 6400 Schroeder Rd., P.O. Box 7895, Madison, WI 53707-7895, or visit the IVCF website at <www.intervarsity.org>.

All Scripture quotations, unless otherwise indicated, are taken from the Holy Bible, Today's New International Version®. *Copyright ©2004 by International Bible Society. Used by permission of Hodder and Stoughton Publishers, a division of Hodder Headline Ltd. All rights reserved. "TNIV" is a registered trademark of International Bible Society. Distributed in North America by permission of Zondervan Publishing House.*

ISBN 978-0-8308-2412-0

Printed in the United States of America ∞

InterVarsity Press is committed to protecting the environment and to the responsible use of natural resources. As a member of Green Press Initiative we use recycled paper whenever possible. To learn more about the Green Press Initiative, visit <www.greenpressinitiative.org>.

Library of Congress Cataloging-in-Publication Data

Tidball, Derek.
  The message of holiness: restoring God's masterpiece / Derek Tidball.
     p. cm.—(Bible speaks today)
  Includes bibliographical references.
  ISBN 978-0-8308-2412-0 (paper - usa : alk. paper)—ISBN 978-1-84474-411-4 (paper - uk : alk paper)
  1. Holiness—Biblical teaching. 2. Holiness—Christianity. I. Title.
  BS680.H54T53 2010
  234'.8—dc22

                                                        2010004098

| P | 18 | 17 | 16 | 15 | 14 | 13 | 12 | 11 | 10 | 9 | 8 | 7 | 6 | 5 | 4 | 3 | 2 | 1 |
| Y | 25 | 24 | 23 | 22 | 21 | 20 | 19 | 18 | 17 | 16 | 15 | 14 | 13 | 12 | 11 | 10 |

Dedicated to
Dr Raymond Brown
in gratitude

Contents

Part 5. Pathways to holiness

Part 6. The destination of holiness

BST | The Bible Speaks Today

GENERAL PREFACE

THE BIBLE SPEAKS TODAY describes three series of expositions, based on the books of the Old and New Testaments, and on Bible themes that run through the whole of Scripture. Each series is characterized by a threefold ideal:

- to expound the biblical text with accuracy
- to relate it to contemporary life, and
- to be readable.

These books are, therefore, not 'commentaries', for the commentary seeks rather to elucidate the text than to apply it, and tends to be a work rather of reference than of literature. Nor, on the other hand, do they contain the kinds of 'sermons' that attempt to be contemporary and readable without taking Scripture seriously enough. The contributors to *The Bible Speaks Today* series are all united in their convictions that God still speaks through what he has spoken, and that nothing is more necessary for the life, health and growth of Christians than that they should hear what the Spirit is saying to them through his ancient – yet ever modern – Word.

ALEC MOTYER
JOHN STOTT
DEREK TIDBALL
Series editors

9

Author's preface

Writing is always a team effort and once again I am grateful to the encouragement of many, especially and as always, to my wife and son; to my former PA at London School of Theology, Jenny Aston, who continues to read and helpfully edit my drafts; to David Peterson, whose own systematic work in this area is extremely valuable, who read the manuscript and made helpful comments leading to one significant change and a number of lesser ones; to Ian Macnair for writing the Study Guide; to Phil Duce at IVP for his perceptive editorial eye, and the team at IVP, with whom it is a pleasure to work; to Colin Duriez, who initiated this series when on the staff of IVP, for skilfully copy editing my manuscript; and to countless others who have spoken to me about the subject and challenged me personally about it.

It is a pleasure to dedicate this work to Raymond Brown, who was my pastor at a significant stage in my life and for whose wonderful Bible teaching in Torquay, as for so much else, I shall always be grateful. Raymond was subsequently Principal of Spurgeon's College. His Cambridge PhD was on the topic of eighteenth-century holiness. I am sure he would have written this book more adequately than me but trust that he will accept it as a tribute and token of gratitude from one who studied at and then became Principal of 'the other place'.

Derek Tidball
June 2009

Abbreviations

AB	Anchor Bible
ABC	*Anchor Bible Commentary*
ABD	*Anchor Bible Dictionary*, ed. D. N. Freedman
BST	The Bible Speaks Today
DPL	*Dictionary of Paul and his Letters*, ed. G. F. Hawthorne, R. P. Martin, and D. G. Reid
IDB	*Interpreters' Dictionary of the Bible*, ed. G. Butterick
ICC	International Critical Commentary
Int	Interpretation Commentaries
Int	*Interpretation*
IVPNTC	IVP New Testament Commentary
JSOTSS	Journal for the Study of the Old Testament Supplement series
KJV	King James' Version
mg.	margin
NAC	New American Commentary
NCBC	New Century Bible Commentary
NIB	*The New Interpreters' Bible*, 12 vols (Nashville: Abingdon, 1994)
NIBC	New International Biblical Commentary
NICOT	New International Commentary on the Old Testament
NICNT	New International Commentary on the New Testament
NIDOTTE	*New International Dictionary of Old Testament Theology and Exegesis*, ed. W. A. VanGemeren
NIDNTT	*New International Dictionary of New Testament Theology*, ed. C. Brown
NIGTC	New International Greek Testament Commentary
NIV	New International Version
NRSV	New Revised Standard Version

NSBT	New Studies in Biblical Theology
SPCK	Society for Promoting Christian Knowledge
TDNT	*Theological Dictionary of the New Testament*, ed. G. Kittel
TNIV	Today's New International Version
TNTC	Tyndale New Testament Commentary
TOTC	Tyndale Old Testament Commentary
TynBul	*Tyndale Bulletin*
WBC	Word Biblical Commentary
ZAW	Zeitschrift für die neutestamentliche Wissenschaft

Select Bibliography

Anderson, B. W., *Contours of Old Testament Theology* (Philadelphia: Fortress Press, 1999)

Anderson, B. W. and W. Harrelson (eds.), *Israel's Prophetic Heritage: Essays in Honour of James Muilenburg* (New York: Harper & Row: 1962)

Arnold, C. E., *3 Crucial Questions about Spiritual Warfare* (Grand Rapids: Baker Books, 1997)

——— *Ephesians: Power and Magic* (Cambridge: Cambridge University Press, 1989)

——— *Powers of Darkness* (Leicester: IVP, 1992)

Averbeck, R. E., *'kpr'* in VanGemeren (ed.), *New International Dictionary of Old Testament Theology and Exegesis*, 3

Ballard, P. and S. Holmes (eds.), *The Bible in Pastoral Practice* (London: Darton, Longman and Todd, 2005)

Barton, S. C. (ed.), *Holiness: Past and Present* (London: Continuum, 2002)

Bassett, P. and W. Greathouse, *Exploring Christian Holiness, 2: The Historical Development* (Beacon Hill Press, 1985)

Bauckham, R., 'The Holiness of Jesus and His Disciples in the Gospel of John' in Brower and Johnson (eds.), *Holiness and Ecclesiology in the New Testament*

Bebbington, D., *Holiness in Nineteenth Century England* (Carlisle: Paternoster, 2000)

Belville, L., '"Imitate me, just as I imitate Christ": Discipleship in the Corinthian Correspondence' in Longenecker (ed.), *Patterns of Discipleship in the New Testament*

Berger, P. L., B. Berger, H. Kellner, *The Homeless Mind* (Harmondsworth: Penguin, 1974)

Blocher, H., 'The Fear of the Lord as the Principle of Wisdom', *Tyndale Bulletin* 28 (1977), pp. 3–28

Bloesch, D., *God Almighty: power, wisdom, holiness, love* (Paternoster, 1995)

———— *The Holy Spirit: Works and Gifts* (Downers Grove: IVP, 2000)

Blomberg, C., *Contagious Holiness: Jesus' meals with sinners*, NSBT (Leicester: Apollos and Downers Grove: IVP, 2005)

Bolt, P. and M. Thompson (eds.), *The Gospel to the Nations: Perspectives on Paul's Ministry* (Downers Grove: IVP and Leicester: Apollos, 2000)

Bonar, H, *God's Way of Holiness* (1864; Evangelical Press, 1979)

Borg, M., *Conflict, Holiness and Politics in the Teaching of Jesus* (Lewiston, Queenston and Lampeter: Edwin Mellen Press, 1984)

Brower, K. E, *Holiness in the Gospels* (Kansas City: Beacon Hill Press, 2005)

———— 'The Holy One of God and his Disciples: Holiness and Ecclesiology in Mark' in Brower and Johnson (eds.), *Holiness and Ecclesiology in the New Testament*

Brower, K. E. and A. Johnson (eds.), *Holiness and Ecclesiology in the New Testament* (Grand Rapids: Eerdmans, 2007)

Brown, C. (ed.), *New International Dictionary of New Testament Theology*, 3 Vols, (Exeter: Paternoster, 1975–78).

Bridges, J., *The Pursuit of Holiness* (London: Authentic Media, 2004)

Bruce, F. F., 'The Spirit in the Letter to the Galatians' in Elbert (ed.), *Essays in Apostolic Themes*

Brueggemann, W., *Theology of the Old Testament* (Minneapolis, MN: Fortress, 1997)

Butterick, G. (ed.), *Interpreters' Dictionary of the Bible* (Nashville: Abingdon, 1962)

Campolo, T., 'Isaiah 58: The Fast God Requires' in Hoek and Thacker (eds.), *Micah's Challenge*

Carson, D. A., *The Farewell Discourse and the Final Prayer of Jesus: An exposition of John 14 – 17* (Grand Rapids: Baker, 1980)

Chester, T., *Good News to the Poor* (Leicester: IVP, 2004)

Copan, V. A., *Saint Paul as Spiritual Director* (Milton Keynes: Paternoster, 2007)

Davies D., 'An Interpretation of Sacrifice in Leviticus' in *ZAW* 89 (1977), 387–399

Dunn, J. D. G., 'Jesus and Holiness: The Challenge of Purity' in Barton (ed.), *Holiness: Past and Present*

———— *The Theology of Paul the Apostle* (Edinburgh: T & T Clark, 1998)

Early Christian Writings, trans. Maxwell Staniforth (Harmondsworth: Penguin Books, 1968)

Eichrodt, W., *Theology of the Old Testament*, Vol 1, (London: SCM, 1961)

Eims, L., *Be the Leader You Were Meant to Be* (Wheaton: Victor Books, 1975)

Elbert, P., *Essays in Apostolic Themes* (Peabody: Hendrickson, 1994)

Elliot, M., *Faithful Feelings: Emotions in the New Testament* (Leicester: IVP, 2005)

Estes, D. J. *Hear, My Son: Teaching and Learning in Proverbs 1 – 9*, NSBT (Leicester: Apollos, 1997)

Fee, G., *God's Empowering Presence* (Peabody: Hendrickson, 1994)

Fiddes, P., *Participating in God: A Pastoral Doctrine of the Trinity* (London: Darton, Longman and Todd, 2000)

Foster, R., *Celebration of Discipline* (London: Hodder and Stoughton, 1980)

Forsyth, P. T., *God: The Holy Father* (1897; London: Independent Press, 1957)

Freedman, D. N. (ed.), *Anchor Bible Dictionary,* 6 vols (New York: Doubleday, 1992)

Gammie, J. G., *Holiness in Israel* (Minneapolis: Fortress Press, 1989)

Guelich, R. A., *The Sermon on the Mount* (Waco: Word, 1982)

Gundry, S. (ed.), and M. Dieter, A. A. Hoekema, S. M. Horton, J. R. McQuilkin, J. F. Walvoord, *Five Views on Sanctification* (Grand Rapids: Zondervan, 1987)

Green, J., *The Theology of the Gospel of Luke* (Cambridge: Cambridge University Press, 1995)

—— 'Living as Exiles: The Church in the Diaspora in 1 Peter' in Brower and Johnson (eds.), *Holiness and Ecclesiology in the New Testament*

Grenz, S. J. and R. E. Olson, *20th Century Theology: God and the World in a Transitional Age* (Downers Grove: IVP and Carlisle: Paternoster, 1992)

Griffiths, M., *Cinderella with Amnesia* (London: IVP, 1975)

Hagner, D. A., 'Holiness and Ecclesiology: The Church in Matthew' in Brower and Johnson (eds.), *Holiness and Ecclesiology in the New Testament*

Harrington, H. K., 'Interpreting Leviticus in the Second Temple Period: Struggling with Ambiguity' in Sawyer (ed.), *Reading Leviticus: A Conversation with Mary Douglas*

Harris, M., *Slave of Christ: A New Testament Metaphor for Total Devotedness to Christ,* NSBT (Leicester: Apollos, 1999)

Hawthorne, G. F., R. P. Martin, and D. G. Reid, (eds.), *Dictionary of Paul and his Letters* (Downers Grove and Leicester: IVP, 1993)

Hauerwas, S. and W. H. Willimon, *Resident Aliens: Life in the Christian Colony* (Nashville: Abingdon, 1989)

Hilborn, D. (ed.), *Movement for Change: Evangelical Perspectives on Social Transformation* (Carlisle: Paternoster, 2004)

Hoek, M. and J. Thacker (eds.), *Micah's Challenge* (Milton Keynes: Paternoster, 2008)

Hughes, D. and J. Grant (eds.), *Transforming the World? The gospel and social responsibility* (Nottingham: Apollos, 2009)

Hughes, G. W., *God of Surprises* (London: Darton, Longman and Todd, 1985)

Hurtado, L. W., *Lord Jesus Christ: Devotion to Jesus in Earliest Christianity* (Grand Rapids: Eerdmans, 2003)

Hunter, J. D., *Evangelicalism: The Coming Generation* (Chicago: University of Chicago Press, 1987)

Jenson, P., *Graded Holiness: A key to the Priestly Conception of the World.* JSOT Supplement Series 106 (Sheffield: Sheffield Academic Press, 1992)

—— 'Holiness in the Priestly Writings of the Old Testament' in Barton (ed.), *Holiness: Past and Present*

Judge, E. A., 'The impact of Paul's Gospel on ancient society' in Bolt and Thompson (eds.), *The Gospel to the Nations*

Kendall, R. T., *God Meant it for Good* (Carlisle: Paternoster, 2003)

—— *Once Saved, Always Saved* (London: Hodder and Stoughton, 1983)

Kittel, G. (ed.), *Theological Dictionary of the New Testament*, 10 Vols. (Grand Rapids: Eerdmans, 1964-76)

Kreider, A., *Journey Towards Holiness: A way of living for God's nation* (London: Marshall Pickering, 1986)

Lewis, C. S. *Mere Christianity* (1952; London: Collins, Fontana Books, 1961)

—— *The Problem of Pain* (1940; London: Collins, Fontana Books, 1957)

Longenecker, R. N. (ed.), *Patterns of Discipleship in the New Testament* (Grand Rapids: Eerdmans, 1996)

Lloyd-Jones, D. M., *The Christian Warfare: An exposition of Ephesians 6:10–13* (Edinburgh: Banner of Truth, 1976)

—— *Darkness and Light: An exposition of Ephesians 4:17 – 5:17* (Edinburgh: Banner of Truth, 1982)

—— *Life in Christ: Children of God*, Studies in 1 John, Vol. 3 (Wheaton and Nottingham: Crossway, 1993)

McDonald, H. D., *Jesus – Human and Divine* (London: Pickering and Inglis, 1968)

Middleton, J. R. and B. J. Walsh, *Truth is Stranger than it Used to be* (London: SPCK, 1995)

Moberly, R. W. L., 'Holy, Holy, Holy: Israel's Vision of God' in Barton (ed.), *Holiness: Past and Present*

Muilenburg, J., 'Holiness' in Butterick (ed.), *Interpreters' Dictionary of the Bible*

Ndungane, N., 'Loving Mercy, Restoring Personhood, Restoring Society' in Hoek and Thacker (eds.), *Micah's Challenge*

Newbigin., L., *The Household of God* (London: SCM, 1953)

Orsutu, D., *Holiness* (Continuum, 2006)

Otto, R., *The Idea of the Holy* (1917; Harmondsworth: Penguin Books, 1959)

Packer, J. I., *'Fundamentalism' and the Word of God* (London: IVP, 1958)

—— *A Passion for Holiness* (Crossway Books, 1992)

—— *Keep in Step with the Spirit* (IVP, 2nd edn. 2005)

Penning J. M., and C. E. Smidt, *Evangelicalism: The Next Generation* (Grand Rapids: Baker, 2002)

Peterson, D., *Possessed by God: A New Testament Theology of Sanctification and Holiness* NSBT (Leicester: Apollos, 1995)

Piper, J., *Tested by Fire* (Leicester: IVP, 2001)

Philip, J., *Christian Warfare and Armour* (Eastbourne: Victory Books, 1972)

Price, C. and I. Randall, *Transforming Keswick* (Carlisle: OM Publishing, 2000)

Putnam, R. D., *Bowling Alone* (New York: Simon and Schuster, 2000)

Purkiser, W. T., *Exploring Christian Holiness, 1: The Biblical Foundations* (Beacon Hill Press, 1983)

Randall, I., *What a Friend We Have in Jesus: The Evangelical Tradition* (London: Darton, Longman and Todd, 2005)

Rowdon. H. (ed.), *Christ the Lord* (Leicester: IVP, 1982)

Ryle, J. C. *Holiness: Its nature, hindrances, difficulties and roots* (Cambridge and London: James Clark, 1956)

—— *Practical Religion* (London: James Clarke, 1959)

Sacks, J., *The Politics of Hope* (London: Jonathan Cape, 1997)

Sawyer, J. F. A. (ed.), *Reading Leviticus: A Conversation with Mary Douglas,* JSOT Supplement Series 227 (Sheffield: Sheffield Academic Press, 1996)

Smail, T., *Reflected Glory* (London: Hodder and Stoughton, 1975)

Stott, J. R. W., *Christ the Controversialist: A Study of the Essentials of Evangelical Christianity* (London: Tyndale Press, 1970)

—— *Issues Facing Christians Today* (London: Marshall, Morgan and Scott, 1984)

Taylor, R., *Exploring Christian Holiness, 3: The Theological Formulation* (Beacon Hill, 1985)

Thomas, G. J., 'The Perfection of Christ and the Perfecting of

Believers in Hebrews' in Brower and Johnson (eds.), *Holiness and Ecclesiology in the New Testament*

Thompson, M. B., *The New Perspective on Paul*, Biblical Series (Cambridge: Grove, 2002)

Thompson, R. P., 'Gathered at the Table: Holiness and Ecclesiology in the Gospel of Luke' in Brower and Johnson (eds.), *Holiness and Ecclesiology in the New Testament*

Tidball, D. J., 'The Bible in Evangelical Spirituality' in Ballard and Holmes (eds.), *The Bible in Pastoral Practice*

—— *Ministry by the Book: New Testament patterns for pastoral leadership* (Nottingham: Apollos, 2008)

VanGemeren, W. A. (ed.), *New International Dictionary of Old Testament Theology and Exegesis*, 5 Vols (Grand Rapids: Zondervan, 1996)

Vriezen, T. C. 'Essentials of the Theology of Isaiah' in Anderson and Harrelson (eds.), *Israel's Prophetic Heritage*

Warner, R., *Rediscovering the Spirit* (London: Hodder and Stoughton, 1986)

Weima, J. A. D., '"How you must walk to please God": Holiness and Discipleship in 1 Thessalonians' in Longenecker (ed.), *Patterns of Discipleship in the New Testament*

Warrington., K., 'Social transformation in the Mission of Jesus and Paul: Priority or Bonus?' in Hilborn (ed.), *Movement for Change*

Webber, R. E., *The Younger Evangelicals: Facing the Challenges of the New World* (Grand Rapids: Baker, 2002)

Webster, J., *Holiness* (SCM, 2003)

Wells, D., *Above All Earthly Pow'rs* (Grand Rapids: Eerdmans and Leicester: IVP, 2005)

—— *God in the Wasteland: The Reality of Truth in a World of Fading Dreams* (Grand Rapids: Eerdmans and Leicester: IVP, 1994)

—— *Losing our Virtue: Why the church must recover its moral vision* (Leicester: IVP, 1998)

Wells, J. B., *God's Holy People: A Theme in Biblical Theology*, JSOT Supplement Series 305 (Sheffield Academic Press, 2000)

Wenham, G. J., 'Christ's healing ministry and his attitude to the law' in Rowdon (ed.), *Christ the Lord*

Wesley, J., *Plain Account of Christian Perfection* (Definitive edition 1777)

White, J., *The Fight: A Practical Handbook for Christian Living* (Downers Grove, Illinois: IVP, 1976)

Wilberforce, W., *Real Christianity* (1797; Colorado Springs: Victor Books, 2005)

Wright, C. J. H., *Old Testament Ethics for the People of God* (Leicester: IVP, 2004)

Wright, D. P., 'Holiness in Leviticus and Beyond' in *Interpretation* 53 (1999), pp. 351–364

—— 'Holiness: Old Testament' in *Anchor Bible Dictionary* 3 (1992)

Wright, N. T., *Justification: God's Plan and Paul's Vision* (London: SPCK, 2009)

—— *The Resurrection of the Son of God* (London: SPCK, 2003)

—— *Simply Christian* (London: SPCK, 2006)

—— *Surprised by Hope* (London: SPCK, 2007)

Introduction

We are all flawed masterpieces. In one way or another, and to one degree or another, the image of God in which we were formed has become marred and corrupted. Holiness is about the restoration of that image. In his innermost nature God is holy and to be fully and truly human is to conform to and reflect his holiness in our lives.

In *Mere Christianity* C. S. Lewis used the parable of reconstructing a building to describe God's work in us, and especially to emphasize its costly nature.

> Imagine yourself as a living house. God comes in to rebuild that house. At first, perhaps, you can understand what he is doing. He is getting the drains right and stopping the leaks in the roof and so on: you knew that those jobs needed doing and so you are not surprised.
>
> But presently he starts knocking the house about in a way that hurts abominably and does not seem to make sense. What on earth is he up to? The explanation is that he is building quite a different house from the one you thought of – throwing out a new wing here, putting on an extra floor there, running up towers, making courtyards.
>
> You thought you were going to be made into a decent little cottage: but he is building up a palace. He intends to come and live in it himself.
>
> The process will be long and in parts very painful; but that is what we are in for. Nothing less.[1]

It is a typically insightful parable which highlights a number of important truths. Nonetheless, I prefer to view holiness as restoring

---

[1] C. S. Lewis, *Mere Christianity* (1952, London: Collins, Fontana Books, 1961), pp. 170–171. Lewis said he borrowed the parable from George MacDonald.

God's image not only because of its biblical basis but because it is more personal. We are living human beings who in our willfulness significantly complicate the task God has in remaking us. Although amateur builders, or cack-handed DIY practitioners like myself, may sometimes doubt it, the materials they have to work with are inanimate and do not have a mind of their own. On the other hand we do, and it is precisely that willfulness that has caused us to need restoring in the first place and which makes the task so prolonged and difficult. Restoring God's image in us leads us to see his work of making us holy (sometimes called sanctification) as a living, dynamic and organic work of the holy Trinity. The result is that we become fully alive human beings in whom Christ has been formed (Galatians 4:19).

1. A disclaimer

I have never been less qualified to write a book than this one. In writing it I make no pretence of having achieved a measure of holiness. I am only too aware of my failings and continuing battle with sin. But two things have given me the courage to tackle such an important subject. First, God's Word is true, no matter what our individual appreciation of or obedience to it might be. The aim of this series is to let that Word speak as key biblical passages are unfolded and applied to today, not to draw attention to the qualifications of its writers. So, I take refuge in sheltering behind the Word God has spoken. Secondly, I had courage to set about the task because it expresses my aspiration, if not my achievement. This study of holiness was designed to teach the author as much as the reader.

I identify with Charles Spurgeon when he said,

> I know nothing about [the] wonderful experience of freedom from conflict and complete deliverance from every evil tendency. I have never won an inch of the way to heaven without fighting for it. I have never lived a day but I have had sorrow over my imperfections. I sometimes get near to God but at that time I weep most for my faults and failings.[2]

That does not say it all, but it says that which is most important.

---

[2] C. H. Spurgeon, sermon entitled 'On his Breast,' preached on 18 Nov. 1888 on John 13:23–26, *Metropolitan Tabernacle Pulpit*, 34 (1888), p. 623.

2. What is holiness?

Definitions can be dangerous for they tend to restrict understanding and encourage a check-list approach to whether or not something conforms to them. Yet they are important in bringing focus and clarity to a subject. Our starting point must be the instruction, repeated four times in Scripture: 'I am the LORD your God; consecrate yourselves and be holy, because I am holy.'[3] According to this fundamental command the essence of holiness is to be found in imitating the character of God. All else flows from this. It means living in his image and overcoming the ways in which his image in us is corrupted by sin. It means combating all that would prevent us from living in his image. It means cultivating all that would reproduce his image in us. It means becoming increasingly God-centred, Christ-like and Spirit-empowered.

In seeking to describe holiness, it is not surprising that some have resorted to full explanations or lists of characteristics.[4] Suffice it to say here, that because the essence of holiness lies in restoring God's image in us, it is as much about what we are as what we do, and it touches every aspect of life. Consequently, holiness can be viewed from many different angles and is multi-faceted in its appearance. It encompasses questions of our relationship with God and with others, our approach to ourselves and creation. It impinges on the inward, personal, social and political dimensions of life. The holiness of God provokes awe and humility, evoking obedience and righteousness; it inspires purity and compassion in equal measure. God's holiness creates a sense of unworthiness and an intense longing for the Spirit to transform us. It calls forth effort on our part, while casting us wholly on the work of God within us.

3. Approaches to holiness

The concern for holiness has been central to the evangelical movement since its inception. Whether one places the origins of evangelicalism in the Reformation and the Puritans, or opts for a later origin in the Evangelical Revival of the 1730s onwards, which was preceded by Wesley's Holy Club that met at Oxford, holiness has always been a high priority on the evangelical agenda. The emphasis,

---

[3] Lev. 11:44; 19:2; 20:26; 1 Pet. 1:16.
[4] Wonderful descriptions by J. I. Packer and J. C. Ryle are given in full later in the book.

however, has classically been on personal holiness and its perspective has sometimes been narrower than that of the Bible itself.

The Bible is a living book written to address a multitude of different situations over a multitude of years, not a systematic textbook. Since its completion, Christians have frequently sought to impose order on it and organize its diverse, but not contradictory, accounts of events or doctrines into some form of systematic framework. Evangelicals have done that with holiness, as much as with other issues.[5] But the result is that the way they have 'understood [it] has been far from uniform'.[6] Three main schools have emerged, each with various sub-schools attached and each with a very different emphasis: the Reformed approach, the Wesleyan holiness stream and the Keswick tradition. To these we should add the more recent Pentecostal and Charismatic perspectives.

These differing views have been much discussed in recent years, and rightly so.[7] The approach one takes has a huge impact on how one interprets one's experience and estimates one's spiritual progress.

In brief, the Reformed view essentially sees sanctification (the process of becoming holy)[8] as arising from justification. Sin is a powerful and persistent enemy and overcoming it is seen as requiring the combined work of God's grace and the Christian's strenuous effort. Together they would produce practical transformation and godliness in a gradually increasing measure. Perfection, however, eludes the Christian while in this world: sin is never completely eradicated and complete transformation awaits the day of Christ.

To Wesley, 'full sanctification' or 'perfect love' was possible in this life, although by this he did not mean sinlessness. It was achieved separately from justification through a second experience of God's grace, and, since the experience could be lost, by subsequent experiences of grace as well. He believed sin could be eradicated through

---

[5] An excellent example of a systematic approach is found in D. Peterson, *Possessed by God: A New Testament Theology of Sanctification and Holiness*, NSBT (Leicester: Apollos, 1995).

[6] I. Randall, *What a Friend We Have in Jesus: The Evangelical Tradition* (London: Darton, Longman & Todd, 2005), p. 111.

[7] Key discussions include, D. Bebbington, *Holiness in Nineteenth-Century England* (Carlisle: Paternoster, 2000), pp. 29–94, S. Gundry (ed.), *Five Views on Sanctification* (Grand Rapids: Zondervan, 1987), J. I. Packer, *Keep in Step with the Spirit* (Leicester: IVP, 2nd ed., 2005) and Randall, *What a Friend We Have in Jesus*, pp. 111–128.

[8] In *Possessed By God*, David Peterson has challenged the common assumption that sanctification is primarily a process, and argued for the 'definitive' or 'positional' nature of sanctification and its implication for the pursuit of practical holiness.

the power of God's Spirit and that the war within might be won, bringing peace.

In the Keswick version of the holiness movement, sin was not so much eradicated as repressed, as one 'surrendered' completely to God and ceased to rely on human striving. Increasingly this 'surrender' was seen as a crisis event, rather than a process. In response to the desperately low level of Christian living which was common, Keswick presented 'victorious living' and 'the higher Christian life' through daily surrender as the norm.

To these approaches we must add that of the Pentecostal and Charismatic traditions. They share much in common with the wider evangelical tradition and are varied in their detailed beliefs about holiness. Nonetheless, Pentecostals believe that justification and initial sanctification are simultaneous. Traditionally many held a second work of grace removed the root of sin while for many charismatics today holiness is associated with the experience of the baptism of the Holy Spirit.

Outlining the different approaches to sanctification suggests major disagreements in the evangelical camp regarding holiness, but the truth is that agreement between evangelicals is more impressive than any disagreement. This becomes apparent in *Five Views on Sanctification*, a book which is devoted to exploring the disagreements between them. In the foreword, as well as on several occasions later in the book, Stanley Gundry, the editor, points out they all agree that the Bible teaches that sanctification is grounded in the past and completed work of Christ, in present experience through the cultivation of a holy life, and in the future return of Christ when 'the effects of sin will be fully removed'. They all agree that believers must express God's love in practice and devote themselves to the spiritual disciplines, rejecting evil and choosing good. Finally, he writes, they 'all agree that the Bible promises success in their process of struggling against personal sin, through the power of the Holy Spirit'.[9] They all share, too, a passion for holiness.

This book will not concern itself directly with these disagreements. The author, like many, is somewhat eclectic in his approach, although his primary stance will inevitably become apparent. Here we seek to engage in biblical theology rather than systematic theology, and expound the key biblical passages on holiness by letting them speak for themselves, rather than seeking to interpret them from the standpoint of one or other of these systematic perspectives.

[9] Gundry (ed.), *Five Views on Sanctification*, pp. 7–8. The fifth view is the Augustinian-Dispensational Perspective which has not been as influential in the UK as in the USA.

Charles Simeon of Cambridge, who was no lover of systematizers, stands as the preacher's ideal in this respect. He 'endeavoured without prejudice or partiality, to give to every text its just meaning, its natural bearing and its legitimate use'. 'My endeavour', he wrote, 'is to bring out of Scripture what is there, and not to thrust in what I think might be there. I have a great jealousy on this head: never to speak more or less than I believe to be the mind of the Spirit in the passage I am expounding.'[10]

In seeking to expound, rather than systematize, I trust these studies will commend themselves across the spectrum of evangelical views rather than be seen as the mouthpiece of any one of them.

4. Wider views of holiness

In the wider church, holiness has been defined and cultivated in even more diverse ways. At one end of the spectrum some see the ideal as to be found in the religious life which withdraws from the world to engage in contemplation and prayer. Others see it as lying in quite the opposite direction and believe it necessitates engagement in social action and political reform. In between there are those who define it in terms of a life of charity and doing good. This is not the place to consider these views which have been competently dealt with by others, although we shall inevitably touch on these perspectives when the scriptures under consideration relate to them.[11]

5. Outline of this book

In aiming to provide a biblical overview, this book begins with examining three vital chapters, two from the Old and the other from the New Testament, concerning God and holiness.

In the next section we select three examples of how the Old Testament understood holiness, envisioning it primarily as purity, or wisdom, or justice.

The third section concentrates on the Gospels which, while using the language of holiness very sparingly, have much to say about it. In this section we first look at Jesus as the embodiment of holiness. Next we view him as the re-interpreter of holiness as we survey the

---

[10] Cited by J. R. W. Stott, *I Believe in Preaching* (London: Hodder and Stoughton, 1982), p. 129.

[11] See A. McGrath, *Christian Spirituality* (Oxford: Blackwells, 1999), and D. Orsuto, *Holiness* (Sheffield: Continuum, 2006).

teaching of the synoptic Gospels about it. The contemporary Jewish concern, even obsession, with holiness as purity, righteousness and as about boundary maintenance are all redefined by Christ. The Gospel of John offers a unique perspective on holiness, as on so much else. Here we see Jesus as orchestrating holiness and explaining it in terms of our relationship with and in the holy Trinity.

The fourth section recognizes that holiness impacts a number of dimensions of our lives. Starting with the inward dimension, we work through what the Bible says about personal holiness, relational holiness within the Christian community and, finally, holiness as a social and political obligation.

The fifth section might be seen as the place where the more traditional evangelical understanding of holiness is to be found. Under the title of 'Pathways to holiness' we review six of the various means God has given us to enable us to grow in holiness. These are the Holy Spirit, the Bible, God's personal discipline, our union with Christ, his provision for us in the battle for holiness, and our need to be distinct from the world in which we live.

The final brief section seeks to put the daunting teaching of Scripture in a future and positive context. Here we are encouraged by our destiny in Christ and reassured by the part God plays in making us holy, which far outweighs our own feeble and patchy efforts.

My objective should be clear throughout. This study is not to inform our heads, although that is important, or even to warm our hearts, which is equally necessary, but to transform our lives, mine as well as yours. I pray that it may enable its readers to reflect the God, whose we are, more perfectly than they would otherwise do.

Part 1
The foundation of holiness

Exodus 19:1–25
1. God of the smoking mountain

With some justice, David Wells has written,

> The fundamental problem in the evangelical world today is not inadequate technique, insufficient organisation, or antiquated music and those who want to squander the church's resources bandaging these scratches will do nothing to staunch the flow of blood that is spilling from its wounds. The fundamental problem in the evangelical world today is that God rests too inconsequentially upon the church. His truth is too distant, his grace too ordinary, his judgment too benign, his gospel too easy, and his Christ is too common.[1]

Israel's God was a God of substance, a God of weight. He summoned his people from beyond the world to encounter him in the world. From the outside he entered space and time and revealed himself to the extent that he chose and to the extent that was sufficient and good for the people he had created. So it was that Israel found itself gathered *on the first day of the month after [they] left Egypt* at the foot of Mount Sinai, where God was to make himself known (1).

It was not the first time God had revealed himself, even in recent memory, for he had shown himself to Moses at Mount Sinai, making himself known in his holiness as 'I AM', and commissioning Moses to deliver Israel from Egypt.[2] It was a result of that that the people of Israel now found themselves at Sinai, ready to witness the major revelation of God in his holiness.

---

[1] D. Wells, *God in the Wasteland: The Reality of Truth in a World of Fading Dreams* (Grand Rapids: Eerdmans and Leicester: IVP, 1994), p. 30.
[2] Exod. 3:1–22.

Contemporary Christianity has turned inwards. Reflecting contemporary culture it has undertaken a subjective turn.[3] Morality is judged by what 'feels good to me'; spirituality caters for 'the inner self' and releasing 'the inner potential'; discipleship has become therapy and is about 'being true to oneself'. Churches serve their own internal agendas and mission has become commercialized and chiefly about the 'here and now'. For a time, in a phase of theology which now looks as out-of date as the fashions of the 1960s, God was said to be not 'out there' but 'the depth of our being'. How different it was for Israel. They were not 'deaf to the summons of the external God'.[4] For them he was a real and holy presence that would summon them from outside their world and whom they only dare approach with care.

The revelation of God at Sinai, as recorded in Exodus 19,[5] is shaped by a three-fold encounter of Moses, who represents the people, with God. The three encounters are marked by an increasing intensity until the God who carried Israel *on eagles' wings* (4) reveals himself at daybreak *on the third day* (16) to be the God of thunder, lightning, cloud, fire and trumpet blast (16–19).

1. Moses' first encounter with God (19:3–8)

As soon as the people came to a stop in the Desert of Sinai, Moses knew his priority was to meet with God (3). There was no expectation that the God who had displayed his awesome power as he delivered Israel from Egypt would come down into the camp itself. He would touch the world where the mountains peaked, where, as it were, earth touches heaven. Mountain-tops became 'places laden with his holy presence'[6] as well as pointing to his transcendence, to the reality of the unseen beyond. Hence, mountains became the setting for revelation, whether it was Moriah, Sinai, Carmel, Tabor, or, greatest of all, Golgotha, or the mountain of ascension in Galilee.

Moses may climb the mountain on his own initiative but once there he is summoned into conversation with God (3). It is the

---

[3] See further, P. Heelas and L. Woodhead *The Spiritual Revolution: Why Religion is Giving Away to Spirituality* (Oxford: Blackwell, 2005).

[4] Wells, *God in the Wasteland*, p. 101.

[5] The complexity of the chapter leads several scholars to conclude that it is a composite chapter, compiled of different accounts. See John Durham, *Exodus*, WBC (Waco: Word, 1987), pp. 258–261, 268–270. But its canonical form is easily accessible and its message coherent to expositors.

[6] W. Bruggemann, 'The Book of Exodus' in *NIB*, *I* (Nashville: Abingdon, 1994), p. 834.

Lord, not Moses, who initiates the conversation – a conversation, not between equals, but between a Lord and his servant. God determines the agenda, which is composed of two items.

a. Their past experienced (19:4)

The covenant God was about to enter with Israel was based on grace, not law; on mercy, not demand. God's grace to Israel was not something they had imagined but something they had experienced. They witnessed with their own eyes the judgment that fell on the Egyptians, and participated with their own feet in the miraculous and hurried escape they made from oppression there. Furthermore, once they had left Egypt, God did not abandon them to fend for themselves in the inhospitable terrain they entered. With great tenderness he *carried [them] on eagle's wings*. His purpose was not to bring them to a place but *to [him]self* (4). The object of his grace was so that they might enter into a relationship, rather than just a land, and be his special people. So, whatever the future relationship was to be, its foundation was that of grace and salvation.

b. Their future envisaged (19:5–8)

They were *now* (5) facing a decisive choice regarding their way forward. What would the future hold? God longed that they should enter into a permanent relationship and issued them with an unprecedented invitation to a binding covenant. Unlike the initial rescue they had experienced which was unconditional, this on-going covenant would be conditional. Adopting the covenant would tie them into not only God's protection but his demands. It would depend on their readiness to listen and obey God. The truth, of course, was that apart from the living God Israel had no future as an independent nation. Had they not been in covenant with him they would have soon perished in the wilderness.

Obedience to the covenant would bestow on them a unique role within the world as well as special privileges. They would be distinguished from other nations as God's *treasured possession . . .* and by being his *kingdom of priests and a holy nation* (5–6). The whole earth belonged to God but out of the whole earth he selected Israel as his 'personal possession'[7] or a 'prized possession'.[8] The term may suggest a royal possession such as precious stones or

[7] A. Motyer, *The Message of Exodus* (Leicester: IVP, 2005), p. 198.
[8] Durham, *Exodus,* p. 263.

metals.[9] They would be valued. They would know the blessings of closeness and intimacy but equally the burden of the responsibility that went with it. As a *kingdom* they were a people who looked to God as their king and he would rule over them without hindrance or qualification. He would be no constitutional monarch but actively hold sway. They would not owe allegiance to any other authority but be exclusively loyal to him.[10] As *priests*, they were to be the mediators between God and the world that he owned. They were his representatives among the nations with a responsibility to model his ways, teach his truth, channel his grace, and pray for his creation. As a *nation* they were, on the one hand, a political entity like other nations, and yet as a *holy nation* they were to be unlike other nations for they were set apart from them to serve God exclusively and display his character in the world. In John Durham's words, they were to be 'a serving nation not a ruling nation'.[11]

These titles, as Jo Bailey Wells suggests, may 'expand and intensify the one before it', but they should be taken as a whole. As his people, in unique and exclusive relationship with him, they have a unique role to play in the world and must live solely for him: a status and a task which has been inherited by the 'new Israel of Christ', according to 1 Peter 2:9.

When the terms of the covenant were put to the people they responded with willing, united and open-ended commitment: *we will do everything the* LORD *has said* (8), they agreed. That, as Terence Fretheim has pointed out, is an indication of how much they trusted God. They showed no fear that God would abuse his position, or demand that which was not in their own best interest in future.[12] Covenants are binding agreements about a relationship in the face of an unknown future (at least, unknown to the human participants) and are open-ended by their nature. This is what distinguishes them from carefully-negotiated contracts with their limited objectives and qualified let-out clauses. Even so, Israel's response to God's call to be his holy people is a sign of the deep gratitude they felt for the amazing salvation they had experienced. If only they had continued to listen to God with such care and responded obediently with such willingness the grief and pain of their future history would have been avoided. But, as H. L. Ellison warned, 'Whenever

---

[9] J. B. Wells, *God's Holy People: A Theme in Biblical Theology* (Sheffield: Sheffield Academic Press, 2000), p. 48.

[10] Wells, *God in the Wasteland*, p. 138–139, citing von Rad, points out this differs from the other nations where the gods 'were on easy terms with one another and left devotees a free hand to ensure a blessing for themselves from other gods as well'.

[11] Durham, *Exodus*, p. 263.

[12] T. Fretheim, *Exodus*, Int (Louisville: John Knox Press, 1991), p. 212.

Israel or the church cease to be holy, set apart from the world for God, they revert to the level of mankind around them.'[13]

2. Moses' second encounter with God (19:9–15)

Moses' second encounter with God begins as he returns to the mountain-top to report the people's response to God. But its concern is not with what Moses said, for his words are left unrecorded, but with what God himself said, which is reported in detail.

a. The revelation God promises (19:9)

God promises Moses that he would shortly reveal himself to the people as a whole, although, for their own sakes, he would be wrapped in cloud as he did so. No one, not even Moses, could see God in his fullness and live.[14] The sight of him in all his glory is too much for a sinful human being to bear and the nature of him in his infinite perfection is too much for a finite human mind to comprehend. God's 'hiding' himself in a cloud is a mercy that protects people and preserves their lives. Yet, what he discloses of himself is both true and sufficient. Even though partial and shrouded in mystery, God reveals enough to serve his purpose and for his people to encounter him without distortion.

Significantly, God's concern is not so much with his appearance as his speech. He comes *so that the people will hear me speaking with you* . . . (9). It is through his words that he chiefly makes himself known. It is true that this particular conversation with Moses is aimed at supporting Moses and authenticating his leadership. Still today, some are persuaded to take a leader seriously because of the connections he or she has. What greater connection can a spiritual leader have than to be shown to be in direct communication with God, as Moses is here?

Yet, as Alec Motyer has commented, there is a wider point to be made. It is an instance of the regular connection between the word of God and the holiness of his people.

By moving directly from the word which God speaks (9) to the holiness which God requires if we are to meet him (10), Exodus reflects the way biblical thinking works. The word of God is

---

[13] H. L. Ellison, *Exodus*, Daily Study Bible (Edinburgh: St Andrew Press & Philadelphia: Westminster Press, 1982), p. 101.
[14] Exod. 33:18–23.

designed to be life-changing and, so the Bible teaches us, nothing is truly 'known' until it permeates from the mind to the heart and will, understood in thought, loved in heart and obeyed in will.[15]

Some stress the apprehension of God is to be found in a wordless vision, when the world is left behind and we are caught up in the spirit into heaven and worship in silent wonder and contemplation. Such experiences of being 'lost in wonder, love and praise'[16] do occur this side of heaven and may be valuable and authentic, as Paul's testimony suggests (2 Corinthians 12:1–5). But the dominant biblical emphasis is that we know God through obeying his words in the body, with our feet firmly planted in the world, not through mystical experiences. So, typically, throughout Exodus 19 we hear the repeated phrase *the Lord said*. When it comes to holiness, his words matter.

b. The requirement God imposes (19:10–13)

When we turn from the act of God speaking to Moses to the contents of what he said, we find the people are instructed to prepare themselves immediately for the descent of God to the mountain that would take place three days hence. The preparations consist of washing their clothes, abstaining from sexual relations and erecting barriers to ensure people keep their distance from the mountain lest they fall foul of God's dynamic holiness.

People instinctively bathe and dress up in clean clothes for a special occasion, especially when invited to meet royalty. Why should God require less? Outward washing, though, is often used throughout this early period to represent the inner cleansing which those who wish to approach God need to undertake.

The command to *Abstain from sexual relations* during this period is not because sex is somehow 'dirty', but because energies should not be diverted from preparing to meet God. Some sports teams find it helpful, even necessary, to separate from their partners before the big match or the big competition in order to focus on the prize ahead. So God's intent in issuing this command is to focus their minds. The command is given 'because the Lord wished to have his people's hearts wholly for himself'.[17]

When God appears he does not, as it were, casually drop in for a cup of afternoon tea. His coming is 'powerful, disruptive,

---

[15] Motyer, *The Message of Exodus*, p. 203.
[16] From Charles Wesley's hymn, 'Love divine, all loves excelling.'
[17] Motyer, *The Message of Exodus*, p. 204

cataclysmic', requiring disciplined preparation and careful cho-reographing, to use Brueggemann's description.[18] He is as much a dangerous God in his holiness as he is a unique God in his grace. His coming needs therefore to be treated seriously and not trivialized in any way.[19] God's holiness communicates itself to the mountain he visits and so, just as people would not touch him, so they cannot touch it either.[20] To do so would be like touching a high voltage electricity cable without any protection. God was awesome in power, pure in essence and majestic in revelation.

There are several explanations as to why any animal or human being who touched the mountain should be executed (12–13). Fretheim[21] argues that the situation here is not parallel to when Uzzah touched the Ark and was instantly slain (in 2 Samuel 6:6–8). He argues rather that this is about the very make-up of creation. God must keep his distance, for if people broke through and 'saw' him they would be denied their human freedom; they could no longer be his voluntary subjects but coerced into obedience as slaves. Not seeing God preserved their humanity. The difference between Exodus 19 and 2 Samuel 6 seems a fine one and the positive-creation argument Fretheim presents is dependent on reading a lot between the lines. It is more likely that this command serves to stress in the most extreme of ways that God's otherness is to be respected. To invade his space or pry into his person is an affront to his majesty. Or, as Ellison explains, perhaps we should understand that, 'If the ban was broken, the man or animal acquired something of the holi-ness [just as the mountain itself did]; since that made them danger-ous to others, he had to be killed.'[22]

Whatever the precise explanation of the command to execute those who infringe the boundary, it is clear that they need to approach the mountain with the utmost caution and only when *the ram's horn sounds a long blast* to summon them (13). The ram's horn was known for its piercing sound rather than its musical tone. Every detail of the preparation emphasizes the awesome otherness of the holy God who descends to the mountain.

[18] Walter Bruggemann, 'The Book of Exodus,' p. 833.
[19] Ibid., p. 836.
[20] Think of the press reports and adverse comments that occur when a visiting dignitary touches the Queen, even if in a well-meaning attempt to provide her with some direction. It is not right to touch 'majesty'. Now magnify this a thousand times and apply it to the King of kings and Lord of lords and you can readily see why God, and that which is closest to him, cannot be touched with impunity.
[21] Fretheim, *Exodus*, p. 218.
[22] Ellison, *Exodus*, p. 103. Words in square brackets are mine.

c. The response God receives (19:14–15)

For a second time the people respond in the right way. They under-stand the importance of treating God with respect and reverent fear. They do not cringe before him, for up to this point they have experienced him as a God of tender mercy and amazing grace. He is the one who sets the oppressed free. But in liberating the underdogs, they had also witnessed his power when he meted out his wrath and judgment on Egypt. They knew enough to know that they could not trivialize their relationship with him, as if he was the boy next door with whom they were going to kick a ball around. Consequently, they respond to God's demands conveyed through Moses, and con-scientiously prepared for his appearance on *the third day.*.

3. Moses' third and the people's first encounter with God (19:16–25)

'Right on schedule, at daybreak',[23] God appears. The time and the day suggest a new chapter in Israel's life is about to begin. But words are stretched to their limit to describe what they experienced that day as they witnessed the revelation of God's fundamental character and as the very essence of his being became, to the extent that it could, visible before them.

a. The revelation of God (19:16–20)

The people experienced the descent of God as if it were a fierce storm. In 'an attempt to describe the indescribable'[24] they recalled his appearance as marked by *thunder and lightening,* as well as *cloud* and *fire,* billowing *smoke,* with the mountain trembling *violently* and a *sound of the trumpet* growing *louder and louder.*

The overall impression left is one of the release of the almighty forces in nature like in a furious storm or through a volcanic erup-tion, as the Creator steps into his creation. Here, undoubtedly, is an encounter with greatness, power and majesty. Several elements of the picture have significance, such as the *thick cloud,* which had guided Israel through the wilderness and in which the Lord had already appeared in the distance in his glory.[25] It speaks of the mystery in which God remains shrouded, impenetrable to the

[23] Durham, *Exodus,* p. 270.
[24] Ibid.
[25] For references to the cloud see Exod. 13:21–22; 14:19; 16:10; 40:34–38.

human mind. But right at the heart of the description we find the statement that *the* LORD *descended on it* [the mountain] *in fire. The smoke billowed up from it like smoke from a furnace, and the whole mountain trembled violently.*

There was already a long association between God and *fire.* When Adam and Eve were expelled from Eden their re-entry was prevented by the gate being guarded by 'cherubim and a flaming sword flashing back and forth' (Genesis 3:24). Fire was the vital ingredient in offering sacrifice, as when Abraham proposed to offer Isaac to God (Genesis 22:6–7) or the Passover lamb was roasted in Egypt (Exodus 12:8–9). It played its part when God entered into covenant with Abraham (Genesis 15:17). Now it is again at the heart of God's revelation of himself. In each case, the fire is linked to the holiness of God. Sinai, then, is about not only power but also purity, a burning purity that consumes all that is unworthy. God's power is not power in itself, amoral in its nature. The fire reveals that there is 'a profound moral aspect to his majesty' and it is this that 'makes him dangerous'.[26] This crucial aspect of God's revelation shows that 'holiness was foundational to God's entire working with [Israel]',[27] as it still is with us. The implications are momentous. God exposes sin for what it is. We can only have to do with him if the barrier of our own sin and impurity is removed. For atonement to happen we ourselves need a priest and a sufficient sacrifice, as well as being a *kingdom of priests.* God's holiness makes him a compassionate saviour who provides the remedy for ills in giving us the sacrifice of his Son. If God were not holy, he could not be gracious, for he can only undeservingly forgive if there is a real offence to forgive in the first place. God moves to transform us from the unholy people we are into the holy people he wants us to be.[28] Our calling to be a *kingdom of priests and a holy nation* is a calling to live a holy life and display his holiness in the world. 'The holiness of God begets and requires in those who approach him the echo of his holiness.'[29] To know God is to know him as a holy God and to grow in him is to grow in holiness.

b. The caution of God (19:21–25)

Such is the awareness God has of his potential to consume his creation in fire, instead of to bless it, that he instructs Moses to descend

---

[26] Wells, *God in the Wasteland,* p. 141.
[27] Ibid.
[28] It should be remembered that God's descent on Sinai is the prelude to and connected with his giving the Ten Commandments (Exod. 20:1–17).
[29] Wells, *God in the Wasteland,* p. 141–142.

39

the mountain again and repeat the warnings already given. This time he adds to his general warning to all a specific warning to the priests,[30] the dealers in holy things whose task it was to draw near to God, who because of their special place might be in danger of presuming the rules didn't apply to them or because of their familiarity with the holy might have been too casual in their approach.

Even at the last moment, as he is going to issue the spiritual and moral charter we call the Ten Commandments (Exodus 20:1–17), God stresses the need for all parts of the community in all respects to fear him and approach him with caution rather than with indifference, presumption or a blasé and casual attitude.

4. Concluding comment

In starting our journey through the biblical teaching on holiness we have necessarily begun with God, who is the source and foundation of all holiness. But we have also entered a very different world: one in which God enters from outside and speaks from beyond, rather than being within. He speaks and we listen. We will not understand the God who has revealed himself as holy if we confine him to the narrow meandering of our own subjective impressions. He comes not as a trickle to flow through the channels we have dug for our own convenience but as a flood that commands attention and that inevitably affects all it touches and proves unavoidable. Before we can discover ourselves, or, more importantly and much better than 'discovering ourselves', before we can be recreated in his image, we must encounter him on his own terms and humble ourselves before his awesome otherness.

Echoing the concerns of David Wells, with which we began, Walter Brueggemann warns of the way in which 'we have trivialised "mountain top" experiences as though they are romantic opportunities for religious self-indulgence. This account', he writes of Exodus 19, 'against any such domestication, portrays the mountain of holiness as a dangerous meeting place that will leave nothing unchanged.'[31] He continues that we

> make God in practice too available, too easy and too immediate. We drop to our knees or bow our heads and imagine that God is

[30] The formal priesthood is yet to be inaugurated but people would have already been acting as priests in Israel. It would be hard to see how any people at the time would function without some kind of priesthood.

[31] Brueggemann, 'The Book of Exodus', p. 838.

eagerly awaiting attention. Or we drop in casually for worship, assuming that God is always there. Most of our worship takes place well short of the mountain, where we can seize the initiative imagining God at our beck and call.[32]

Any rediscovery of power in our enfeebled church will begin not with the adoption of new techniques, music or language, but with adopting the stance of Israel who 'saw the thunder and lightning and heard the trumpet and saw the mountain in smoke, [and] trembled with fear [and] stayed at a distance' (Exodus 20:18). Although as disciples of Christ we should draw near confidently[33] to God, we should never draw near casually. Our God remains 'a consuming fire' (Hebrews 10:29) for whom it is still true that 'without holiness no-one will see the Lord' (Hebrews 12:14).

We need to restore 'weight' to God, to learn to stand at the foot of the mountain, listening attentively and humbly to the voice of God calling us to be his holy people, transformed, and transforming, for the sake of his world.

[32] Ibid., p. 839.
[33] Heb. 10:22.

Isaiah 6:1–13
2. God in glory

Was Isaiah expecting anything extraordinary to happen when he visited the temple *in the year that king Uzziah died* (1)? Was it just a routine visit to do 'business as usual' with God or was it a special festival he attended, connected, perhaps, with the death of the monarch who had reigned for fifty years? We do not know. But we do know that his visit was to have a life-changing effect as he encountered the holiness of God in all its fullness.

Holiness starts with God, not with us. Our concern with holiness arises because the God we serve is holy.[1] Ever since God appeared to Moses at the burning bush he had made himself known as one who is holy.[2] It is his essential nature, the essence of his being. His very name, as Isaiah, 'the prophet of holiness'[3] repeatedly insists, is 'the Holy One of Israel'.[4] His name is qualified by the adjective 'Holy' more than all the other adjectives that accompanies it in the Old Testament put together.[5] Not only is he holy in himself, but that which belongs to him or is connected with him is described as holy whether it is the city, the temple or the people of Israel.[6] Their relationship with God makes them holy by their very constitution, even if they fall short of God's holiness in practice and prove themselves unworthy of the claim. But God provides a way of dealing with their failures and of making them to be the people they are called to be.

It is impossible for us adequately to describe God in human language and therefore we usually resort to speaking of him in

[1] Lev. 11: 44–45; 19:2; 1 Pet. 1:15–16.
[2] Exod. 3:5.
[3] A. Motyer, *The Prophecy of Isaiah* (Leicester: IVP, 1993), p. 17.
[4] Isa. 1:4; 5:19, 24; 10:20; 12:6; 17:7; 29:19, (23); 30:11, 12, 15; 31:1; 37:23; 41:14, 16, 20; 43:3, 14; 45:11; 47:4; 48:17; 49:7; 54:5; 55:5; 60:9, 14.
[5] Motyer, *The Prophecy of Isaiah*, p. 77, n. 1.
[6] See further p. 70.

metaphors: God is our Father, Shepherd, Rock or Light. To speak of God as holy, however, is not to speak in a metaphor. It is, as Walter Brueggemann has written, 'the only theological term in Israel that is not derived from other parts of life and so alone is not metaphorical'.[7] As such it is the ultimate definition of God, a definition that stretches the imagination as we seek to understand it. The only way to comprehend it is to look at how the biblical writers used the term and how people experienced it.[8] If we do so, we discover it has to do with God's altogether different nature, his transcendent separateness, his exalted majesty, his awesome power, his absolute purity, his immeasurable brightness, his unfathomable glory and also his redeeming salvation. It is shorthand for the excellence of his perfection. Just as it is difficult to grasp simultaneously every element of a brilliant firework bursting into glorious life high above us in the sky, it is as impossible to hold every aspect of this constellation of God's attributes in our hearts and minds at once. Consequently, the people and the prophets of Israel latched on to different aspects of God's holiness as their circumstances required, without detriment to the whole.[9]

Isaiah 6 is said, with justice, to 'represent the most emphatic statement concerning God's holiness found anywhere in the Old Testament',[10] so it is an appropriate starting point for our exploration of the theme of holiness. This single vision in which Isaiah encounters God's holiness emphasizes three aspects of God's nature: his sovereign transcendence, his moral purity and his costly grace.

1. God's holiness as sovereign transcendence (6:1–4)

a. The setting

Isaiah's vision took place *in the year that King Uzziah died* (1). King Uzziah, also known as Azariah, had reigned from 792–740 BC, beginning at the early age of sixteen. The record of his kingship states that 'he did right in the eyes of the Lord' and points to his many accomplishments in strengthening the kingdom of Judah.[11] But his was not an unblemished record and towards the end of his

---

[7] W. Brueggemann, *Theology of the Old Testament* (Minneapolis: Augsburg, 1997), p. 288.

[8] See P. Jensen, 'Holiness in the Priestly Writings of the Old Testament' in S. Barton (ed.), *Holiness Past and Present* (London: Continuum, 2002), pp. 93–121.

[9] Brueggemann, *Theology of the Old Testament*, p. 292.

[10] J. B. Wells, *God's Holy People: A Theme in Biblical Theology* (Sheffield: Sheffield Academic Press, 2000), p. 148.

[11] 2 Kgs 15:1–7; 2 Chron. 26:1–23.

life 'pride led to his downfall'[12] with the result that he was inflicted with leprosy. As a consequence, he lived in isolation and his son, Jotham, shared the last decade of his reign as co-regent. Isaiah's visit to the temple, then, occurred in the midst of transition and uncertainty. An era of stability had passed. Judah's nervousness at the death of Uzziah was compounded by the increasing aggression of Assyria and its inroads into neighbouring territories.[13] It was at the point when the transience and weakness of earthly thrones was all too apparent, that Isaiah was granted a vision of the one who is the real Lord of all, whose reign was both permanent and powerful.[14]

b. The vision

Earth and heaven merge giving Isaiah a sight of *the Lord seated on a throne* (1). The vision is both visual and aural. What he sees and what he hears reinforce each other.

(i) What he sees

His eye is drawn upwards to the elevated position of the throne which is *high and exalted* (1). God's throne is not on a level with earthly thrones, whether it be the throne of his chosen Uzziah or Jotham, or of the up-and-coming Assyrian, Tiglath Pileser III, but higher than theirs. Its very distance above the temple speaks of his supremacy over the earth and over all human rulers, who rise and equally fall at his command. His surpassing greatness was the bedrock of Israel's faith. The constant cry of the psalmists for the Lord to 'be exalted'[15] was not intended to imply a need to elevate God to a position he did not already occupy, for they knew that 'God reigns over the nations; God is seated on his holy throne. . . . the kings of the earth belong to God; he is greatly exalted.'[16] Rather it was a prayer that they, and others, might bow in recognition of the status that was already his. God's throne was inviolable whatever circumstances his people were undergoing as they worshipped him. Even when the nation has apparently come to an end and its people were suffering in exile, Daniel still spoke of God as 'the Most high God' who was 'sovereign over the kingdoms on earth and gives them to anyone he wishes'.[17]

[12] 2 Chron. 26:16.
[13] 2 Kgs 15:17–38.
[14] John Goldingay, *Isaiah*, NIBC (Peabody: Hendrickson and Carlisle: Paternoster, 2001), p. 58.
[15] E.g., Ps. 18:46; 21:13; 57:5, 11; 108:5.
[16] Ps. 47:8–9.
[17] Dan. 4:2, 25. See also Dan 4:34–35.

The throne is surrounded by the trappings of majesty. The royal robe reaches from heaven into the temple. Its extensive length captures the grandeur of God's sovereign rule but also, by providing contact between God's throne and the earth, suggests that God is not remote from or indifferent to the struggles of his subjects below. The robe specifically *filled the temple* – not the palace, the seat of power, nor the courts, the seat of law – but the temple, the place of sacrifice where atonement was made, further suggesting God's desire to overcome his people's lack of holiness by providing them with a means of cleansing, forgiveness and reconciliation with himself.

Attendants surround the throne of any earthly sovereign and here the *seraphs* (2) attend the King of kings. These mysterious creatures are mentioned only here in the Bible, although other angelic beings are said to serve in God's heavenly court elsewhere. They are 'the fiery ones',[18] but not even they can look directly on God. Hence *with two wings they covered their faces* (2). Why they should also cover *their feet* is uncertain. Some argue that *feet* is a euphemism for their sexual organs which it would be unseemly to display in the presence of majesty.[19] But such an explanation is ill-suited to the context. Alec Motyer's comment that they covered their feet because they 'disavowed their intention to choose their own path' is more apt.[20] The other pair of wings they used to fly, since they were constantly ready to do the bidding of their Lord. Their ears, it should be noted, were not covered by their wings as their duty was to listen to God's command and obey.

When such creatures were mentioned in Egypt it is said that their responsibility was to spread their wings to protect their gods, like modern FBI agents interposing their bodies between the President of the USA and any potential assailant. But the seraphs who attended the living God of Israel are the ones in need of protection.[21] Their wings do not cover him but themselves, in view of his awesome holiness.

(ii) What he hears

Isaiah's attention shifts from what he sees to what he hears. *And they were calling to one another: Holy, holy, holy is the* LORD

---

[18] For an explanation of the connection between their name and serpents or 'fiery ones' see J. N. Oswalt, *The Book of Isaiah: Chapters 1–39*, NICOT (Grand Rapids: Eerdmans, 1986), pp. 178–179.

[19] Oswalt, p. 179, J. D. W. Watts, *Isaiah 1–33*, WBC, 24 (Waco: Word, 1985), p. 74.

[20] Motyer, *The Prophecy of Isaiah*, p. 76.

[21] Wells, *God's Holy People*, p. 149.

Almighty; the whole earth is full of his glory (3). The song is something of a surprise. Since the picture has been one of sovereignty, one might expect a song that celebrated the legitimacy of God's rule, his power, strength or authority. Instead they celebrate his holiness. They are not content to mention it and pass on, or even to mention it twice, which would be the usual Hebrew way of providing emphasis, but they repeat their cry three times. God's holiness is such that a 'super-superlative'[22] has to be pressed into use to explain it. Walter Moberly thinks that even more than this might be intended and the repetition may involve an increasing intensity.[23] He is, as it were, utterly, thoroughly utterly, perfectly utterly, holy. Here is, says Moberly, 'an emphatic formulation [that] is tantamount to a definition of the nature of YHWH'.[24]

The earlier chapters of Isaiah lead up to this proclamation where from the start, in 1:4, God is referred to as 'the Holy One of Israel'. The rest of Isaiah works through the implications of the claim not only for Israel but also for the nations of the world. His holiness may focus on his otherness, his brilliance and the brightness of his being, but it also stresses his moral integrity. This is seen in the previous chapter where Isaiah had used language similar to the vision saying, 'But the LORD Almighty will be exalted by his justice, and the holy God will be proved holy by his righteous acts' (5:16). The meaning of his holiness is neither ethereal nor abstract but practical and active in relation to his people.

The second line of the song of the seraphs takes us further and defines the sphere in which this holy God operates. His glory, that is, the manifestation of his divine attributes, is to be seen throughout the world. Isaiah encounters him in the temple, but he is not limited to the temple. In the words of Micah, one of Isaiah's contemporaries, 'Look! The LORD is coming from his dwelling place; he comes down and treads the heights of the earth' (Micah 1:3). Isaiah may represent the children of Israel, but his sovereignty is not limited in scope to his covenant people. Just as his signature is found throughout his creation[25] so too may his law be known throughout the earth[26] and his works observed by the nations. In Paul's words, 'since the creation of the world God's invisible qualities – his eternal power and divine nature – have been clearly seen, being understood from what has been made, so that people are without excuse' (Romans 1:20).

---

[22] Motyer, *The Prophecy of Isaiah*, p. 77.
[23] R. W. L. Moberly, 'Holy, Holy, Holy: Isaiah's Vision of God', in S. Barton (ed.), *Holiness Past and Present* (London: Continuum, 2002), p. 126.
[24] Ibid.
[25] Ps. 19:1–6.
[26] Ps. 19:7–9.

The God whom the seraphs worship is no petty tribal deity, limited in authority to a small group of people in Judah, but one whose holiness is displayed in the theatre of the whole world.

c. The effect

It would have been surprising if this breaking-in of divine power – 'highly active, energetic, dynamic even threatening' power[27] – had not had an immediate impact on the place where it took place. Isaiah records the classic signs of a visitation from God in terms of *the doorposts and the thresholds shook* (4) as if an earthquake was occurring and *the temple was filled with smoke* (4). As Moses spoke with God on Sinai when Israel was commissioned to be 'a kingdom of priests and a holy nation' (Exodus 19:6) 'smoke billowed up from it like smoke from a furnace, and the whole mountain trembled violently' (Exodus 19:18). Here was the God of the exodus and the God of Sinai revealing himself once more at a crucial point in Israel's history and here were the outward signs that the vision of his sovereign transcendence was authentic.

2. God's holiness as moral purity (6:5)

a. The impression on Isaiah

It goes without saying that such an out-of-the-ordinary experience would have proved profoundly disturbing, 'arousing both fascination and dread'.[28] We are not surprised to read that Isaiah's response was to cry out, *Woe is me! . . . I am ruined!* (5). But little is made of his emotions. We do not read of him shaking, showing signs of panic, being confused, lying prostrate, going into a trance or adopting any defensive position as he cried out. Rather, to our astonishment, the text takes us for a second time in an unexpected direction. He is able to articulate the cause of his fear and it lies not in his emotional terror in the face of the power that has confronted him, but his personal unworthiness in the face of the holiness he encountered. His response is to say that his fate is sealed because *I am a man of unclean lips, and I live among a people of unclean lips, and my eyes have seen the King, the LORD Almighty* (5).

Having encountered holiness, Isaiah realizes that his own life is far

---

[27] B. W. Anderson, *Contours of Old Testament Theology* (Philadelphia: Fortress Press, 1999), p. 43f.
[28] Ibid.

from clean; in fact, about as far removed from holiness as it is possible to get.[29] His confession centres on his lips for a number of reasons. First, the seraphs' lips had proclaimed the holiness of God and he becomes aware, by contrast, that his own lips had failed to witness to the perfection of God. Second, as a prophet his lips were the chief instrument he used to fulfil his calling and it would be natural, therefore, to focus on them. They symbolized his identity. In confessing that he was *a man of unclean lips*, he was not referring to swearing or filthy conversation. He was confessing that unworthy messages had passed his lips, perhaps having their origin in his own imagination, frustrations, temper, or perhaps desire for compromise. Thirdly, given the setting in the temple where words and song were central to the liturgy, it was natural for him to think of his speech. Perhaps he had spoken cynically of the liturgy or voiced the contempt that comes from over-familiarity. Whatever the precise meaning, he was not alone in his guilt. The rest of the nation were just as culpable, probably by making light of God's Word and his law. Fourthly, and most significantly, the lips give expression to the mind and the heart. They reveal the otherwise silent thoughts of those who speak. In focusing on his lips, then, Isaiah is not majoring on the sins of speech at the expense of other sins but rather using the lips to symbolize that his whole life and the total lives of those among whom he lives are out of sync with God. He is saying he is wholly unfit to serve a holy God.

b. The implication of Isaiah

It is hard to overestimate the significance of Isaiah's response for our understanding of holiness. Some, following Rudolf Otto, have tried to reduce religion to an emotion and have stressed that 'the idea of the holy' lies in a feeling of creatureliness which causes us to tremble in awe before the mystery of 'the wholly other'. We find, Otto argues, the experience of the *numinous* compelling, attractive and fascinating, and before it we instinctively react by devaluing the self. Isaiah's response, he says, is typical, as was Peter's in the face of Christ's miraculous provision of abundant fish when he begged Jesus, 'Go away from me, Lord; I am a sinful man' (Luke 5:8). These self-deprecating reactions Otto described as 'immediate, almost instinctive, spontaneity . . . a direct reflex movement . . . [which] does not spring from the consciousness of some committed transgression'.[30]

---

[29] Moberly, 'Holy, Holy, Holy: Isaiah's Vision of God,' p. 128.
[30] Rudolf Otto, *The Idea of the Holy* (1917; Harmondsworth: Pelican Books, 1959), p. 65.

It would be patently foolish to deny some element of emotion when God reveals himself in his awesome holiness as he did to Isaiah. But it is grossly inadequate to say that emotion alone explains the response of Isaiah, not least because it ignores the substance of Isaiah's response. It is not mystery but morality that characterizes Isaiah's reaction to this in-breaking of overwhelming power. And there are good reasons why it should be so. Isaiah's schooling in the Torah, his personal formation as a member of the covenant community, the setting in the temple where atonement was made for failure to observe the law, and the song of the seraph which draws attention not to God's power but to his holiness, all combine to make his reaction one of confession of sin. As Oswalt says, 'for Isaiah the announcement of God's holiness meant that he was in the presence of One distinct from – other than – himself. But for Isaiah as a Hebrew, it also meant that the terrifying otherness was not merely in essence but in character. Here was One ethically pure, absolutely upright, utterly true.'[31] The one who is wholly other relates to his people in very down-to-earth ways and looks to them 'to act justly and to love mercy and to walk humbly with [their] God' (Micah 6:8), as Micah so strikingly put it.

If Isaiah's reaction was instinctive it was because it was an expression of the person he had been made as a child of Israel. If it was self-deprecating it was because he was measuring himself correctly in the light of his encounter with the Holy One. To quote Oswalt again,

> The content of this experience is not merely numinous, emotive, nonrational. Had God only wished to convey his otherness to Isaiah, that could have been done without words. But here a cognitive and rational element is introduced, providing one more indication that revelation does not come merely through raw experience, but also through divinely given cognitive interpretation of that experience.[32]

Other deities would make themselves known as 'raw power' but the God of Israel was unique: his holiness was not only power but morality, not only transcendence but ethics. Other gods may have given their people laws but those laws did not necessarily reflect their own characters.[33] The God of Israel required his people to live in such a way as to mirror his own character. They were called to live in imitation of him. They were to be holy – to live ethically –

[31] Oswalt, *The Book of Isaiah*, p. 181.
[32] Ibid, p. 180.
[33] Ibid.

49

because he was holy, a being of absolute moral perfection.[34] Isaiah's response, therefore, was entirely appropriate and exactly right.

3. God's holiness as costly grace (6:6–13)

Isaiah's vision reveals a third dimension of God's holiness, that of costly grace. Christians are apt to contrast God's holiness with his love, pitting law and grace, judgment and salvation over against each other. Isaiah would have no truck with such a view. It is because he is the Holy One of Israel that he exercises compassion on his less-than-holy people, providing salvation for them and inviting them to enjoy being reconciled to him. 'The Holy One of Israel' is also said to be their helper (40:14); their Saviour (43:3; 52:10); and, most frequently, their Redeemer (43:14; 47:4; 48:17; 49:7; 54:5). As Isaiah 30:15 advises: 'This is what the Sovereign LORD, the Holy One of Israel, says: "In repentance and rest is your salvation, in quietness and trust is your strength. . .".'[35]

The costly grace of God is manifest in Isaiah 6 in three ways: it is seen in the cleansing of the prophet, the chastening of the people and the choosing of a remnant.

a. The cleansing of God's prophet (6:6–8)

In response to Isaiah's confession *one of the seraphs flew to me with a live coal in his hand which he had taken with tongs from the altar. With it he touched my mouth and said, 'See, this has touched your lips; your guilt is taken away and your sin is atoned for.'* Though we might fear that the touching of Isaiah's lips with a burning coal might disfigure them it does nothing of the sort. Rather, it cleanses them, which only makes sense in the context of Israel's sacrificial understanding of worship.

There is a strong connection between holiness and fire.[36] God often reveals himself in fire;[37] it frequently displays his judgment[38] and plays an obvious role in offering sacrifices. All three of these are inherent in the live coal being taken from the altar. We do not know from which altar the coal was taken. It may have been the altar of burnt offering, signifying the renewed commitment into

---

[34] Lev. 11: 44–45; 19:2; 1 Pet. 1:15–16.
[35] Motyer, *The Prophecy of Isaiah*, p. 18.
[36] J. Muilenburg, 'Holiness', *IDB*, pp. 617–618.
[37] E.g., Exod. 3:2–3; 19:18; 24:17; Deut 4:12, 24; Ezek. 1:4–28; Hab. 3:3–4.
[38] Lev. 10:1–3; Is. 34:8–10; Zeph. 1:18.

which Isaiah was entering.[39] More likely it was the altar of incense[40] which stood in the holy place and played a crucial role in the annual atonement ceremony.[41] The mention of smoke, suggesting the presence of incense, may indicate that. Whichever, through his identification with the sacrifice offered, Isaiah is pardoned and his sin atoned for.[42] Coal was frequently used in the process of purifying metals and was now being used to cleanse the prophet and make the unfit fit for service again.[43] Here God's holy purity is satisfied and his holy grace is manifest. The penalty of sin is met and the sinner is cleansed.

In touching Isaiah's *mouth*, God is not only dealing with Isaiah at his expressed point of need but touching him, as we have seen, at the place which symbolizes his calling as a prophet. His unclean lips have not been injured but equipped and Isaiah correctly understands this act not only as one of salvation but of commissioning. Immediately following his cleansing God speaks (8) and Isaiah readily makes himself available to God once more. His life is no longer his own. Just as God's holiness marks his separateness, so now the prophet is separated from ordinary affairs to be wholly available to do God's bidding. It was good that the commitment was made so firmly and in circumstances that were so unmistakable, for Isaiah was to face the most challenging of all prophetic callings, to speak to an audience that were profoundly and steadfastly deaf to God.

b. The chastening of God's people (6:9–12)

Isaiah's preaching was not to result in the people turning to God but the fault did not lie with him. It was not because he lacked skill in communication or urgency in speech that the people failed to hear. It was part of God's plan, for though in his holiness he is a God of grace and salvation, he is not a God of cheap grace or cut-price salvation. To offer cheap grace is incompatible with his holiness, as well as failing to meet the true needs of a sinful people. Blanket forgiveness coupled with easy repentance would prove worthless. It would neither lead to a genuine reconciliation between a holy God and his sinful people, nor to a real transformation in their lives.

---

[39] Exod. 27:1–8; 38:1–7.
[40] Exod. 30:1–10; 37:25–29.
[41] Lev. 16:1–34.
[42] The word atoned for (*kipper*) may mean to cover over, to ransom or to wipe clean, which has given rise to wide discussion. See R. E. Averbeck, '*kpr*' in *NIDOTTE* 3, pp. 689–710.
[43] Num. 31:22–23, Moberly, 'Holy, Holy, Holy: Isaiah's Vision of God,' p. 130.

Grace is not only costly to God, in that he provides the sacrifice for atonement, but also to sinners in that there must be evidence of a changed way of life.

Consequently, before God could bring about salvation for Israel, it was necessary for him to subject them to a period of chastisement so that they could face up to the seriousness of their sin and the cost involved in renewing grace. P. T. Forsyth, a prophet who lived much nearer our own times than Isaiah, understood this well. He taught us that we may treat God too lightly if we see him only as a father for, in truth, he is the Holy Father. He complained that Christians in his day had discovered much about God as love but not thought deeply enough about its meaning. God's love, he argued, is inseparable from his holiness which is the ultimate claim we make about God. 'You can go behind love', he wrote, 'to holiness but behind holiness you cannot go.'[44] He explained further, '"God is love" is not the whole gospel. Love is not evangelical till it has dealt with holy law. In the midst of the rainbow is a throne.'[45] It is this that makes the cross necessary. Forgiveness does not occur without cost for 'the soul of divine fatherhood is forgiveness by holiness'.[46] 'Forgiving is not just forgetting. It is not cancelling the past. It is not mere amnesty and restoration. There is something broken in which a soul's sin shatters the world.'[47] It cannot, then, be repaired on the cheap.

Isaiah was to learn this the hard way: he was to preach to an unresponsive audience. Indeed, his preaching was to make them even more unresponsive than they already were. It was not that he was to cause their hearts to be calloused towards God. They already were. But he was to draw their hardness out, just as a bruise comes out before it heals. They were just like Pharaoh of old whose heart towards God was already hardened before the plagues were activated against him.[48] Those miraculous judgments revealed what was already in his heart and merely brought it to such a climax that God could finally act.

No wonder Isaiah asks how long this 'stupefying, dulling, and blinding'[49] ministry is to last (11), although he cannot have gained much comfort from the answer (11–12) which bound him to the task until the exile occurred and Israel was, in effect, no more.

[44] P. T. Forsyth, *God: The Holy Father* (1897; London: Independent Press, 1957), p. 5.
[45] Ibid.
[46] Ibid.
[47] Ibid., p. 9.
[48] Exod. 7:1 – 11:10.
[49] Moberly, 'Holy, Holy, Holy: Isaiah's Vision of God,' p. 132.

Isaiah's experience typifies a recurring pattern of ministry. Jesus quotes Isaiah 6:9–10 more than once, not least to explain his use of parables.[50] And Paul uses the same words to justify his preaching of the gospel to the Gentiles.[51] God's severe mercy,[52] it seems, reflects his holy love in bringing people to an end of themselves, to an end of their excuses and self-justification before they are ready to receive the remedy of his salvation, secured, ultimately, at the cost of the sacrifice of his son.

c. The certainty of God's grace (verse 13)

Exile is not the end of the story. God's aim is to chasten Israel so that they, or at least a purified remnant of them, might be restored to their homeland. God alone determines when the process of refinement is complete and the new exodus will take place.

Verse 13 is a difficult verse to interpret because the Hebrew is uncertain but the majority believe it points to hope beyond the exile. A minority believe it speaks of the need for Israel to be continually subject to burning, that is God's chastening and purifying work, even if only a stump of them remains.[53] But even they see it as hopeful, for God's purpose remains one of refinement not destruction. But most point to the survival of the stump as the key image and argue that just as the stump of a felled tree breaks forth into new life, so the stump of Israel that returns from exile will be the bearers of a new hope and heralds of a new beginning.

The majority interpretation of verse 13 is certainly consistent with several of the other prophets of Israel who, having warned of coming catastrophe, end with a note of grace. Hosea promised that God would not 'devastate Ephraim again' (Hosea 11:9). Amos spoke of David's fallen shelter being restored (Amos 9:11–15). Micah spoke of God as unique in pardoning sin and hurling all their 'iniquities into the depth of the sea' (Micah 7:19). God's grace is never facile. The demands of holiness need to be satisfied, and then the other facet of his holiness, that of redemptive and costly grace, can come to the fore.

---

[50] Matt. 13:13–15; Mark 4:12; 8:17–18; Luke 8:10; John 12:40.

[51] Acts 28:26–27.

[52] *A Severe Mercy* is, of course, the title of Sheldon Vanauken's autobiography (1977).

[53] Moberly, 'Holy, Holy, Holy: Isaiah's Vision of God,' pp. 134–136. For a good discussion see R. E. Clements, *Isaiah 1 – 39*, NCB, (Grand Rapids: Eerdmans and London: Marshall Morgan and Scott, 1980), p. 78.

4. Concluding comment

Eager worship leaders often hold up Isaiah's experience in the temple as the template for regular worship. It is true that our weekly worship is often pitifully poor and totally lacks ‘the dynamic of God's living and holy presence. But, truth to tell, Isaiah records this vision of God precisely because it was not routine, because it did not happen to him every time he went to the temple. It was exceptional, if not unique and unrepeatable. But even if it only occurred the once, it was enough to fashion him as ‘the prophet of holiness’. From then on he lived to proclaim that the Holy One of Israel was a God of awesome majesty and of sovereign transcendence, of moral perfection and of absolute purity, and equally of costly grace and severe mercy. And though it only happened once, the same God presides unseen over our worship, calling forth from us submission to his sovereignty, trembling before his purity and trust in his cleansing.

1 Peter 1:1-2, 13-21
3. God in Trinity

We cannot help it. We constantly send out subtle signals that let others know where we come from, even when we try not to, which, naturally enough, become especially evident when we are in a foreign culture. The clothes, the accent, the style, the way we respond to things all reveal that we have been shaped by particular cultures to make us the people we are. Our understanding of those from other cultures is often based on a stereotype, but stereotypes have some basis in reality. It is probably true that the English form a queue even if they are on their own!

The Christians to whom Peter wrote stood out as not quite belonging to the culture in which they lived. Scattered throughout four provinces of Asia Minor, since their conversion to Jesus Christ they had lived as resident aliens in a society that was ignorant of God (14). Their description as 'strangers' (KJV), *exiles, foreigners*, and even 'homeless', captures the uncomfortable nature of their situation (1, 17).[1] Although attempts have been made to argue that these labels refer to their social and political position as 'displaced persons' who were facing 'debilitating economic circumstances',[2] most reject this and believe the labels are primarily metaphorical descriptions of their spiritual situation as those who were not quite at home in an unbelieving culture.[3] It is their commitment to Christ, not their position in the social pecking order, that places them

[1] These words are variously used to translate the terms *parepidēmos* and the *paroikia/paroikos* word group, found together in 2:11 and separately elsewhere. *Paroikos* is an alien in residence and *parepidēmos* a settler or displaced person.

[2] J. H. Elliott, *A Home for the Homeless: A Sociological Exegesis of 1 Peter. Its Situation and Strategy* (London: SCM, 1982), p. 72. Elliott is the chief proponent of this position.

[3] J. B. Green, *1 Peter*, Two Horizons New Testament Commentary (Grand Rapids: Eerdmans, 2007), pp. 15-16.

on the margins of mainstream society. Metaphorical or not, this unpopular commitment had some very real consequences as they were the subject of suspicion, slander and persecution – concerns which claim major attention in Peter's letter.

What was it that marked them out as different? The differences were not superficial, such as to do with dress or language, but fundamental, having to do with ethics and lifestyle. The anonymous *Epistle to Diognetus,* written early in the second century, showed a sharp insight in summarizing the differences:

> The difference between Christians and the rest of mankind is not a matter of nationality, or language, or customs. Christians do not live apart in separate cities of their own, speak any special dialect, nor practise any eccentric way of life. . . . They pass their lives in whatever township – Greek or foreign – each man's lot has determined; and conform to ordinary usage in their clothing, diet, and other habits. Nevertheless, the organisation of their community does exhibit some features that are remarkable, and even surprising. For instance, though they are residents at home in their own countries, their behaviour there is more like that of transients; they take their full part as citizens, but they also submit to anything and everything as if they were aliens . . . Like other men they marry and beget children, though they do not expose their infants. Any Christian is free to share his neighbour's table, but never his marriage-bed. Though destiny has placed them here in the flesh, they do not live after the flesh; their days are passed on earth but their citizenship is above in the heavens. They obey the prescribed laws, but in their own lives they transcend the laws. They show love to all men – and all men persecute them. They are misunderstood and condemned; yet by suffering death they are quickened to life.[4]

What brought about the difference, in a word, was 'holiness'. They were called by a holy God to live a holy life. Holiness is foundational to all that Peter writes by way of encouragement to his homesick readers. In line with the rest of Scripture his exposition of holiness is threefold. Holiness first describes the nature of God. Secondly, holiness defines the status of believers. And only then, thirdly, does holiness become an appeal to believers. The first and second of these are found in Peter's opening greeting and the first and third are found as he introduces the subject of holy living more fully later in his first chapter.

---

[4] 'The Epistle to Diognetus,' in M. Staniforth (trans.), *Early Christian Writings: The Apostolic Fathers* (Harmondsworth: Penguin Books, 1968), pp. 176–177.

1. The Trinitarian call of God, 1:2

Faced with persecution the early Christians needed some explanations. The pressures on them to conform to mainstream living were great and unless Peter could help them understand how their suffering fitted with their calling as God's children, they might be tempted to give up and return to their pagan ways. Much of Peter's letter sets their suffering in the context of the suffering of God's people, and especially of his Son, down the ages. But before he explains that, he takes them back to the beginnings so that they might have a fresh understanding of their distinct identity. Their calling goes back to God himself and is one in which each member of the Trinity plays a part in bringing about their destiny. Peter shows little interest in the internal relationships of the Trinity since he is more interested in the role each member of it plays, albeit in cooperation with each other, in relation to the Christian's vocation.[5] In that regard the Father, Spirit and Son have distinct, if complementary, roles in initiating Christians into a holy status and to holy living.

a. Chosen by God the Father (1:2)

To the establishment elites and trendsetters of Asia Minor, the Christians may be of no significance. But to God they have immense value, for they *have been chosen according to the foreknowledge of God the Father* (2). Their status, worth and destiny are determined by God not by earthly powers or social trends, and his choice was not made on the basis of their social standing, economic prosperity, political power, ethical achievements or religious observance but according to his own *foreknowledge*. Peter's intention in referring to this is not to give rise to theoretical debates about predestination. 'To know' is a relational term[6] and 'to know beforehand' draws attention to the Father's loving commitment to them before the world was made.[7] Peter is reminding them that 'their inclusion in the people of God is no accident, no afterthought, but God's purpose from the beginning'.[8] His providential care has been watching over them since eternity past, when he appointed them to his service and to be the recipients of his grace.

---

[5] See further J. R. Michaels, *1 Peter*, WBC (Waco: Word, 1988), lxvii.

[6] John 10:14; 1 Cor. 8:3; 2 Tim. 2:19. See Wayne Grudem, *1 Peter*, TNTC (Grand Rapids: Eerdmans and Leicester: IVP, 1988), p. 50.

[7] 1 Pet. 1:20. See also Rom. 8:29 and 11:2.

[8] Edmund Clowney, *The Message of 1 Peter*, BST (Leicester: IVP, 1988), p. 33.

The God who has called them in this way has made himself known as a holy God and their calling is inextricably bound up with his character (15). Before long Peter is reminding them of Leviticus 11:45 and 19:2: *Be holy, because I am holy* (16). Like Paul, who told even the wayward Corinthians that they were 'called to be [God's] holy people' (1 Corinthians 1:2), Peter knows that the privilege of election goes hand in hand with the responsibility to live a holy life and to reflect the character of the God to whom they belonged in the world in which they lived.

Some find that the root idea of the Hebrew word for holiness lies in the concept of 'separation' or of being 'set apart'. Thus, as we saw in chapter 2, God is set apart from his creation and altogether different from sinful human beings, exalted in his majestic purity.[9] By extension, those objects and people that God calls into his service are also 'marked off, separated, withdrawn from ordinary use'.[10]

Being chosen by God, then, exerts a double influence on Christian believers. On the one hand, they are significant and secure for no one less than the Lord God of the universe has chosen them. On the other hand, they are no longer their own to live as the rest of humankind does, but, though their lives inevitably continue to be entangled with those of their unbelieving neighbours, they are marked out as belonging to God alone and to serve only him.

b. Sanctified in God the Spirit (1:2)

This calling takes effect *through the sanctifying work of the Spirit* (2). Working in harmony with the other members of the Trinity, the Holy Spirit is *sent from heaven* (1:12) to make preachers of the gospel productive in their work of bringing people to Christ. He never works independently, always being intimately related to the Father (4:14) and the Son (1:11).

The Holy Spirit takes the calling of God that occurred in eternity and actualizes it in people who live in a particular time and space. Peter writes of those who lived in first century Asia Minor but the Holy Spirit has operated in the same way in the lives of all who have come to believe down the centuries and around the world.[11] Paul makes exactly the same point in very similar words in 2 Thessalonians 2:13, where he says the Thessalonians were chosen

---

[9] Exod. 15:11; Hos. 11:9.

[10] W. Eichrodt, *Theology of the Old Testament*, Vol. 1 (London: SCM, 1961), p. 270. Eichrodt discusses the value and limitations of this idea.

[11] Jesus speaks of his role in relation to his own teaching in similar terms in John 16:12–16.

'as firstfruits to be saved through the sanctifying work of the Spirit and through belief in the truth'.

The conciseness of the statement in Greek[12] makes for differences in the precise interpretation of the Spirit's work, although all agree that the Holy Spirit is the agent of sanctification, that is, of making people holy and of consecrating them to God. The original almost certainly means that the Holy Sprit brings people out of the realm of evil and relocates them *into* 'the realm of holiness'.[13] The emphasis is on people's initiation into the Christian life and on their becoming God's chosen people rather than on the Spirit's continuing work of refining people's lives and building holiness in them. Our position, thanks to the work of the Holy Spirit, is one of sanctification.[14]

However, while the focus is on people's new position or status as they have been brought under God's rule, the Spirit's work does not end there. After all, as Howard Marshall says, transferring people to God's ownership necessarily has implications for people's behaviour.[15] When a country is taken over by a new power, wholesale changes often follow: cities are renamed, signs are redone, customs are reconsidered, the economy is revamped, taxes are redirected, expectations are revised and sometimes even the language is replaced. So it is with the Holy Spirit. He works both to secure a new position for believers and a new practice in their lives as well.[16] He is inducting people into 'the new way of life that should characterize the children of God'.[17] Consequently, he is not only concerned about the cleansing of past sins but the growth of present and future Christlikeness. His power is bent on bringing about obedience to Jesus Christ, as Peter goes on to say.

c. Obedient to God the Son (1:2)

As the *Spirit of Christ* (1:11), the purpose of the Spirit's work is to bring people *to be obedient to Jesus Christ and sprinkled with his blood* (2). Both these phrases have rich resonances with other parts of Scripture that help us understand their meaning. Obedience

[12] *en hagiasmō pneumatos.*
[13] For a discussion see Green, *1 Peter,* pp. 19–20.
[14] D. Peterson, *Possessed by God: A New Testament Theology of Sanctification and Holiness,* NSBT (Leicester: Apollos, 1995), p. 27.
[15] I. H. Marshall, *1 Peter,* IVPNTC (Downers Grove: IVP and Leicester: IVP, 1991), p. 31. Wayne Grudem is somewhat unusual in interpreting the phrase as exclusively referring to the continuing sanctifying work, *1 Peter,* p. 51.
[16] 1 Thess. 4:8.
[17] Marshall, *1 Peter,* p. 31.

is a key theme in the New Testament but when Paul uses it in Romans[18] and Thessalonians,[19] he often uses it of people's coming to accept the gospel, rather than of their on-going obedience to Jesus as Christians. Peter uses it in this way himself in 1:22, when he says to his readers, *you have purified yourselves by obeying the truth.* In line with what we have seen here of the work of the Father and the Spirit, this focuses on people's coming to faith. In doing so they have changed allegiance and responded positively to the summons of grace, placing themselves under the authority of Jesus Christ.

Yet, again, even if Peter focuses on the start of the Christian's calling, it is unwise to think the Spirit has achieved his objective simply when people are converted. There are plenty of occasions when the word 'obedience' clearly does not refer to the convert's initial obedience to the gospel but to other forms of on-going obedience.[20] It would lead down the dangerous path of antinomianism if it left the impression that continuing obedience was unimportant. It would lead to the sort of gospel preaching that looks merely for a decision rather than a transformation. Neither of these would have been Peter's intention. The obedience that inaugurates the Christian life flows naturally into a life of obedience. There is, in any case, an element of forward thrust when Peter writes that believers are chosen *to* [*eis*][21] *be obedient to Jesus Christ,* as if they are always advancing (1:2) until complete obedience is attained at the end of time.

At first sight the sprinkling of Christ's blood seems an obvious reference to his cleansing people from sin. Those who had recovered from serious skin diseases and sought to re-enter the camp in early Israel were sprinkled with blood as an act of cleansing.[22] And Aaron sprinkled sacrificial blood on 'the atonement cover' and the altar in the Holy Place on the Day of Atonement to cleanse Israel from their sin and the sanctuary from its defilement.[23] Peter, then, is surely saying that Christians need continually to be forgiven for their sin and that their relationship with God is in need of continuous repair because of sin, and that, thankfully, in God's grace, this is possible through Christ's shed blood being 'figuratively sprinkled

[18] Rom. 1:5; 15:18; 16:26.
[19] 2 Thess. 1:8.
[20] Rom. 5:19; 6:16; 2 Cor. 7:15; 10:5–6; Phlm. 21; Heb. 5:8. See Grudem, *1 Peter,* p. 52.
[21] Grudem, *1 Peter,* p. 52, believes *eis* has the sense of 'towards'.
[22] Lev. 14:6–7.
[23] Lev. 16:15–19.

over them'.[24] A life of holiness is characterized by a life of continuous repentance and cleansing.

Even here, however, some argue Peter has something rather different in mind as he uses this phrase. In Exodus 24:6–8 Moses dashes blood against the altar and sprinkles the spectators with it in the process of confirming their covenant with God. Hebrews takes up this picture and makes much of 'the blood of the covenant' in 9:18–22 and 12:24. If this is the background Peter was drawing on, then *sprinkled with his blood*, like the earlier phrases, primarily stresses our entering the new covenant through Christ.

This opening greeting of Peter's letter remind his readers that although it is a sociological fact that they live on the despised margins of mainstream society, there is a greater theological reality to which they should firmly hold. They have been chosen in eternity by a holy Father to belong to him. His Spirit has made them holy, setting them apart as his 'special possession' (2:9). This happened when they came to obey his Son and enter into a blood covenant with him. They have been the recipients of the gracious power of the triune God who cooperates to equip them for their heavenly destination (1:4). But in each case, these claims merely open the way to a new mode of living in which the Father's holiness is reproduced in their lives, and the Spirit's refining makes them increasingly obedient to the Son who, in his extraordinary and patient grace, goes on cleansing them from sin as they have need. The Trinity is truly a holy trinity.

2. The outworking of the call of God (1:13–21)

That the Trinitarian God should *elect* the likes of these dispersed exiles, or us, into his service is astonishing and Peter naturally turns this thought into doxology as he praises God for the 'new birth', the 'living hope' and the heavenly 'inheritance' that is theirs, and ours (3–5). This provides Peter with the context he needs briefly to introduce the question of their suffering (6). Praise puts their suffering in context, a massive context which reaches forward to glory that they will enjoy on the day when Jesus Christ returns (9) and backwards to the prophets as witnesses to the authenticity of their faith (10–12). All that he has written to this point has ramifications for the way his readers should live and takes him back to the subject of holiness. *Therefore*, in verse 13, he tells us that even in a hostile environment the consequence of God's election and mercy on them should be the pursuit of practical holiness.

[24] Grudem, *1 Peter*, p. 53.

Four basic lessons on holiness are taught in verses 13-21

a. The battle for holiness requires determination (1:13)

As exiles and strangers the pressures on Peter's readers to forsake their own beliefs and behaviour patterns and adopt the majority world-view and more socially accepted life-styles were intense. Such pressure is a constant in the Christian experience. Sometimes pressure is exerted as a direct offensive but more often than not it presents itself more subtly, just chipping away at Christian distinctives and causing a gradual erosion of holiness. Few enjoy the discomfort of being a non-conformist (though, some naturally awkward people might!) and therefore we find the path of assimilation to the godless culture that surrounds us attractive. Maintaining holiness is a battle in which we can never afford to relax, which is why Peter's first instructs them to be fully alert and focused in the battle they face.

TNIV's *with minds that are alert and fully sober* (13) hardly does justice to his command. Referring to the familiar custom of tucking one's long robe into the belt or tying it up round the waist when it was time to get into action,[25] Peter tells them to do the same with their minds. In contemporary terms it means take off your coat and roll up the sleeves of your mind.[26] Casual, lazy, relaxed attitudes will never safeguard holiness, still less nurture it. The urgency of being alert is underlined as he adds 'and with full attention'.[27] Some translations interpret the Greek word *nēphrontes* as 'be sober' and that, indeed, picks up the sense of it since drunken people are not aware of the dangers around them and not in control of themselves, let alone their situation. By contrast, the Christian's mind needs to be characterized by self-discipline and vigilance.

Peter's next command instructs us to maintain focus on the hope of *the grace to be brought to you when Jesus Christ is revealed at his coming.* Successful athletes knows the importance of bracketing out distractions, whether they come externally from the crowd or internally in the mind, as they race toward the finishing tape. The goal becomes all-absorbing and causes them to perform to the best that their abilities and training will allow. Christians are encouraged to develop the same focus on the end times, not only so that they might persevere in spite of distractions but also so that they may progress towards being like the Christ they will meet on his return.

[25] Luke 12:35.
[26] C. E. B. Cranfield, *I & II Peter and Jude* (London: SCM, 1960), p. 47.
[27] Michaels, *1 Peter*, p. 55.

b. The practice of holiness involves transformation (1:14)

Having defined Christians at the start of his letter as *obedient* (2) because of their positive response to the gospel message, Peter now spells out to them the implications of that obedience. Because they are obedient their lives will undergo a transformation that means they conform less and less *to the evil desires* they once had when they *lived in ignorance* (14).

Desires can be neutral but New Testament writers more usually employ the term negatively to refer to the longings we have as members of a fallen humanity and the evil impulses within, over which we struggle.[28] What makes desires evil is that they take what is good and distort it until it becomes idolatrous, as happens with materialism; or, that they are destructive in their effect on others, as happens with sexual lust or anger; or, that they debase our true humanity by becoming cravings we cannot control, as happens with our addictions and besetting sins. Peter lists some of these evil desires later in his letter and includes 'malice' and 'deceit, hypocrisy, envy and slander' (2:1) as well as 'debauchery, lust, drunkenness, orgies, carousing and detestable idolatry' (4:3). But 'to conform to these desires is to slip right back into the life-style that the Christian should have abandoned at conversion'.[29]

These evil desires may be natural enough for a fallen humanity but Peter points out that their fires are stoked by a philosophy of *ignorance* (14) and lead to an *empty way of life* (18). This ignorance cannot be so much a lack of knowledge or absence of information for, as Paul argued in Romans 1:18–20, all human beings have, though creation, a basic and sufficient knowledge of God to follow after him. This ignorance is moral and spiritual rather than intellectual. It is either, as Joel Green argues, 'a faulty pattern of thinking', misunderstanding rather than not understanding,[30] or it is a more culpable ignorance in which people ignore what is plain for them to know. Whatever the degree of culpability, the consequence of ignorance is serious as individual lives and whole societies get shaped as if there was no God, and are rendered futile.[31]

Though in some respects Christians cannot completely disentangle themselves from the 'real' world and must remain enmeshed in

---

[28] P. H. Davids, *The First Epistle of Peter,* NICNT (Grand Rapids: Eerdmans, 1990), p. 68, cites Rom. 1:24; 6:12; Gal. 5:16; Eph. 2:3; Titus 2:12; 1 Pet. 2:11; 4:2–3; 1 John 2:16–17.
[29] Ibid.
[30] Green, *1 Peter,* p. 270.
[31] Eph. 4:17–19.

wider society, Peter, like Paul,[32] calls on them both to think and live as nonconformists, refusing to yield to the pressures that would lead them to unholy living.

c. The nature of holiness consists in imitation (1:15–16)

If from a negative viewpoint Christians are not to conform to the world around them, from a positive viewpoint they are to conform to the God above them. The essence of holiness lies in the imitation of God. Since he is holy by nature, our calling is to be holy in practice, giving the world a glimpse, however limited, into his character. This is not a new calling but one which has always been a happy obligation laid on God's people, as Peter's quotation of Leviticus 11:45 and 19:2 shows. The setting of those verses makes clear that holiness affects the whole of life and not just the religious dimension of it. It has as much to do with social ethics and community relationships, as personal purity, all of which are addressed in 1 Peter.[33] If his initial exposition of holiness in verse 14 may be said to concentrate on its personal dimension, in chapter 2 he addresses the corporate holiness of the church, and from then on how one engages as holy people in the world. The challenge of holiness is more comprehensive than is often presented when evangelicals dwell almost exclusively on its personal dimension. Biblical holiness is never about withdrawing from the world in order to keep oneself from being contaminated; it is always about engaging in the world and its relationships in a way that displays the character of God.[34]

Yet, Peter gives this ancient call a new impetus elsewhere in his letter by also presenting Christ as a model for us to imitate, as for example, in 2:21, when he writes of the suffering of Christ. Under the new covenant, then, holiness has become the imitation of God in Christ.

Two things are worth observing about this. Firstly, the call for us to imitate God in Christ is grounded on our being made 'in the image of God' (Genesis 1:27). Without that premise, the command for us to *Be holy, because I am holy* would be made in vain. It is possible because we are both born originally and born again into his family, and we share the family image. That image became marred through sin but holiness is the adventure by which that broken image is being

---

[32] Rom. 12:2 is the only other place in the New Testament where the verb 'do not conform' is used.

[33] See D. Tidball, *The Message of Leviticus*, BST (Leicester: IVP, 2005), and C. J. H. Wright, *Old Testament Ethics for the People of God* (Leicester: IVP, 2004), pp. 38–39.

[34] Green, *1 Peter*, p. 44.

restored in our lives. In conversion we have, and in daily consecration we need to, 'put on the new self, which is being renewed . . . in the image of its Creator' (Colossians 3:10). The work of the Holy Spirit is to repair the damage done by sin so that we attain to our full humanness once again as those created in God's image.

Secondly, 'imitation' does not mean slavish 'repetition' or a mere reduplication of particular actions. It is bigger than that. After Billy Graham's visits to Britain in the 1960s any number of British evangelists imitated him by preaching with a mid-Atlantic accent, using the phase 'The Bible says. . .', and by making an appeal for people to 'make a decision'. But they would also have been imitating him, and almost certainly more effectively, if they had not adopted these incidental aspects of his preaching but had the same confidence as he had in the Word of God and the same passion to see people saved through a clear preaching of the gospel, mediated through their own personality, which invited some response. Since we live in a very different world from that in which the early Christians lived – most of us, for example, do not suffer as slaves at the hands of unjust masters, although some do – our imitation of Christ will be the same but different from theirs. Joel Green explains that imitation calls for 'a creative performance' of the script that Christ has provided, not a wooden repetition of it, so that we bring his holiness alive in our day and apply it to the form of 'ignorant' culture in which we live.

d. The pursuit of holiness necessitates motivation (1:17–21)

The combination of the high standards we are called to reach and the fierceness of the battle which we fight means that we need good motivation if we are to persevere in holiness. Peter provides this as he points to the fear of God and the redemption of Christ.

While many would deny it today, the proper kind of fear can be healthily motivational. The wrong sort can paralyse rather than enable. A cringing fear of the judgment of a distant God with whom one has no relationship may prove terrifying, rather than be an inspiration to better things. But this is not the sort of *reverent fear* (17) that Peter uses to encourage Christians to holiness. That fear is the respectful fear that arises from a good relationship with God whose fatherly care is known. Furthermore, Peter draws attention to the fact that their Father is not on the side of the rich and powerful, who are the source of some of their problems, for he *judges each person's work impartially* (17). So, although they may be made to feel they are a waste of space by their earthly leaders, the one who really counts has no such prejudice and as a result they can *live out* their lives before God with confidence.

The second incentive for persevering in a holy life arises from the redemption price that was paid to secure release from living an *empty way of life* (18). Their freedom from futility, and ours, was gained at the cost of *the precious blood of Christ, a lamb without blemish or defect* (19). The provision of this perfect sacrifice, like the choice of God (1), was no afterthought or second-best plan of God but one that he had planned out of his self-giving love *before the creation of the world* (20). The right and natural response when someone dies to save another person's life is to express deep gratitude for the sacrifice made. And the right and natural response to the death of Jesus Christ for us is to live gratefully before him. Living a holy life is a mark of that gratitude.

3. Concluding comment

One of the wonders to me of being a parent was to observe the marvel of all the potential locked up in our baby's life gradually unfold. It was astonishing. How could that tiny lump of helpless, inarticulate flesh develop into an intelligent, communicative, athletic, responsible, autonomous and relational adult? Truly we are 'fearfully and wonderfully made' (Psalm 139:14). Of course, the progress required human effort, but it was essentially an unfolding of the person God had made. So it is with holiness. Made in the image of God and chosen by him to be his holy people, his Spirit lives within and has put within us the potential of growing into holiness, which is to be obedient to and like Christ. Holiness is about being what we are.

Part 2
Visions of Holiness

Leviticus 11:1–47
4. Holiness as purity

Some of the most sublime theological claims in Scripture are made in the most mundane of contexts.[1] It is like unexpectedly stumbling across a diamond when doing the housework. The command *be holy, because I am holy* (11:44, 45) does not first appear as the preface to what we know as the great charter of ethical living, Leviticus 19,[2] but towards the end of the laws about clean and unclean animals, laws which we find among the strangest in the book. It is a 'breathtaking' command which calls on Israel to reflect the character of God and to do what he would do.[3] 'Holiness', writes Chris Wright, 'is the biblical "shorthand" for the very essence of God.'[4] That makes it especially hard to understand why holiness has to do with whether we eat pork or octopus, yet this is the context where we first encounter the call to imitate God's holy character.

1. The perspective of the priests

The overwhelming theme of Leviticus is the call to be holy.[5] It presents a particular vision of holiness, that of the priests, although

---

[1] A New Testament example is 2 Cor. 8:9 or 9:15 which occurs when Paul is talking about the collection, or Phil. 2:6–11 which arises from Paul's concern about relationships in the church.

[2] Lev. 19:2.

[3] C. J. H. Wright, *Old Testament Ethics for the People of God* (Leicester: IVP, 2004), p. 39.

[4] Ibid. Wright continues, 'No less breathtaking, of course, was Jesus' own echo of the verse to his disciples: "Be perfect, therefore, as your heavenly Father is perfect" (Matt..5:48).'

[5] For a full exposition see the author's *The Message of Leviticus,* BST (Leicester: IVP, 2005), and A. P. Ross, *Holiness to the Lord* (Grand Rapids: Baker Academic, 2002).

as we shall come to see, it should not be contrasted with other standpoints too strongly.[6] The priests saw the world as an orderly creation in which everything had its place and in which boundaries should not be crossed.[7] God presided over his creation in awesome majesty and those who encountered his holiness encountered 'a force which actively opposes impurity'[8] and so were exposed to danger unless they themselves were pure and protected. The tragic deaths of Nadab and Abihu[9] and the rituals of the Day of Atonement bear this out in different ways.[10]

The camp, with the tabernacle at its centre, representing 'the presence of God in his holiness and glory', was a microcosm of the orderly world.[11] At its heart was the most holy place, surrounded in ever widening circles by the holy place; the courtyard; the camp itself, which was clean territory; and finally, the wilderness, which was unclean and symbolized the territory of disease, demons and death. People like priests, objects like offerings, the furniture and utensils of the tabernacle, property like the sanctuary and dedicated houses, and time, like the sabbath and the festivals, all partook of the quality of holiness.[12] God made his ways known to the children of Israel by the way the camp was laid out and how it operated. God taught his people not just through words but through the drama of life and its rituals.

A number of questions were thrown up by this orderly view of the world. What happened when boundaries were crossed? How could breaches be repaired? Was there a way of restoring the balance? Holy people and objects were liable for a variety of reasons to become contaminated. How could the 'unholy' be made holy again, if at all, and how could the ritually impure be cleansed?[13] The

---

[6] See J. B. Wells, *God's Holy People: A Theme in Biblical Theology* (Sheffield: Sheffield Academic Press, 2000), p. 81.

[7] Good summaries are found in J. G. Gammie, *Holiness in Israel* (Minneapolis: Fortress, 1989), P. Jenson, *Graded Holiness: A key to the Priestly Conception of the World*, JSOTSS 106 (Sheffield: Sheffield Academic Press, 1992), Wells, *God's Holy People*, pp. 58–96, and G. Wenham, *The Book of Leviticus*, NICOT (London: Hodder and Stoughton, 1979).

[8] H. K. Harrington, 'Interpreting Leviticus in the Second Temple Period: Struggling with Ambiguity' in J. F. A. Sawyer (ed.), *Reading Leviticus: A Conversation with Mary Douglas*, JSOTSS 227 (Sheffield: Sheffield Academic Press, 1996), p. 216.

[9] Lev. 10:1–5.

[10] Lev. 16:1–34.

[11] Gammie, *Holiness in Israel*, p. 16.

[12] For full details see D. P. Wright, 'Holiness: Old Testament', *ABC* 3 (1992), pp. 237–249.

[13] In Leviticus, the terms 'holy' and 'clean', and 'unholy' and 'impure' are not synonyms but neither are they unrelated. For details see Tidball, *The Message of*

priestly view of the world was as concerned with moral failure and wrong done to one's neighbours as it was about questions of ritual purity. Sin disrupts the good order of God's creation and threatens to destroy it. So how could humans, whose lives have been polluted by sin and whose relation with God had been disrupted, be made clean and restored to harmony with him?

For each of these questions God provided an answer: cleansing was available. Depending on the nature of the offence, the offering of a blood sacrifice or undertaking of a ritual of cleansing was the means by which harmony with God, harmony between neighbours, harmony in the community and harmony in the world could be restored.

All this, and more, lies behind the way the priests viewed the world that the holy God had made.

2. The principles of holiness (Leviticus 11:1–47)

A close-up view of holiness, from a priestly perspective, can be seen in examining the laws concerning clean and unclean food. Leviticus 11:39–45 will be our focus. Our interpretation of the food laws, and the purity regulations generally, raises any number of questions that it is not possible to deal with here and which I have dealt with elsewhere.[14] Whatever the problems in understanding these laws, those who wrote Leviticus clearly understood them to teach important lessons about holiness, through using, as it were, a sort of visual aid. Leviticus does not explain the reason for the dietary laws in terms of hygiene but in terms of holiness. Once we make that connection a number of principles regarding holiness follow.

a. Holiness is a question of obedience (11:41–43)

Various explanations are advanced as to why God set out these particular rules for Israel. Clean animals do appear generally to mirror

---

Leviticus, pp. 27–28. Richard Bauckham helpfully writes, '. . . holiness expresses what God intrinsically is, distinct from all creation, and yet it is also shared – in varying degrees – by all that belongs to God . . . Purity, on the other hand, is what creaturely persons and things have when they are not defiled by such things as death, sexual emissions. . . . Impurity of this kind – ritual impurity – is more like dirt than sin. . . . However, there is also another type of defilement – moral impurity – that results from immoral behaviour' ('The Holiness of Jesus and His Disciples in the Gospel of John' in K. E. Brower and A. Johnson [eds.], *Holiness and Ecclesiology in the New Testament* [Grand Rapids: Eerdmans: 2007], pp. 95–96).

[14] Tidball, *The Message of Leviticus*, pp. 141–157.

what one would expect as normative or whole for a particular kind of animal, while unclean animals seem to be exceptions or deficient in some way. The rules may have had hygienic benefits or even ascetic value. They might well have marked Israel out as distinct, a sign of separation from their neighbours.[15] Whatever the explanation, the bottom line is that God has commanded them and his people are called to obey. Verses 41–43 instruct Israel as to what they are to think and what they are to do. It is not for Israel to question God's wisdom or motives, but rather to obey him. Obedience, on this occasion, will guard their ritual purity. On other occasions obedience will guard their moral purity. Both of these are aspects of holiness.

It is significant that these rules have to do with what Israel is to eat. Cultures are often distinguished by their different diets and eating customs so, in one sense, this is fairly normal and quite understandable. But making Israel's menu a matter of holiness teaches us something else of importance. It suggests that God is not a God to be kept confined to the tabernacle but a God who has relevance for every area of life. Holiness is as much to do with what happens in the kitchen as the tabernacle. And as the rest of Leviticus demonstrates, it has as much to do with the maternity unit and the market place, the sick room and the bedroom, the law court and the farmyard as it has to do with the sanctuary. God looks for holiness in every dimension of our lives.

b. Holiness is a matter of ownership (11:44)

A reason is given as to why God should expect Israel to *consecrate [them]selves and be holy*. It is because he is their God. Other nations are identified with other gods but Israel had entered a covenant relationship with Yahweh. In saying *I am the LORD your God*, he is not vaunting his rights but reminding them of that loving relationship and their mutual commitment. The covenant they have entered is a two-sided commitment whereby he provides them with peace, prosperity, protection and blessing in return for their obedience and walking in his ways.[16] Different gods would act very differently towards their people, have different standards, and require different signs of loyalty. But Israel had made Yahweh their God and come

---

[15] This explanation has particular merit given the close connection between holiness and separation. Gammie says, 'Holiness demands separation'. And, 'The notion of separation is pervasive in the priestly tradition . . . ' (*Holiness in Israel,* pp. 9, 11).

[16] There are various versions of the covenant. The crucial summary in Leviticus is found in Lev. 26. See also Exod. 24; Deut. 27 – 28. The covenant with Israel was based on God's earlier covenants with the patriarchs (Exod. 2:24).

under his protection, and, therefore, ownership. God declares, 'I have set you apart from the nations to be my own' (Leviticus 20:26). They are no longer free to live as they wished, but have agreed to live in accordance with his declared will. Paul makes exactly the same point about our membership of the new covenant in saying to the Corinthians, 'You are not your own; you were bought at a price. Therefore honour God with your bodies' (1 Corinthians 6:19–20).

In days when we prize individualism and independence, the thought of being owned by someone seems strange and fearsome. It conjures up thoughts of being 'owned' by the company we work for, which for many is a less-than-happy experience. But what better than to be owned by the God of the universe who, by definition, as our Maker, knows best how we should live in his world? Actually, in the very next verse, Leviticus tells what is even better than that.

c. Holiness is a response to grace (11:45)

Even better than our Maker being the one who owns us because he has a sovereign right to do so, is the fact that his ownership of us is confirmed because of his saving grace. To the claim *I am holy*, made in verse 44, he adds, in verse 45, another *I am* claim – *I am the LORD, who brought you up out of Egypt to be your God* – before reiterating his holiness. Israel entered into a covenant with the God of holiness because he came to their rescue when they were slaves, breaking the bars of their yoke, and overthrowing their oppressors. His purpose was to set them free to enjoy the liberty of being his people rather than Pharaoh's chattels, and to live as a community that was characterized by righteousness rather than injustice. With backs that were no longer bent to bear the lash of the whip, and wills that were no longer forced to do the whim of the taskmaster, they could 'walk with heads held high' (Leviticus 26:13). The God who had acted so decisively for their salvation was a God who deserved to be served with gratitude. Their service was forever coloured by the assurance that he would never be the means of their oppression. To be grateful was to be holy. The call to holiness, then, is inherent in the work of grace and not disconnected from it.

d. Holiness is an objective to attain (11:45)

The command to *be holy* clearly implies that Israel cannot take their holiness for granted or else it would be redundant. Even if they attained to holiness on occasions, the command suggests they had not yet reached a steady-state of holiness in practice.

The repetition of the command makes this point fundamental.[17] The idea of holiness is complex. It describes the innermost nature of God and the status of his people as those set apart for him (Leviticus 20:26). But the word also applies to the spiritual and moral standard of life which God's people were expected to attain. God is realistic enough to know that as fallen creatures in a fallen world, and subject to the malign influence of Satan, we will not always reach the goal. Nonetheless, God does not accommodate his standard to our failures. Rather he uses his standard as our incentive to aspire to better things, while making it possible for us to deal with our failing to meet the mark through the offering of sacrifices of atonement.

e. Holiness is a relationship to be repaired (11:24–40)

In a priestly understanding of holiness, purity is maintained by separating oneself from what is unclean. But what happens if the boundaries are not maintained? With regard to the food laws, a person may break them in a number of ways and become unclean. Someone might eat forbidden food unwittingly, or, more likely, as this chapter indicates, comes into direct or indirect contact with something that is dead and so become defiled (11:24–40). Then what happens?

The answer is simple: for every cause of uncleanness there is provided a ritual of cleansing. In these cases, the infringement is temporary and so the way of dealing with it is for those concerned to *wash their clothes, and they will be unclean till evening* (verses 25, 28, 39). More long-lasting defilement, like those spoken of in the chapters that follow, requires more serious rituals of cleansing. Offences against God and against neighbours required the services of a priest and the offering of blood sacrifices, as set out in Leviticus 1 – 7, in order to make amendment and restore the relationship that had been disrupted.

God's grace was not a one-off but extends beyond Israel's deliverance from Egypt to embrace their on-going deliverance from sin and impurity. Through the various rituals of cleansing, people who have fallen short of God's expectations are restored to their position of holiness, so that once again they can strive in practice to live up to their status as his special people.[18]

Although the food regulations no longer apply to Christians,[19] we still defile ourselves with sin and fail in the battle to live up to our true identity as a holy people. As John wrote, 'If we claim to be

---

[17] In addition to here, there is Lev. 19:2 and similar commands in 20:7, 26.
[18] Lev. 20:8; 21:8; 22:9, 16, 32.
[19] Mark 7:1–23; Acts 10:1–48.

without sin, we deceive ourselves and the truth is not in us' (1 John 1:8). For us, too, there is a way of repairing our broken relationship with God and restoring it when we have failed, for as John continued, 'If we confess our sins, he is faithful and just and will forgive us our sins and purify us from all unrighteousness' (1 John 1:9). God does this not solely because of our confession but because 'Jesus Christ, the Righteous One . . . is the atoning sacrifice for our sins' (1 John 2:1–2).

3. The practice of holiness

The priestly vision of holiness is often presented in a distorted way as if it is only concerned with minute and arcane issues of separation from impurity and the maintenance of ritual purity. To present it in this way, however, is to convey 'a misleading caricature'.[20] Leviticus is a book of two halves – chapters 1 – 16, sometimes known as the Priestly Torah, and chapters 17 – 27, usually known as the Holiness Code – which relate closely to each other, even if they speak the same language with a different accent. They both concern the call to be holy. The first half is more concerned with how holiness relates to the work of the priest and affects the cult. It was the priest's task, for example, not only to offer sacrifices but also 'to distinguish between the holy and the common, between the unclean and the clean' (10:10). The second half concerns the outworking of holiness as people lived their lives in the community. This covers not only a variety of moral issues but also issues of how to organize one's time so that there is holy space for God.

In a detailed examination of how these two halves relate to each other, David Wright has concluded:

> Holiness is a fundamental theological principle in both the Priestly Torah and the Holiness School. The Holiness School's concern for holiness grows out of its dependence upon the Priestly Torah. But the Holiness School also transforms and expands this basic doctrine of the Priestly Torah. One of the Holiness School's main interests is constructing a system in which obedience to God's commandments is logical and compelling for its audience . . . In short, while the Holiness School does not revolutionize the Priestly Torah tradition, it explains, adapts, updates and reformulates it.[21]

[20] Gammie, *Holiness in Israel*, p. 34.
[21] D. P. Wright, 'Holiness in Leviticus and Beyond', *Int*, 53 (1999), p. 363.

In both halves holiness is presented in very practical terms. It is not some mystical state, achieved by some degree of unearthly or disembodied sanctity, but about the down-to-earth concerns of daily living. It is as basic as what to do when the body functions in a certain way or what holds the family together. In Leviticus, the call to holiness is a prism through which the colours of holiness refract. The spectrum covers the spiritual, ritual, physical, ethical and social colours of our lives. A brief review of these underlines the comprehensive claim of holiness upon us.

a. Holiness and the heart

It is far from true that the priestly vision of holiness is one which is only concerned with external rituals. They have their part but they are always seen as expressions of the heart, an outward demonstration of an inward attitude. Worshippers were required to lay their hands on their offerings as a sign that the offerings were standing in their place and bearing the penalty which they acknowledged as due for their sin. There was no atonement for those who sinned in a defiant and rebellious manner but only for those who sinned 'unintentionally'.[22] The inward attitude was significant. The sin offering atones for acts of omission, such as when someone doesn't speak up when they should (5:1), as well as sins of commission. Whether someone was faithful or not is the issue underlying the guilt offering (5:14–17) and is really concerned about someone's attitude both to God and their neighbour.

The inner workings of the heart are brought out into the open in chapter 19. There, attitudes of discrimination and prejudice (19:15), hatred and courage (19:17), revenge and grudge-bearing (19:18) and respect for others (19:14, 32), are all explicitly mentioned, as well as the plea to 'love your neighbour as yourself' (19:18). Holiness certainly has to do with the heart!

b. Holiness and the spiritual

'Above all', Donna Orsuto writes, 'holiness is ultimately measured by one's love for God and neighbour' (19:18).[23] Although loving God and one's neighbour are inseparable, they are also

---

[22] The word 'unintentionally', used in Lev. 4:1, 13, 22, 27; 5:15, 18, is debated but many believe it covers all the usual sins and lapses in holiness if one's basic intention in life is to be obedient to God. See discussion in Tidball, *The Message of Leviticus*, pp. 71–73.

[23] D. Orsuto, *Holiness* (Sheffield: Continuum, 2006), p. 17.

distinguishable. We do not only love God through loving our neighbour but we also love God in and for himself. The sacrifices of Israel perhaps demonstrated that most in the priestly understanding of holiness. The first sacrifice Leviticus mentions is that of the burnt offering. It is a voluntary offering (1:1–17) which may be offered in a number of ways to bring it within the reach of everyone. Although it has some role in making atonement for people (1:4), its essential purpose seems to lie elsewhere. It creates 'an aroma pleasing to the LORD' (1:9, 13, 17) as his people, through the medium of the sacrifice, offer themselves again to God. The total consumption of the offering by fire symbolizes that they belong wholly to the Lord. That this is the first sacrifice to be mentioned and the most frequent to be offered suggests that being wholly available to the Lord is the default position of the children of Israel.

God is worshipped in the grain offering (2:1–16) as the people offer him the fruit of their labour. The fellowship offering (3:1–17) enables people to celebrate the ordinary events of life and family with gratitude in the presence of God, rather than presuming they are a right and arrogantly ignoring the one who gives 'every good and perfect gift' from above.[24] The sin (4:1 – 5:13) and guilt offerings (5:14–19) were required when sin had been committed, while the annual Day of Atonement (16:1–34) cleansed Israel from their general defilement as a sinful people. These restored the sinner's individual and corporate relationship with God and renewed their status as his holy people.

If elsewhere, there is a greater stress on intimacy with God,[25] it is not altogether absent in the priestly writings. We catch a glimpse of it in Leviticus 10 in the aftermath of the death of Nadab and Abihu, and in the high priest going into the very presence of God on the Day of Atonement (16:11–18). But the more fundamental concern is how a people who have been delivered by God maintain fellowship with him in spite of their uncleanness.

c. Holiness and the body

It is amazing that this ancient manual on holiness contains so much about the very basic functions of our bodies. Evangelical Christians have perhaps been in denial about the body, following in the footsteps of Augustine and the Puritans, although a younger generation of Christians are less inhibited in this area. But the Bible is nothing if not realistic and the topics raised in the chapters on purity, chapters 11–15, are about the physical conditions and functions of life.

[24] Jas 1:17.
[25] E.g., Exod. 33:7–11.

After dealing with the diet (chapter 11), the priests give instruction about a woman's recovery after giving birth (chapter 12), what to do about skin diseases in people and mould in buildings (chapters 13 – 14), before concluding with the subject of discharges from the body, some of which are routine and some of which signify illness (chapter 15).

The Christian attitude to the body has been influenced by a wrong understanding of these chapters where we have frequently taken 'unclean' to mean 'dirty' or 'evil'. Several factors need to be borne in mind if this mistake is to be avoided. First, declaring an animal, or a woman who had just given birth, unclean was a protective mechanism. Unclean animals became protected species who could not be killed for food or commerce, and new mothers were being given the chance to restore their strength before men would make them the objects of their desire again. Regulations about defiling skin diseases and mildew in various materials have the obvious social benefit of preventing the diseases from spreading throughout the camp. Bodily discharges fit into both of these groups, offering time for restoration and preventing the spread of ill-health.

There are, however, other things to understand about these regulations as well. The use of the word 'unclean' is not to be equated with 'unholy'. In these cases, the purification required when one suffered from an uncleanness was not a moral cleansing but a ritual one. In Leviticus, God teaches his people about himself and the holiness he requires not just through rational instruction but by providing analogies, so that people can learn through an association of ideas. What they experience in their social life becomes a mirror for spiritual realities. So, the unclean animals, a loss of blood or fluid from the body, or an invasion of disease represent the forces that threaten to destroy God's good creation and lead it on the path to death.[26] But God gives life. It is Satan who destroys it. So to be his is to be on the side of life. To be holy, as he is, is to take steps to prevent the onset of chaos and destruction and to recover purity where it had been lost.

d. Holiness and the ethical

The second occurrence of the command to *be holy because I am holy* comes in Leviticus 19:2, at the start of a chapter which, by common consent, is one of the great ethical writings of the world. Though complex and seemingly random in composition, it not only integrates the priestly and more ritual concerns of Leviticus with

[26] See Tidball, *The Message of Leviticus*, pp. 22–23.

its moral and ethical concerns, but establishes a clear connection between being holy and living an ethical life. The string on which all its varied beads hang together is the string of respect. It begins with respecting God's law (19:3–8, 11–12) and returns to that periodically (as in 19:26–28, 30–31). It mostly consists of inviting respect for others: for parents (19:3); for the poor (19:9–10); for neighbours (19:13, 16–18); for employees (19:13); for the disabled (19:14); for justice (19:15); for creation (19:19, 23–26; for slaves (19:20–22); for family (19:29); for the elderly (32); for immigrants (19:33–34); and for customers (19:35–36). What a wonderfully wholesome society would be created if we lived in accordance with the invitation to imitate God's character in the way we relate to one another.

e. Holiness and the community

The focus of Leviticus 19 might be said to be on personal ethics, although since, in the words of the famous saying, 'no man is an island,' our living always impacts others. If we live well we enhance the society in which we live, while 'all sin is sin against the society of which the sinner is a part'.[27] A society that could count on its citizens to live like that would be one at ease with itself and be rich in social capital.[28] Even so, by comparison, the surrounding chapters become much more focused on the community than the individual. Each of these chapters is aimed at building strong, compassionate and clean societies, while they also help individuals to live righteously before God.

In these chapters, holiness requires Israel to live ethically and distinctively (18:3) in relation to creation (chapter 17); to the family (chapter 18); to justice (chapter 20); to spiritual leadership (chapters 21–22); to our use of time (chapter 23); to the service to God (chapter 24); and to economics (chapter 25). The theme of respect, which we saw in chapter 19, applies to these chapters as well.

A deeper look at chapter 18 illustrates the social dimension of holiness. God commands Israel to reject the sexual practices of the surrounding cultures, not because he is a killjoy, but because he knows how best to build stable and lasting families, which are the basic building blocks of any society. So, the practices outlawed in this much-maligned chapter, namely incest (18:6–18), adultery

---

[27] H. H. Rowley quoted in D. Davies, 'An interpretation of sacrifice in Leviticus' in *ZAW*, 89 (1977), p. 393.

[28] Sociologists increasingly recognize the need for societies not only to have financial capital and a physical infrastructure to function but also social capital. See Robert D. Putnam, *Bowling Alone* (New York: Simon and Schuster, 2000), pp. 18–24.

(18:20), child sacrifice (18:21), homosexuality (18:22), and bestiality (18:23), are those that would erode the family, threaten its well-being, and probably cause its disintegration.

Here, then, is a holiness that impacts the social dimension of our lives. It is about how we live as fathers, mothers, children, citizens and neighbours. It is about our responsibility for the environment, for the home, for the financial system, our work place and our leisure hours. Down-to-earth holiness is about our social responsibilities as much as our personal purity.

4. Concluding comment

Philip Jenson has described the priests' idea of holiness as 'subtle, diverse and richly developed'.[29] To him, the best framework for understanding this perspective on holiness is neither separation, nor power, nor the 'wholly other', nor God's character but that which 'belongs to God's realm or sphere'.[30] The priestly view is indeed complex, but rich. Holiness 'belongs to God alone' and his overpowering glory consumes that which enters his presence in a state of unworthiness.[31] Yet he makes his people holy and calls them to a life of holiness and purity. He makes provision for them when holiness lapses and impurity threatens so that they can rediscover and live out their true identity. The priest's preoccupation with order and boundaries symbolizes God's order in his good creation and society. When the order is disrupted or the boundaries are breached atonement is necessary. Many and varied channels are used to communicate that message: the rules about sacrifices, the regulations about purity in diet and body, the rituals of atonement and the plain-speaking laws about life. The priestly vision blends the ritual with the ethical, the personal with the social, the internal with the external. It does all this to one common end: that God's people might reproduce his holiness in his world.

---

[29] P. Jenson, 'Holiness in the Priestly Writings of the Old Testament' in S. Barton (ed.), *Holiness Past and Present* (London: Continuum, 2002), p. 121.

[30] Jenson, 'Holiness in the Priestly Writings,' p. 105.

[31] D. Orsuto, *Holiness* (Sheffield: Continuum, 2006), p. 17.

Proverbs 2:1–22
5. Holiness as wisdom

It's possible to play the same music in more than one way. The rhythm can change and the key can be transposed. At first sight, it is foolish to turn to Proverbs for an understanding of holiness, since the nearest Proverbs gets to using the language of holiness is twice to refer to God as the 'Holy One' (9:10; 30:3). Yet the book dances to the tune of holiness. Here, Israel's commitment is made over into another key. Here, holiness is transposed into wisdom.

In common with the priestly literature examined in the last chapter, the wisdom books[1] see the world as created and ordered by one God. 'By wisdom the LORD laid the earth's foundations, by understanding he set the heavens in place; by his knowledge the deeps were divided, and the clouds let drop the dew' (Proverbs 3:19–20). Unlike the priests, this does not lead to a concern about maintaining ritual purity or boundaries so much as how to live in the ordinariness of everyday life in harmony with the way God has appointed. Living wisely means to live with the grain of our world, rather than to cut across it. So, Proverbs is concerned about words and integrity, wealth and poverty, parents and children, friends and enemies, neighbours and naggers, time and space, industry and laziness, joy and grief, planning and spontaneity, alcohol and health, patience and pride, and peace-makers and mischief-makers. The list could go on![2]

---

[1] That is Job, (some) Psalms, Proverbs and Ecclesiastes, among which Proverbs is central.

[2] For a survey from the viewpoint of contemporary scholarship see R. E. Clements, *Wisdom in Theology*, The Didsbury Lectures (Carlisle: Paternoster and Grand Rapids: Eerdmans, 1992), and from a more devotional viewpoint K. T. Aitken, *Proverbs*, The Daily Study Bible (Edinburgh: Saint Andrew Press and Philadelphia: The Westminster Press, 1986).

No single passage encapsulates all its teaching, but Proverbs 2 has 'a programmatic character'[3] to it and enables us to examine some of the key principles that are then unfolded and applied in the rest of the book. Proverbs 2 is the second of several messages of instruction to a young man that form the first nine chapters, before the pithy precepts we associate with the book kick in. It is an acrostic, composed of one long single sentence but divided in the middle. The first half, verses 1–11, has, according to Bruce Waltke, to do with the development of a person's character and the second, verses 12–22, to do with deliverance from wickedness.[4] Each half is composed of two stanzas, although we shall divide it a little differently.

The melody line throughout is that of wisdom and, while the music, like a good symphony, makes a clear progression from one phase to another, themes surface more than once. This type of teaching is not common in the Old Testament but neither is it unique. It particularly resonates with some of the wisdom psalms to which we shall refer.

1. The quest for wisdom (2:1–4)

Proverbs 1 – 9 record the instructions given by a father to his son, so chapter 2 typically begins, *My son, if you accept my words, and store up my commands within you* . . . It quickly becomes evident that the father is an expert, schooled both by experience and the tradition of Israel, and one who expects to have his words taken seriously and to be obeyed. Yet he avoids being authoritarian and purely directive, which would have had the result of making his pupil merely a passive recipient of his wisdom. His strategy is that of a facilitator who 'creates conditions that are conducive to the learner's independent growth'.[5] He teaches by 'indirection' as much as by offering direction and often by placing concrete examples from life before the learner and enabling the learning to 'infer the principle which they teach'.[6]

[3] R. E. Murphy, *Proverbs,* WBC (Nashville: Thomas Nelson, 1998), p. 17.
[4] B. K. Waltke, *The Book of Proverbs, Chapters 1 – 15*, NICOT (Grand Rapids: Eerdmans, 2004), p. 216. For further on the literary structure see Leo Perdue, *Proverbs*, Int (Louisville: John Knox Press, 2000), p. 88, who particularly draws attention to the 'if . . . then' structure of verses 1, 3, 4, 5, 9.
[5] D. J. Estes, *Hear, My Son: Teaching and Learning in Proverbs 1 – 9*, NSBT 4 (Leicester: Apollos, 1997), p. 134.
[6] Ibid., p. 103.

a. Wisdom needs to be internalized (2:1–2)

The goal of any good education is surely that pupils imbibe what is taught so that it becomes a part of them, shaping their attitudes and reactions instinctively. It is a failure of education when things are superficially lodged in the mind only to be forgotten the moment the lesson has ended. A certain amount of information has to be given as a basis for wisdom but it is important that these instructions are internalized, so the son is instructed to *store up my commands within you.* The next verse amplifies the point: turn *your ear to wisdom and* apply *your heart to understanding.* Proverbs is concerned with the whole person and an integrated life, not one where the head says one thing and the heart another with the result that the feet walk in foolish paths. 'Above all else', it teaches, 'guard your heart, for everything you do flows from it' (Proverbs 4:23). David recognizes the same need when, in Psalm 51:10, having confessed his sin with Bathsheba,[7] he prays, 'Create in me a pure heart, O God, and renew a steadfast spirit within me.' If one is to live wisely, wisdom has to be assimilated deep within.

This commitment to the formation of character stands in sharp contrast to the values of our own day where personality and celebrity status rather than character is prized. David Wells argues that an abrupt change of focus from character to personality occurred around 1890. 'The adjectives most commonly used to describe personality', he writes, quoting Warren Susman,

> became *'fascinating, stunning, attractive, magnetic, glowing, masterful, creative, dominant, forceful.'* None of these words could easily be used to describe someone's character. Character is not stunning, fascinating, or creative. Character is good or bad, while personality is attractive, forceful, or magnetic. Attention therefore was shifting from the moral virtues, which need to be cultivated, to the image, which needs to be fashioned. It was a shift away from the invisible moral intentions towards the attempt to make ourselves appealing to others, away from what we actually are and toward refining our performance before a public that mostly judges the exterior.[8]

Wisdom concerns the cultivation of character. Proverbs is not intended as a reference book to consult each time one meets a new situation to find out how one should behave. It is a workbook

---

[7] 2 Sam. 11:1 – 12:25.
[8] D. F. Wells, *Losing our Virtue: Why the church must recover its moral vision* (Leicester: IVP, 1998), p. 97.

instructing people in the art of living wisely so that in every situation, whether familiar or unknown, whether mentioned or unaddressed, we are trained to know how to react in a wholesome way. Moreover, it is concerned with who one is and not merely with what one does. In developing godly character, one of the foundation stones on which wisdom builds is that 'the all-knowing divine majesty requires purity of heart and inner integrity'.[9]

b. Wisdom is insight (2:3)

Several words are used to explain the meaning of wisdom. It is *understanding* or *insight*. If it is to do with the acquisition of knowledge it is about knowledge that is applied and practical rather than abstract and intellectual. Our world has never had such easy access to immense amounts of information as we have today, where millions of pieces of 'knowledge' are instantly available to us through the Internet. Yet, arguably, the increase in knowledge has been in inverse ratio to the increase of wisdom. The more we know, the less we know how to handle it. The more research we undertake, the less we know how to solve the ills of our society and the problems that confront us. Our world is dying, our societies fragmenting and our families struggling, not for a lack of knowledge but for a lack of wisdom.

William Cowper's poem, *The Task*[10] helpfully distinguished between knowledge and wisdom like this,

> Knowledge and Wisdom, far from being one,
> Have ofttimes no connection. Knowledge dwells
> In heads replete with thoughts of other men;
> Wisdom in minds attentive to their own.
> Knowledge, a rude unprofitable mass,
> The mere materials with which Wisdom builds,
> Till smooth'd and squared and fitted to its place,
> Does but encumber whom it seems t' enrich.
> Knowledge is proud that he has learned so much;
> Wisdom is humble that he knows no more.

c. Wisdom is elusive (2:4)

Wisdom is treasured and therefore not spread around 'as common as muck', as they say in Yorkshire. It is not to be undervalued or

---

[9] J. G. Gammie, *Holiness in Israel* (Minneapolis: Fortress, 1989), p. 126.
[10] *The Poetical Works of William Cowper, Vol II* (London: William Pickering, 1830), p. 164.

taken for granted. It is not to be picked up and used, and then just as easily discarded, when it has served our utilitarian ends. It is about moulding us to be the people that otherwise we would not be. Therefore God does not make wisdom freely available to all but he does make it readily available to those who demonstrate their desire for it. In this way he tests the genuineness of those who search for it. Genuine seekers will search for it as if searching for *silver* or *hidden treasure* and treat it as just as precious when it is found.

Many of the things we prize in life are valued because we worked or struggled patiently for them until the day came when we could afford them or achieved them. We generally do not value that which falls into our laps. The very act of struggling means our appreciation of them reaches a dimension we would otherwise miss. So it is with wisdom: we appreciate its lessons most when we strive to attain it. Since we are human beings, having moral responsibility, God looks for our cooperation and determination in the battle for wisdom. He does not remove a defective chip from our brains and reprogram us with a perfect, moral chip. That would makes us robots rather than human moral agents. Consequently, wisdom is something we should search for with all our might.

Psalm 84:2 echoes this longing for wisdom in saying, 'My soul yearns, even faints, for the courts of the LORD [where wisdom is to be found]; my heart and flesh cry out for the living God.'

2. The gift of wisdom (2:5–8)

The teacher shifts his focus from his son to his Lord, who becomes the subject of the next section. This corrects a false conclusion that may be drawn from the first stanza. Although we need to seek diligently, when we find wisdom it is not because of human intelligence, rational enquiry, or our own effort, but because God has revealed it to us. It reminds me of the small child hunting for the hidden Easter egg whose parents are willing her on and nudging her in the right direction before, in the end, showing her where it was all along. So God by his Spirit nudges us towards wisdom and reveals it to us when he knows our search has been genuine. Attaining wisdom is never our own achievement, nor is wisdom the property of those who teach us and mediate it from God. Still less is it our private possession. It is never other than a gracious gift bestowed by God.[11]

---

[11] Waltke, *The Book of Proverbs, Chapters 1 – 15*, p. 223. Waltke stresses that this means 'the Lord alone has access to wisdom' and he, not Solomon or 'the father', is the source of it.

From that primary principle a number of other aspects of God's relation to wisdom flows.

a. Wisdom begins with the fear of God (2:5)

Recalling Proverbs 1:7, 'the fear of the LORD is the beginning of knowledge [wisdom]', we are reminded that the starting point for acquiring God's gift of wisdom is to fear him. It is the 'first and controlling principle' which one never leaves behind.[12] It might be translated that 'the essence of wisdom is to fear the Lord'. Put simply, this is what wisdom is.

But what does it mean to 'fear the Lord'? Undoubtedly, there is an emotional element to it. Fear does not mean the cringing fear of a young child abused by an alcoholic father. It does mean having a sense of reverence and proportion before a mighty and transcendent God. To fear God is to recognize our limitations in contrast to his greatness: our smallness, our dependence, our ignorance, our lack of experience, our transience. It leads to humility, without which we can neither be wise nor holy. 'The principle of wisdom', Henri Blocher writes, 'is the renouncing of autonomy, and trusting acknowledgment of the LORD at every step of one's practical or intellectual progress.'[13]

Fearing the Lord equally involves being teachable about what he reveals as his law, commandments and statutes. So it goes beyond emotion and has substance to it. God has given a general wisdom to all. The farmer, for example, has knowledge of how to sow and reap and how to care for animals. But fearing the Lord in this context refers to taking God's specific revelation of his will, which comes through his servants like Moses or Solomon, seriously.[14] Fearing him means listening to and complying with his will.

b. Wisdom leads to a knowledge of God (2:5)

The benefit of fearing God is that in doing so we will *find the knowledge of God*. To know God is not to know about him, to collect facts that have purely intellectual fascination, but to know him personally, to have a relationship with him and a degree of intimacy with him. Such intimacy is the other side of the awe which is inherent in

---

[12] D. Kidner, *Proverbs*, TOTC (London: Tyndale Press, 1964), p. 59. The phrase also occurs in Prov. 9:10; 15:33; Ps. 111:10; Job 28:28.

[13] H. Blocher, 'The Fear of the Lord as the Principle of Wisdom,' *TynBul*, 28 (1977), p. 18.

[14] See Waltke, *The Book of Proverbs, Chapters 1 – 15*, pp. 100–101 and 223–224.

fearing God. God can never be known if we put ourselves on a par with him and even less if we feel ourselves to be superior to him, as modern human beings often seem to think. A warm, loving, faithful and committed relationship is initiated in fear and equally continues to grow as we continue to stand in awe and learn humbly of him.

c. Wisdom releases blessing from God (2:6–7)

A number of blessings flow from knowing God. It is not that they are mechanical rewards like the parents promising (bribing?) their children that if they pass the exam they will be rewarded with a new bicycle. No, these blessings are the inherent consequence of knowing God. They flow implicitly from the relationship. Without knowing God we sentence ourselves 'to stumble and blunder through life blindfold, as it were, with no sense of direction and no understanding of what surrounds [us]'.[15] When we know him we have *knowledge and understanding* to guide us through life.

Furthermore, God *holds success in store for the upright.* The storing up of wisdom in the son's heart (verse 1) is matched by the storing up of success that God gives to the upright (verse 7). We should, of course, be careful as to how we interpret this. This is no blank cheque guaranteeing prosperity for those who keep God's laws. They have their share of heartache and suffering as much as others in our fallen world and the wisdom literature is fully aware of this, especially in the books of Job and Ecclesiastes. Nonetheless, it is a general truth and orienting promise. There is a correlation between knowing God and a richly resourced life.[16] Life with God is smoother, easier, more sustainable, more profitable, more hopeful, more blessed than life without him.[17] It stands to reason that it should be so. Since he is the God who made us, and the physical, moral and social world we inhabit, living in this world his way is likely to prove far more beneficial than trying to devise our own ways or, worse still, flying in his face.

The psalmists knew what it was to celebrate 'the good life' that those who walked with God could enjoy. Psalm 37, for example, in spite of David's struggle with the apparent prosperity of the wicked, knows that true security and blessing is found in trusting in God. Those are the ones whose steps the Lord makes firm. Psalm 112 is

---

[15] J. I. Packer, *Knowing God* (London: Hodder and Stoughton, 1973), pp. 14–15.
[16] Waltke, *The Book of Proverbs, Chapters 1 – 15*, p. 225, quotes Michael Fox as translating 'success' as 'resourcefulness'.
[17] Prov. 8: 35.

even more unqualified in its rejoicing. Taking up the phrase 'fear the LORD', it celebrates the way in which God-fearers enjoy a good reputation, have children who bring them honour, benefit from wealth and generosity, and enjoy security even when bad news comes. They exhibit a righteousness that not only brings them respect now but one that 'endures for ever'.

d. Wisdom results in protection by God (2:7–8)

This section ends by introducing another blessing that comes from being wise and knowing God: *he is a shield to those whose way of life is blameless, for he guards the course of the just and protects the way of his faithful ones.* Introduced here, the theme of God's protection is going to be replayed in verse 11 and illustrated in verses 12–22. There we see the kind of protection that God provides. But we should note that this promise applies to the *blameless* and the *faithful ones.* Does this mean that sinless perfection is required before we can know God's protection on our lives? Such a thought has bred many an insecurity in Christian believers, resulting in the promise having the exact opposite effect to the one it was intended to have. The terminology used here is not that of sinless perfection but of covenant loyalty. Today the promise is for all those who are living faithfully as members of the new covenant initiated by Jesus Christ.[18] Living within the covenant relationship means that they have no desire to sin and that they will not habitually do so, even if, on occasion, they fall.[19] Here, then, is a word of promise that all conscientious disciples of Jesus may trust, even if God still has more perfecting and refining to do in their lives yet.

3. The fruit of wisdom (2:9–11)

Two themes in this section replay notes that have been sounded earlier, although they bring a somewhat different emphasis to them. But the section as a whole is introduced by a new theme, that of the practical outworking of wisdom.

a. A new theme (2:9)

Wisdom has moral consequences and to be wise is to lead an ethical life. The point is underlined by the use of three similar but distinct

[18] Jer. 31:31–34; 2 Cor. 3:7–18; Heb. 8:1–13.
[19] See 1 John 3:6, 9; 1:8 – 2:2.

words in verse 9 which had previously been used as an explanation of prudent behaviour in 1:3. Through wisdom, the teacher asserts, *you will understand what is right and just and fair – every good path. Right* is that which is right according to the laws of God. *Just*, which often goes hand in hand with righteousness, relates not so much to our relationship with God but to our treatment of our fellow human beings. *Fair* suggests 'words or actions that are honest and truthful'.[20] The virtues are brought together with a metaphor, that of the *good path*, which is going to become increasingly prominent as the chapter concludes. Living wisely, in the fear and knowledge of God provides a good way to walk, a good way forward in life, free from the fears of it leading nowhere, or that life will prove dangerous and its obstacles insurmountable.

Wisdom, it tells us, is to be measured neither by emotional well-being, nor the giving of lofty but detached advice, nor by shifting cultural norms, nor by pragmatic tests of what works,[21] but by how closely one lives in obedience to God. The test of wisdom is ethical.

Here is the sort of life described in a different way by Psalm 15 when it asks who is fit to enter the Lord's presence in Jerusalem. The psalm not only repeats the need for the virtues we have met in Proverbs 2 – those of wholeheartedness, righteousness and truthfulness – but also points to the need for those who come into God's presence to live ethically in every dimension of their lives, whether that be in the community, the moral, the religious, the commercial, or the social and political aspects of living.

b. Repeated notes (2:10–11)

Two themes that have been heard before follow in verses 10 and 11. The need for wisdom to *enter your heart* is mentioned again. Waltke[22] sees here not just a repetition of what was said in verse 2 but a reference to the transformation of the heart as prophesied by Jeremiah[23] and Ezekiel[24] and as became possible in Jesus.[25] To live wisely we need more than education; we need regeneration, the life-giving transformation of our dead hearts by the Spirit of God.[26] When wisdom become part of us – 'your own way of thinking, and

[20] Estes, *Hear, My Son,* p. 51.
[21] Ibid.
[22] Waltke, *The Book of Proverbs, Chapters 1 – 15,* p. 227.
[23] Jer. 24:7; 31:31–34; 32:37–41.
[24] Ezek. 36:26–27.
[25] John 3:5–8.
[26] Eph. 2:4–5.

your acquired taste'[27] – then other ways of thinking and acting lose their appeal and we gain an appetite for living to please God.

The function of wisdom as standing guard over our lives is the second theme to be repeated here. This time the new element is the focus on how God, the protector of verses 7 and 8, does his work. Protection comes from God by our learning *discretion* and *understanding*. They prove to be watchful sentries by alerting us to the difference between right and wrong, encouraging us to shun the temptation to do wrong, and building into our lives godly habits that, while they do not makes us immune from sin, act substantially as preventative medicine and cause us to live healthy lives for God.

4. The antithesis of wisdom (2:12–19)

Like a good teacher, Proverbs not only sets out the lesson positively but drives it home by illustrating it negatively. Neatly balanced, the teacher refers to wicked men (12–15) and an adulterous woman (16–19). The catchwords throughout have to do with the paths we tread.

a. Wicked men (2:12–15)

The description is general so as to encompass any number of people whose words lack integrity, whose behaviour is undesirable and whose ways are devious. The people are readily recognized by the way they are described further in the Psalms.[28] They speak well of you to your face but ill of you behind your back. They are plausible friends on the surface while stabbing you in the back. They seem pillars of the community but everyone knows in truth that they are parasites in the community, living off the blood of others. They promise everything while delivering little. They seem so caring while being heartless, putting the poor and unprotected out on the streets. Their way of life seems so patently evil that one wonders what the attraction is, especially to one who has had a half-decent, moral education. But sin would not be a problem if it were not pleasurable, and these men are seduced by the thrill of the hunt, the buzz of the game, the power they can wield and the fortunes they can accumulate. Their life-style, self-confidence and apparent autonomy can prove seductive to anyone who is not fully committed to searching out wisdom.

[27] Kidner, *Proverbs,* p. 62.
[28] See, for example, Pss 10; 11; 36; 37; 58; 73.

Furthermore, this path may be *dark* and *crooked*, but we don't always appreciate that to begin with. Our first hesitant steps down the path of evil often lie in the semi-light and before the path twists too much. But before long, we find ourselves trapped by those first few feet and unable to retrace our steps to the light. It is better to erect a big 'no entry' sign at the entry to the path and to avoid falling into the wrong company in the first place, just as Psalm 1, the introduction to the whole of the Psalms, taught so forcefully.

b. An adulterous woman (2:11–19)

Given the power of our sexual drives, the ability of an adulterous woman to seduce a man may seem more intelligible than the ability of the men we have just mentioned to tempt people into other kinds of wickedness. The frequency with which sexual sin is mentioned in Proverbs 1 – 9[29] testifies to the way in which it was, and still is, a common human failing. But while it might be more understandable, it is no less disastrous. It is not right to dismiss sexual dalliance as a one-night fling, an unfortunate trifle, or a purely physical but otherwise meaningless act. Proverbs goes to the heart of the matter. The adulterous woman *has left the partner of her youth and ignored the covenant she made before God.* The same, of course, is true of the male in the illicit partnership, assuming he is married. The issue cannot be dealt with as a discussion about mechanical sex; it has to be dealt with as a discussion about faithfulness and integrity, obligation and responsibility, and it involves God as well as other people.

As before, the simple first steps may well lead to the point of no return and then, far from making life richer, its only destination is death. Wisdom dictates this as a path to be avoided.

5. The value of wisdom (2:20–22)

The image of the path, which has been in the background to this point, now comes centre-stage. In words that are reminiscent of Psalm 1, the father encourages his son to *walk in the ways of the just and keep to the paths of the righteous.* The teaching of Proverbs will prove a sure guide in the journey of life and departure from it is likely to lead one into danger. Hill climbers face enough perils due to changing weather conditions or the sudden descent of fog without endangering themselves by striking out on an uncharted

---

[29] Prov. 5:1–14, 19–20; 6:20–35; 7:1–27; 9:13–18. This promiscuous woman stands in contrast to the Lady Wisdom of Prov. 8.

path of their own. That route leads to disaster and the need to call out the mountain rescue team. So why risk it? There is wisdom in keeping to 'the ancient paths'.[30]

The picture of walking, with its emphasis on activity, gives way to the picture of dwelling, with its emphasis on belonging. *For the upright will live in the land, and the blameless will remain in it.* No doubt this originally applied to the promise given to the children of Israel of the land of Canaan but it may rightly be taken to be a wider metaphor.[31] The path of life will be safe if one walks in the way of wisdom but better even than that, the experience of life will be settled because we enjoy the security of being 'at home' in God's world. Not for nothing have modern people been described, by respected and perceptive commentators, as suffering from 'homeless minds'.[32] Unlike the wicked who have no long-term future (22), and unlike the restless who are desperately looking for guidance everywhere except where it may be found, those who pursue wisdom are people who enjoy stability, even, as Psalm 112:6–7 points out, when bad news comes.[33] They are content without being complacent, and steadfast without being arrogant, for they know how much more wisdom they have yet to learn. They live in God's world as he intended, and are at home with him. Home is where they belong.

6. Concluding comment

Proverbs provides us with a variation of the theme of holiness. Far from being concerned with the superficialities of life or with providing commonplace mottos for the day, its real concern is with the development of godly character. The essence of wisdom is to fear the Lord. Without that no progress can be made in developing godliness. The lessons have to go deep, entering our heart, and not lie on the surface of our lives. True godliness does not arise from legalistic obedience to external rules but from the formation of characters moulded by wisdom. What is in the heart must then work itself out in everyday living, in the conduct of an ethical life and the avoidance of temptation and folly. Wisdom is something we must vigorously pursue, and yet remains a gift from God, just as holiness is both

[30] Jer. 6:16.
[31] Waltke, *The Book of Proverbs, Chapters 1 – 15*, p. 234. On the question of land, see, L. Perdue, *Proverbs*, pp. 87, 93–95 and C. J. H. Wright, *Old Testament Ethics for the People of God* (Leicester: IVP, 2004), pp. 182–211.
[32] P. L. Berger, B. Berger and H. Kellner, *The Homeless Mind* (Harmondsworth: Penguin, 1974).
[33] See also Prov. 1:33.

something we pursue and a gift from God. It is the path to knowing him and enjoying his blessings on our lives. Proverbs shows us what holiness looks like in our working clothes rather than our 'Sunday best'. To be wise is to be holy. To be holy is to be wise.

Isaiah 58:1–14
6. Holiness as justice

Along with the siren call of Amos to 'let justice roll on like a river, righteousness like a never-failing stream!'[1] and the penetrating interrogation of Micah, 'And what does the LORD require of you? To act justly and to love mercy and to walk humbly with your God,'[2] Isaiah 58 provides us with a classic statement of a prophetic understanding of holiness. 'Few passages in . . . Isaiah', writes Paul Hanson, 'reach across the centuries with as much power as this chapter. It requires no fancy interpretive ploys. Its message addresses the heart as passionately today as it did in the sixth century B.C.E. One cannot read these fourteen verses without the sense of having been addressed by God . . .'[3]

Throughout the prophecy of Isaiah the holiness of God is the warp and the obligation of justice the weft of the fabric of Israel. They are, as it were, as inseparable as salt and pepper, fish and chips, or a horse and carriage. When Isaiah thinks of one, he automatically thinks of the other. As we saw in chapter 2, Isaiah is 'the prophet of holiness'[4] who, more than any other, sees God as in essence holy. Isaiah 57:15 characteristically presents God as 'the high and exalted One . . . who lives for ever, whose name is holy'. A holy God requires a holy people and to be holy is to display compassionate justice in our dealings with others.

Isaiah 58 is an extended commentary on the call that comes at the beginning of Isaiah to 'Stop doing wrong, learn to do right! Seek justice [*mišpāṭ*],[5] encourage the oppressed. Defend the cause of the

---

[1] Amos 5:24.
[2] Micah 6:8.
[3] P. D. Hanson, *Isaiah 40 – 66*, Int (Louisville: John Knox Press, 1995), p. 207.
[4] See p. 42 for details.
[5] 'This justice was not merely civil righteousness, but right judgment in every sphere of life. The *mišpāṭ* is the judgment which has been pronounced in accord-

fatherless, plead the case of the widow' (Isaiah 1:16–17). A critique of religious observance, which is divorced from ethical obedience, is implicit throughout. Given the parallels with Nehemiah, many scholars believe this prophecy is addressed to specific issues of economic instability and social fragmentation that arose after the exile when Israel was restored to its own land.[6] Such a concrete setting prevents us from reading this as merely poetic idealism. At the same time, however, the prophecy contains truths that need to be heard by every generation of believers.

For all its passion, the prophecy is not an undisciplined eruption of unconnected thoughts but a carefully structured address that may be understood as follows:

A God speaks (1)
   B False fasting exposed (2–5)
      C True fasting explained (6–7)
         D The rewards of true worship (8–9b)
      C[1] True fasting emphasized (9c–10b)
         D[1] The rewards of true worship underlined (10c–12)
   B[1] True feasting commended (13–14c)
A[1] God has spoken (14d)

1. God speaks (58:1)

God's voice pierces the silence like a trumpet blast, condemning his people for their *rebellion* and *sins,* which are set out in what follows. The harsh tone recalls the earlier voice of the prophets who condemned Israel before the exile,[7] reminding the people that even when the dreadful experience of the exile is over, they cannot take their obedience to God for granted and are required to serve him on his terms, not their own.

The directness of the speech, however, should not be confused with a scornful attitude. Over a century ago, George Adam Smith viewed this chapter as a master class in preaching and commented:

ance with the absolute will of the LORD and is, therefore, right judgment in accordance with strict justice and truth.' E. J. Young, *The Book of Isaiah,* Vol. 1, NICOT (Grand Rapids: Eerdmans, 1965), p. 73.

[6] P. D. Hanson, *Isaiah 40 – 66,* p. 204, J. D. W. Watts, *Isaiah 34 – 66,* WBC (Waco: Word, 1987), pp. 265–267, 271. Some conservative scholars insist Isaiah 58 was addressed to an earlier context in Jerusalem rather than being addressed to a post-exilic audience.

[7] The words used are similar to Hos. 8:1 and Mic. 3:8.

Perhaps no subject more readily provokes to satire and sneers than the subject of this chapter, – the union of formal religion and unlovely life. And yet in this chapter there is not a sneer from first to last. The speaker suppresses the temptation to use the nasal tones, and utters, not as the satirist, but as the prophet. For his purpose is not to sport with his people's hypocrisy, but to sweep them out of it. Before he has done, his urgent speech, that has not lingered to sneer or exhausted itself in screaming passes forth to spend its unchecked impetus upon final promise and gospel. It is a wise lesson from a master preacher, and half of the fruitlessness of modern preaching is due to the neglect of it. The pulpit tempts men to be either too bold or too timid about sin; either to whisper or to scold; to euphemise or to exaggerate; to be conventional or hysterical. But two things are necessary, – the facts must be stated, and the whole manhood of the preacher . . . brought to bear upon them.[8]

2. False fasting exposed (58:2–5)

The popular mind associates the word 'holy' with words like 'religious', or 'pious', or 'church'. Ironically, the address God delivers through Isaiah dispels any thought of an automatic connection between them. The people Isaiah addresses were certainly religious and outwardly displayed all the hallmarks of piety. Their worship was regular: *day after day they seek me out* (2). Their worship was sincere: *they seem eager to know my ways . . . They ask me for just decisions and seem eager for God to come near them* (2). The word *seem* should not be read as casting doubt on their sincerity but rather as emphasising their desire.[9] Their worship was fervent, since they were *eager* to find out God's ways.

The impression that their worship was assiduous is further underlined by their practice of fasting. Fasting had been reserved for occasions of national calamity but after the exile fasts were observed regularly four times a year to commemorate episodes in the downfall of the nation.[10] During the fast they lamented their situation and prayed for the restoration of Israel to its former glory. Like other religious observances they were punctilious in keeping the fasts and

---

[8] G. A. Smith, *The Book of Isaiah XL – LXVI*, The Expositor's Bible (London: Hodder and Stoughton, 1890), p. 417.

[9] J. Goldingay, *Isaiah*, NIBC (Peabody: Hendrickson, 2001), p. 325 and A. Motyer, *The Prophecy of Isaiah* (Leicester: IVP, 1993), p. 479.

[10] The four episodes were the day when the siege began; the fall of Jerusalem (2 Kgs 25:3–21); the destruction of the temple (Jer. 52:12–13); and the murder of Gedaliah (2 Kgs 25:23–25). See Watts, *Isaiah 34 – 66*, p. 273.

yet they could tell for themselves that it was to no purpose. God had not apparently taken any notice of their prayer-filled self-denial as they might reasonably have expected him to (3). Their worship seemed to be futile.

Their worship was indeed an empty and worthless act and the prophet proceeds to explain to them why. What may have begun as a time for doing serious business with God, soon degenerated into a public holiday in which worship receded into the background. It became a day in which *you do as you please* (3) with the result that it ended in *quarrelling, strife* and violence (4). Those whose ostensible business was prayer had turned into the sort of brawling mob we are used to seeing at some contemporary sports fixtures. But there was an added dimension to their stupidity in that on the very day when they fasted they also exploited their workers (3).[11] They may have found the days pleasurable but their workers found them days of further weary toil. Given the precarious economic circumstances they faced, it was easy to victimize the weaker members of society and take advantage of cheap labour to further the interests of the more powerful.[12] The employers were riding roughshod over the sabbath principle, which was designed in part to protect the interests of workers and prevent their exploitation,[13] with the result that they condemned their employees to a new slavery. It is a matter to which Isaiah will return at the end of his address (13–14).

So, Isaiah patiently explains that they cannot *expect [their] voice to be heard on high,* for God is against all oppression, whatever its source, whether Egypt, Assyria, Babylon or Israel itself. The fast has no intrinsic merit in its own right. The rituals of bowing one's head, like a wilting plant without water[14] and abasing oneself in *sackcloth and ashes* give God no pleasure as such. Like a reduced student rail fare, where the ticket is only valid if accompanied by a correct student identity card, so their fasts only have value when accompanied by a life of compassionate justice. God is looking for more than *only a day* (5) on which people go through these religious rituals. He is looking for a life, lived in daily obedience and considerate righteousness.

---

[11] Watts offers a minority translation of 'exploit all your workers' as 'you suppress all your pains' and writes of fasting as giving the people escapist pleasure as envisaged in Marx's view that 'religion is the opiate of the people' which acts as a sedative to disguise the true misery of their situation. Watts, *Isaiah 34 – 66*, p. 274.

[12] Neh. 5:1–19.

[13] Exod. 20:8–11; Deut. 5:12–15.

[14] Watts, *Isaiah 34 – 66*, p. 274.

3. The nature of true worship (58:6–7)

From negative condemnation, Isaiah turns to a positive explanation of the sort of religious observance, symbolized by fasting, that
causes God pleasure. Pleasing God involves the creation of a just
society, caring for vulnerable individuals within it and accepting
one's family obligations.

'Doing justice', Walter Brueggemann explains, 'is not simply
keeping the rule, but consists in the venturesome enactment of
positive good.'[15] The obligation of Israel to practise justice was not
about the duty to mete out retributive justice on criminals but about
creating the conditions in society that would enable every member
of the community to be treated with dignity and to sustain a life free
from exploitation. Verse 6 focuses on this element of the fast God
chooses as it calls 'for the abolition of every way in which wrong
social structures, or wrongdoers in society, destroy or diminish the
due liberty of others' and 'the need to eliminate every way in which
people are treated like animals'.[16] Amelioration is not enough.
Nothing less than the abolition of injustice is required.

Nehemiah 5 gives a powerful example of how detailed economic
and political policy can accomplish these ends. When wealthy Jews
greedily exploited the economically vulnerable around the partly-
restored Jerusalem, Nehemiah told them they should walk in the fear
of the Lord, insisted they stopped charging interest and immediately
return property and interest that they had unjustly taken. Although
the Governor, he himself set an example by refusing to use his
various entitlements 'out of reverence for God' (Nehemiah 5:15).

Verse 7 gives some individual examples of those who would be
in special need of care – the hungry, the homeless and the naked –
without feeling the need to analyse what had caused them to be in
this condition in the first place. The reference to not turning *away
from your own flesh and blood* may be a general reference to humans
all being made in the creator's image but is more likely to highlight
the particular responsibilities that family members had towards
other family members who had fallen on hard times, as is beautifully
illustrated in the book of Ruth. This is yet another example of the
Bible's consistent witness to '*a radical sensitivity to suffering* that
pervades the biblical narrative from the exodus to the cross'.[17]

---

[15] W. Brueggemann, *Theology of the Old Testament: Testimony, Dispute,
Advocacy* (Minneapolis: Fortress Press, 1997), p. 461.

[16] Motyer, *The Prophecy of Isaiah*, p. 481.

[17] J. R. Middleton and B. J. Walsh, *Truth is Stranger than it Used to be* (London:
SPCK, 1995), p. 87. Italics theirs.

The positive call to act in the interests of liberty and to work for the overthrow of injustice necessarily carries with it a critique of the way many then and now live. In Brueggemann's words,

> Such a command, understood as a poignant reflection of Yahweh's own way in the world (as evidenced in the Exodus), clearly is intrusive in and critical of a life of self-protection, self-sufficiency, and self-indulgence. The mandate marks Israel as a community that practises intense openness to the neighbour, and it balances the openness by a keen sense of self-criticism about sociopolitical-economic advantage. That is, the function of these commandments is not to protect acquired advantage, but to call that advantage into question when it does not benefit the community.[18]

4. The rewards of true worship (58:8–9b)

In a chiastic structure[19], like this prophecy, the crossover point is usually where the most important element of the teaching is to be found. It invites attention as everything before it leads up to it and everything after it leads away from it. So, in Isaiah 58, it is not condemnation which is the key message but the longing of God to renew 'free-flowing fellowship'[20] with his people. Having ignored 'the law that gives freedom' and having turned it into an instrument of oppression, the supercilious fasters might have expected to be judged without mercy. But once more, 'Mercy triumphs over judgment.'[21]

A host of blessings will be unleashed on them as soon as Israel starts to live as God requires. A new day will dawn and a new phase in life begin as *light will break forth like the dawn* (8). *Healing* of past sicknesses caused by their foolish way of life *will quickly appear* (8) so they need no longer be dogged by the failures or guilt of yesterday. They will experience God's protection as Israel had done before when they travelled through the wilderness.[22] On this occasion, righteousness would be their advance guard, going before them 'to meet Yahweh as a kind of ambassador to plead their cause'.[23] God himself, then, in all his glory would be their rear

---

[18] Brueggemann, *Theology of the Old Testament,* p. 423.

[19] A chiastic structure is X-shaped, where the first part crosses over with the second part, or the first part is mirrored in the second part.

[20] Motyer, *The Prophecy of Isaiah,* p. 482.

[21] Jas 2:12–13.

[22] Exod. 13:21–23.

[23] R. N. Whybray, *Isaiah 40 – 66,* NCBC (Grand Rapids: Eerdmans and London: Marshall, Morgan and Scott: London, 1981), p. 216.

guard.[24] Added to all this would be the benefit that *you will cry for help, and he will say: here am I* (9). The long hours of the night when God was silent would have come to an end and once more they would experience easy communication with their Lord.

5. The nature of true worship re-iterated (58:9c–10b)

On the surface the next section is a repetition of verses 6 and 7, but although the thrust of the message is the same, there are differences. These verses start with the *If . . .* part of an *if . . . then* sandwich with the *then* part coming half way through verse 10. The image of the fast has been left behind but the image of the *yoke* is picked up from verse 6 and, if anything, is intensified in the phrase *yoke of oppression*. The *pointing finger and malicious talk* are novel but could be another way of talking about the *quarrelling* which was mentioned in verse 4. The *pointing finger*, however, might imply something more than a mere gesture of rudeness and indicate that the one pointing was seeking to invoke evil on his opponent by using magic.[25]

The real difference between this and the previous comment on the nature of true religion is that this paragraph personalizes it more. The earlier comment was largely a statement of principle. This is unavoidably a statement of personal practice. There can be no sheltering behind social policy here or arguing that injustice in society is someone else's fault. *You* is intentionally personal. It comes as a warning against having merely a theoretical interest in world poverty but then ignoring the homeless people on your own doorstep. The *you* of these verses is inclusive of us all. If every member of the church took these words seriously, community transformation would begin. Nearby there are people wanting a listening ear and practical support. Tim Chester has estimated that 'within a short walk of the average town church in the UK there are likely to be 10,000 people including:

- 1,200 people living alone, 580 of whom will be of pensionable age
- 1,500 people who talk to their neighbours less than once a week
- 50 people who have been divorced in the last year
- 375 single parents
- 18 pregnant teenagers
- 150 recent or contemplated abortions

---

[24] Exod. 16:10.
[25] Whybray, *Isaiah 40 – 66*, p. 217. See Prov. 6:13.

- 250 people who are unemployed
- 1,700 people living in low income households
- 1,100 people with some kind of mental disorder
- 100 bereavements within the last year
- 2,700 people living in households without a car
- 60 people in a residential care home
- 1,280 people caring for a sick, disabled or elderly relative or friend
- 2,800 people who have been victims of crime in the past year
- 40 homeless people in temporary accommodation
- 15 asylum seekers.'[26]

We cannot do it all, but we can start somewhere. Isaiah's call is not only to challenge oppression but, more than that, to live in such a way ourselves that we do not perpetuate it. To *spend yourselves on behalf of the hungry* means that generosity must replace greed, open-handedness must displace acquisitiveness, and practical compassion must supplant merely theoretical interest.

6. The rewards of true worship underlined (58:10c–12)

The *then* part of the sandwich begins with the familiar imagery of verses 8 and 9. The blessings of living righteously are once again mentioned as *light* rising and dispelling the *darkness,* and The LORD being a guide through the wilderness. But Isaiah now develops the image of the wilderness, leading to a new idea being introduced as a promise for the future and then to a second promise which is particularly apt for those who would one day return from exile.

The wilderness is *a sun-scorched land.* Both stamina and water are needed if Israel was to negotiate its way through the wilderness successfully. Hence God promises to *strengthen your frame* and to make them *a well-watered garden, like a spring whose waters never fail.* The image of the parched and barren ground being revived and becoming fruitful again, because of the irrigation of God's Spirit, is a familiar one in Isaiah, and understandably so, given how much they depended on water for their sheer survival.[27] But it also had particular significance because it was a reminder that in an earlier chapter of their nation's history, God had miraculously provided for them. 'They did not thirst when he led them through the deserts;

---

[26] Tim Chester, *Good News to the Poor* (Leicester: IVP, 2004), p. 132.

[27] Isa. 12:3; 27:3; 32:2; 33:16; 35:6–7; 41:18; 44:3; 49:10. The metaphor was not limited to Isaiah. See especially Ezek. 47:1–12 and Zech. 14:8. Jesus applies the latter to himself in John 7:37–39.

he made water flow for them from the rock; he split the rock and water gushed out' (Isaiah 48:21).[28] What God had done for his needy people before he would do for his repentant people now, if only they would amend their lives.

A picture from the wilderness gives way to a picture from the city. The ability of God to bless his people was not limited to the early days of the wilderness but was equally sufficient for their need in the urban setting of the Promised Land, to which they had been restored. Although the need for water remained constant, their more immediate concern was that the city that had housed God's dwelling place now lay in ruins. Isaiah promises that it will not always be so but that they would *rebuild the ancient ruins and will raise up the age-old foundations*. Deserted streets would again become bustling with life and empty shells restored as family homes. They would recover from past disasters and know the blessing of God leading them into a joyful future.

7. The feast God commends (13–14c)

Isaiah then takes what looks like a sudden change of direction, but isn't. In what is clearly a new section, he continues his *if . . . then* approach but the *if* now concerns the observance of the sabbath. The immediate impression is that he is about to undo all that he had achieved to this point. Had he now been trumpeting the message that religious worship in and of itself is of no value? If so, why is he now cautioning them against *breaking the Sabbath* (13)? Is that not to fall into the very trap of pious legalism and of potential external hypocrisy he has been condemning?

To read it this way is to miss the point. These verses respond to the puzzles raised in verses 2–5, as not only the substance but also the vocabulary suggests. On their fast days they found pleasure in doing as they pleased (3). By contrast the sabbath was a day when they were required to abstain from *doing as you please* (13) because it was a day set apart for God. It was his pleasure, not theirs, that should be uppermost. One way in which they pleased themselves was by working on the sabbath, despite God's clear instruction to the contrary.[29] Moreover, if they sought to please God, there would be no room for the *quarrelling and strife* of verse 4, or *the point-ing finger and malicious talk* of verse 9. Rather they would live in harmony with each other.

[28] The background is found in Exod. 17:1–7 and Num. 20:1–13.
[29] Goldingay, *Isaiah*, p. 327.

There is also an unexpressed, but no less important, assumption here that is germane to the complaint God has against them. If they were to honour the sabbath as God intended, they would be prevented from exploiting their workers.[30] The sabbath legislation was never designed as a tyranny that imposed a rigid inactivity on people, thereby reducing them to a state of mind-numbing boredom. It was meant to ensure freedom from the tyranny of labour and space to restore balance in life. As Jesus reminded the people of his day, 'The Sabbath was made for people, not people for the Sabbath' (Mark 2:27).

The Mosaic legislation emphasized that the sabbath laws covered servants and foreigners. The leisure of the seventh day was not to be enjoyed by the rich at the expense of the poor. All were to enjoy the day off. In a society where the demands of land and flock could be relentless, it created a pause and acted as a relief. One purpose of the sabbath law was to ensure that the Israelites never treated others as they themselves had been treated in Egypt: 'Remember that you were slaves in Egypt' (so, no sabbath there!) 'and that the LORD your God brought you out of there with a mighty hand and an outstretched arm' (so, do not subject others to that awful experience of slavery).[31] But that, according to verse 3, was the very sin they were committing in the name of observing a sacred fast. In reinforcing the sabbath law, then, Isaiah in not inviting them to practise pharisaic legalism but liberating social justice.

The *if*, of verse 13, is followed by the *then*, of verse 14. Obeying God's law is found to be the true source of *joy*. True pleasure is not to be found in doing as one likes but in walking humbly before one's Maker. True success is to be found on the same paths. The busy merchants of Israel who feared that taking time off for proper worship might lead them to lose business and give the edge to their competitors, had to learn that the reverse was true. Those who obeyed God rather than served self would, says Isaiah, using the words of Deuteronomy 32:13, be caused *to ride in triumph on the heights of the land* (14). Many a businessman could testify to the truth of these words. Honouring God rather than merely going with the drift of tyrannical (and sometimes dishonest) business practices leads to true prosperity and a satisfied and motivated workforce.

---

[30] Ibid., p. 328. Goldingay argues that the focus is on the sabbath as holy and therefore as developing proper attitudes to God, rather than on the well-being of the people. In strict terms he is right but there is surely no need to divorce the twin aspects of the sabbath legislation from each other, which is both holy to the Lord and beneficial to the people, especially in view of the context here.

[31] Deut. 5:15.

Continuing the reference to Deuteronomy 32:13, the climax of God's blessing in Israel is being invited not to a fast but to a feast: *to feast on the inheritance of your father Jacob* (14). 'The Lord', as Alec Motyer has rightly said, 'is more interested in enjoyment of his blessings through obedience than in self-imposed deprivations.'[32]

Isaiah, then, does not seek to do away with the rituals of worship, but only to invest them with true meaning. They are empty rituals unless the worshipper lives a life full of compassionate justice. This means, as Tony Campolo has recently suggested, 'the prophet would have strong words for those in our present world who are heavily into worship but, like those in ancient Israel, have done little in working for social justice. Worship', he writes, 'which has become the dominant part of the life of evangelical and Pentecostal churches, must be coupled with not only loving charity, but also to justice on behalf of the poorest of the poor of the world.'[33]

8. God has spoken (14d)

The prophecy ends where it began. The prophet was instructed to *Shout it aloud, do not hold back. Raise your voice like a trumpet* (1). Having done so, the people are reminded that these are not his word but words that *the mouth of the LORD has spoken* (14).

9. Concluding comment

The message is plain. Holiness is not synonymous with religion, or adequately expressed merely in devotional piety. More than ritual observance is required. A holy God requires a holy life and a holy life requires that we spend ourselves in the cause of justice and avoid living in a way that perpetuates injustice. In the complex world in which we live, which has now shrunk to a global village, we in the West are more aware of the cost of our lifestyles to others than earlier generations. This can lead to being overwhelmed with the immensity of the task and to paralysis of action. But in recent years the churches have taken some bold initiatives that have put them in the forefront of seeking to overcome poverty and combat AIDS. There are now plenty of avenues by which we can fulfil the mandate of Isaiah 58 both individually and as local churches, from

[32] Motyer, *The Prophecy of Isaiah*, p. 483.
[33] T. Campolo, 'Isaiah 58: The Fast God Requires' in M. Hoek and J. Thacker (eds.), *Micah's Challenge* (Milton Keynes: Paternoster, 2008), p. 94.

buying Fair Trade goods to becoming a Jubilee or Micah Challenge church.[34] As it was for Isaiah's original hearers, so it is for us. The real challenge is whether or not we will obey the word the Lord has spoken.

[34] Details can be found on various related websites or in Hoek and Thacker (eds.), ibid., pp. 164–199.

Part 3
The transformation of holiness

Luke 1:35; 4:1, 34; 23:41
7. Holiness personified

Jesus is holiness personified. In him, holiness ceases to be an unattainable ideal and becomes a reality; it ceases to be an aspiration and becomes an actuality. Academic discussions about the nature of holiness and hidebound rules are totally eclipsed by the sight of one who is holy through and through. Holiness is exhibited in his every move. It is displayed in his every conversation. If we want to understand what it is to be holy, we need do no more than look to Jesus Christ. In fact, there is nowhere else we can look and see perfect holiness.

There is no single discussion of the holiness of Jesus in the Gospels, and the word 'holy' and associated words are rarely used. Holiness is rather woven into the fabric of the Gospels and to pull the thread of holiness is not to remove an element of his life but to cause the whole of it to unravel. It is possible to see the different nuances of holiness being emphasized by the different Gospel writers. Matthew, with his emphasis on righteousness, presents Jesus as the one who fulfils all righteousness.[1] Mark, with his emphasis on the arrival of the kingdom and the resulting conflict of powers, shows him as exhibiting the awesome power of God.[2] Luke, with his emphasis on the Holy Spirit and compassion for sinners, displays him as the fulfilment of the prophetic vision of holiness as justice.[3] John associates holiness with the glory of God and presents Christ as both glorifying his Father on earth and being glorified by his Father.[4]

Rather than ranging over the four Gospels, however, I have chosen some references in Luke's Gospel as the framework for considering the holiness of Jesus.

[1] E.g., Matt. 3:15.
[2] E.g., Mark 1:24; 8:38.
[3] E.g., Luke 4:16–21.
[4] E.g., John 17:1–5.

1. Holiness and the uniqueness of Christ (Luke 1:35)

The angel said to her, 'The Holy Spirit will come upon you, and the power of the Most High will overshadow you; therefore the child to be born will be holy; he will be called Son of God' (NRSV).[5]

Luke sets out his stall right at the beginning. Before Jesus is born, an angel announces to his virgin mother that he would be *holy*. Immediately we are confronted with the special nature of this baby and the special relationship he enjoys with God the Father. The high priests of Israel were made holy through ordination and others became holy as they were separated from ordinary people and dedicated exclusively to the service of God. But this child was not to become holy, or to be made holy but, from the beginning, he was to be holy. It was his nature and character to be separate *from* others, whilst being fully human and sharing human life without reserve. It was his nature to be separate *for* God and always to say an unqualified 'Yes' to God's will though his fellow humans were less than totally obedient to that will.[6] Some choose to draw the sting of these verses by arguing that every firstborn son was holy and, according to the law,[7] was consecrated to God, until a redemption price was paid. Furthermore, the addition of the title *Son of God* does little, they say, to mark him out as unique, for are we not all sons of God born in God's image; were not the covenant people of God all sons of his; and is not the title used to designate other servants of God in the Old Testament?[8]

The dilution of the uniqueness of Christ as contained in these verses, however, is to be resisted on two grounds. First, there can be no doubt that the cumulative effect of all that is said in verses 29–37 is meant to signal that he is unmatched by anyone else. He is 'the Son of the Most High' (1:32), whereas John, his cousin, is only 'a prophet of the Most High' (1:76). He is to inherit the throne of David from which he will rule not for a limited time but eternally (1:32–33). The Holy Spirit is to play a unique role in his generation.[9] He is to be born to a virgin, not by natural human

---

[5] The verse may be translated either as in TNIV or NRSV. NRSV is to be preferred in making *holy* the object of the verb *called*, making *Son of God* an additional explanation, rather than making *the holy one* the subject of the sentence as in TNIV. See J. Nolland, *Luke 1 – 9:20,* WBC (Dallas: Word, 1989), p. 55.

[6] Luke 22:42; John 4:34; 6:38.

[7] E.g., Exod. 13:1–13, cf. Luke 2:23.

[8] E.g., Exod. 4: 22; Deut. 1:31; 14:1; 2 Sam 7:14; Ps. 2:7; Hos. 1:10.

[9] Richard Bauckham says, 'Jesus' origin is unparalleled in previous human history since Adam and Eve.' Cited by K. Brower, *Holiness in the Gospels* (Kansas City: Beacon Hill Press, 2005), p. 46.

conception (1:35–36).[10] While his cousin John is called to prepare the way for the message of salvation (1:76), his very name, Jesus, points to him being the saviour (1:31). The second reason why the minimalist interpretation of these words is unacceptable is because of the way in which we see his sonship developing in Luke. In his case, to be a son evidently meant something special and out of the ordinary.[11]

There can be no doubt that Luke intends us to know that the one called *holy* is in a class of his own. He is the Son of God in the fullest sense as John expressed it in the introduction of his Gospel; 'the one and only [Son], who is himself God and is in the closest relationship with the Father. . .' (1:18). His sonship affects the very essence of his being, not just his role on earth.[12] He has 'a uniquely favoured status and relationship to God'[13] which is well described not only by his being designated *Son* but by his also being called *holy.* He is set apart to be the one means of salvation from sin.

The word *holy,* as we have discovered, is a complex word which has many aspects to its meaning. One aspect of holiness is separation. Traditionally, this was, in fact, considered the essence of holiness since the root of the Hebrew word lies in 'that which is marked off, separated, withdrawn from ordinary use'.[14] In describing Jesus as *holy* before he was born, the angel was stressing the aspect of holiness that relates to his separateness. It does not yet relate to his ethical goodness, though that will emerge from it.[15] It does not relate to his power over evil, though his holy and majestic power over all evil and impurity are inherent within it and will become apparent. It does not involve a claim to sinlessness, though his moral perfection is evident throughout his ministry. The angel's claim does not exhaust all that the Gospels portray about the holiness of Jesus from Nazareth. But it is the essential soil through which the other aspects surface. Jesus is without equal, anointed by God and, in an unparalleled relationship with him as his Son, he is called to live as a 'son of Adam' (3:38). And yet he is separate from other human beings, and so fulfils the unique mission of being the saviour of fallen humanity.

---

[10] On the virgin birth see L. W. Hurtado, *Lord Jesus Christ: Devotion to Jesus in Earliest Christianity* (Grand Rapids: Eerdmans, 2003), pp. 327–330.

[11] Luke 3:21–22, 38; 4:1, 3, 9, 14 and 18.

[12] Joel Green, *The Gospel of Luke,* NICNT (Grand Rapids: Eerdmans, 1997), p. 91, writes, 'though Luke is not working with Johannine or later trinitarian categories, he is nonetheless moving toward a more ontological (and not only a functional) understanding of Jesus' sonship'.

[13] Hurtado, *Lord Jesus Christ,* p. 108.

[14] W. Eichrodt, *Theology of the Old Testament,* Vol. 1., trans. J. A. Baker (London: SCM, 1961), p. 270.

[15] R. H. Stein, *Luke,* NAC (Nashiville: Broadman Press, 1992), p. 85.

Ironically, it is the combination of his separateness from and his identity with humans that is going to overcome the separation between human beings and God which sin had caused.

2. Holiness and the goodness of Christ (Luke 4:1)

Jesus, full of the Holy Spirit. . .
It is not long in Luke's Gospel before we are acquainted with another aspect of Jesus' holiness, that of his ethical goodness.

a. The temptations (Luke 4:1–13)

The very first episode in the ministry of Jesus after his baptism sees him facing down the temptations that Satan puts to him in the wilderness. This was no accident for Luke stresses that he *was led by the Spirit into the wilderness* (4:1) and, though physically weakened by hunger, was *full of the Holy Spirit* when he met the devil. It was necessary for him to be tested if he was to prove to be the saviour of the world. The temptations were real, not fictional. Jesus lives under the same conditions as any human being. He has no special protection that insulates him from sin's seductive power. He cannot retreat behind his divinity so that the temptations glide off him like water off a duck's back. He meets the temptations like any other human being, feeling the full force of Satan's barely-resistible attractions. In this he proves his true humanity and only by undergoing this to the fullest extent could he be qualified to redeem our humanity. We are only able to be certain that he atoned for our sin and not his own because he proved his ability in the wilderness to refuse sin when it attacked him full-on at a vulnerable time.

The temptations (4:1–13) particularly relate to Jesus' special calling, although in other forms they appeal to us all. In being invited to turn stones into bread, Jesus who was to feed the hungry with the bread of life, faced the temptation of self-protection. The quest for comfortable satisfaction is within us all. In being invited to worship Satan in return for authority over the kingdoms, Jesus, who had laid aside his majesty, faced the temptation of self-seeking. The quest for power lurks within us all. In being invited to cast himself down from the pinnacle of the temple, Jesus, who was to destroy the temple and rebuild it again, faced the temptation to self-display. The quest to draw attention to ourselves is within us all.[16] Had he

---

[16] Some appear not to draw attention to themselves but often do so perversely by being needy, problem-centred or even merely shy.

succumbed, Jesus would have abused his power and given false legitimacy to Satan's attempt at usurping God's power. He would also have disqualified himself from ever being our saviour. But each is resisted and in each case he shows active and total obedience to God, a major facet of holiness.

What was the secret of Christ's ability to resist temptation? His knowledge of the Scriptures and his wielding of the sword of the Word of God is one secret.[17] But Luke's double reference to the Holy Spirit in verse 1 and his comment immediately after the temptations that 'Jesus returned to Galilee in the power of the Spirit' suggests that his relationship with the Holy Spirit was the key.

b. The Holy Spirit

The Spirit had descended on Jesus at his baptism (3:22), anointing him for the ministry about to commence and assuring him of his sonship. After the opening episodes in his ministry the Holy Spirit is only mentioned explicitly a couple of times as empowering Jesus.[18] But Luke is giving us a narrative account of Jesus' ministry, not a theological analysis, and from the references he makes to the Holy Spirit he means us to see the whole of his ministry as Spirit-empowered.[19]

Peter commented on this when later he was evangelising Cornelius. 'God anointed Jesus of Nazareth', he said, 'with the Holy Spirit and power, and . . . he went around doing good and healing all who were under the power of the devil, because God was with him' (Acts 10:38). A few sentences earlier, Peter had declared Jesus to be 'Lord of all' (Acts 10:36). But now he draws the attention of Cornelius and the others listening to Jesus' humanity and stresses his earthly existence. This 'Lord of all' was none other than Jesus from Nazareth, a human being like you or I, and yet one empowered by God, who anointed him with the Holy Spirit to do good and work miracles. He therefore fulfilled what they expected of the coming Messiah and his claim, made in the synagogue at Nazareth,[20] that the prophecy of Isaiah 61 was being realized in him, found ample justification in his actions.

[17] Eph. 6:17. He quotes Scripture in verses 4, 8 and 12.
[18] Luke 4:1, 4, 18; 10:21 and 11:20.
[19] J. Green, *The Theology of the Gospel of Luke* (Cambridge: CUP, 1995), p. 45. Green stresses that Luke is writing 'a narrative account' of Jesus' ministry and his 'profound emphasis' on the Holy Spirit at the start of the ministry applies to all that follows.
[20] Luke 4:14–29.

Much is made of the spectacular healings and exorcisms, and rightly so, but little attention is given to his 'doing good' (*euergetōn*). F. F. Bruce[21] points out that the same word is used by Jesus in Luke 22:25 when he says, somewhat tongue-in-cheek, that the kings of the Gentiles 'call themselves Benefactors'. By contrast, Jesus truly was a benefactor of mankind, doing good, not just in the spectacular encounters with evil but in the ordinary encounters with friends and followers. He did good, because he was good.

Here, then, is a second aspect of Jesus' holiness. Because of his 'intimate relationship with the Father through the Spirit',[22] though fully human, he is empowered to live a life of victory over sin and of perfect obedience to the will of God, as is manifest in the sheer goodness of his life. Hebrews reflects on Christ's perfect holiness from a different angle. Using sacrificial language, we read there of God's desire to find a human being who could live in flawless conformity with his covenant.[23] He longed to receive the sacrifice of an unblemished life to be offered, rather than receiving an atoning sacrifice which was offered as a substitute by those whose lives were blemished by sin. In the man Jesus of Nazareth, his Son, his desire was met. His active obedience to God meant he could offer the unblemished sacrifice that the covenant sought, while his passive obedience that led him to Calvary meant he could offer himself as a sacrifice for sinners. Jesus was the perfect 'son of Adam' who uniquely demonstrates what God's masterpiece should truly look like. In him the image of God was uncorrupted, and God's intention in creating human life revealed.

3. Holiness and the power of Christ (Luke 4:34)

I know who you are – the Holy One of God!

A third aspect of holiness relates to the majestic and awesome power of God.

The demons he exorcized from their victims proclaimed that Jesus was holy in the most forthright way. Early in his ministry Jesus visited the synagogue in Capernaum where he met a man who was possessed by a demon. The evil spirit knew immediately that he had met his match in Jesus and in a strong voice from deep within the possessed man he cried out, *What do you want with us, Jesus of*

[21] F. F. Bruce, *The Acts of the Apostles, The Greek Text* (Grand Rapids: Eerdmans and Leicester Apollos, 1990, 3rd ed.), p. 263.
[22] Brower, *Holiness in the Gospels*, p. 59.
[23] Heb. 10:5–7.

Nazareth? Have you come to destroy us? I know who you are – the Holy One of God![24]

To speak of Jesus as *the Holy One of God* is very rare, at least at this stage of things.[25] It was to become more common later in the earlier church but had not become so yet.[26] For now it was more likely that Jesus would have been referred to as the Son of God,[27] even though Luke, as we have seen, connects Jesus' sonship with his holiness.[28] The demons, however, have supernatural insight into the identity of Jesus which human beings, as yet, have not attained.[29]

The Holy One of God is a very perceptive choice of title for the demons to use. They know their doom is sealed because the holiness of God is both powerful and pure. In the Old Testament, God's holiness was frequently manifested in powerful acts, such as at the exodus, and in awesome theophanies, like that at Mount Sinai, or in Isaiah's vision in the temple. That same divine power was now being manifest through Jesus in the synagogue at Capernaum where his supernatural and holy power clashes with the supernatural but evil power of the demon. The power of holiness here and throughout the Gospels is always the stronger power that overcomes the destructive power of Satan and his allies. It is never an equal conflict. What happened in Capernaum is a small revelation of God's holiness which through Jesus 'involves the total destruction of the demonic world'.[30]

But, as in Isaiah's vision, this revelation of God is not just about power; it is also inevitably about purity. Isaiah's reaction to seeing God's majesty was to despair of his own uncleanness. When Peter witnessed the miracle of a large catch of fish, his first reaction was to cry, 'Go away from me, Lord; I am a sinful man!' (Luke 5:8). When Christ's true identity was manifest to the select band of disciples at the transfiguration, the disciples reacted with fright.[31] Others too could find the very person of Christ awesome and shrink back from

---

[24] The parallel in Mark 1:21–28 uses identical words. The 'us' is likely to be a reference to the demon and the man he possessed since on this occasions the possession is by a single demon.

[25] The title is so rare that it is 'hardly a Christological title' according to J. D. G. Dunn, 'Jesus and Holiness: The Challenge of Purity' in S. C. Barton (ed.), *Holiness Past and Present* (London: Continuum, 2002), p. 170.

[26] Acts 3:14; 4:27, 30; although note John 6:69.

[27] Mark 3:11; 5:7.

[28] Luke 1:35.

[29] R. T. France, *The Gospel of Mark*, NIGTC (Grand Rapids: Eerdmans, 2002), p. 104.

[30] Nolland, *Luke 1 – 9:20*, p. 207. See Heb 2:14.

[31] Mark 9:6.

him in fear.[32] The sheer force of his being, in which his awesome power and astonishing purity blended, caused people to realize their own impurity and unworthiness.

The demon-possessed man did not need to encounter Jesus to discover he was unclean. His condition made that all too obvious and, according to the rules of the day, this man should have been excluded from worship, from his family and the community for fear that his impurity might contaminate others. But Jesus removes his impurity and makes him pure by the miracle of exorcism, thereby enabling him to take his place in the synagogue and community without fear. The holiness of Jesus is seen, then, not only in the power he exercised but the purity he brought about. Jesus' mission was both to teach and exemplify a redefinition of holiness whereby the unclean would be made clean, as will be explored further in the next chapter. This man in Capernaum was an early signal of that redefinition.

This exorcism demonstrates a further aspect of holiness which we find in Isaiah's temple vision.[33] Isaiah not only came into contact with the awesome power of God and his need for cleansing but also encountered the compassion and grace of God, as firstly he was cleansed and then, beyond his ministry, even the stiff-necked people who were experiencing God's judgment in exile were given a promise of hope. Here, too, as so often in Luke, this miracle displays the compassion of God as the evil squatter is ejected from this man and he is restored to wholeness. Of the power of God, there can be no doubt. But remarkably, it is power that does not crush but is channelled into people's lives in love and compassion. It is the power of grace.

4. Holiness and the perfection of Christ (Luke 23:41)

But this man has done nothing wrong.

Like a well-cut diamond, the beauty of holiness radiates not just from one aspect but from many facets of the beautiful life of Jesus. From holiness as separation, as sheer goodness and as liberating power, we turn to the aspect of Jesus' sinlessness, which is implicit in Luke's Gospel.

The dying thief probably did not realise the full significance of what he was saying as he chided his fellow criminal with the words, *We are punished justly, for we are getting what our deeds deserve.*

[32] See also Mark 4:41; 5:14–16;10:32; John 18:6.
[33] See chap. 1.

116

But this man has done nothing wrong. No doubt in his mind he meant that Jesus was being executed unjustly because he had not committed any criminal offence. But the words are the keyhole through which we can view the whole life of the one who was without sin.

Unlike writings elsewhere in the New Testament where the absence of sin in Christ was explicitly stated,[34] the Gospel writers do not claim that he was sinless in so many words. But his triumph over Satan in the wilderness shows the strength of his resistance to sin, and his sinlessness, at least during that severe test. And, when Jesus throws down the challenge to the Pharisees, 'Can any of you prove me guilty of sin?' (John 8:46), his critics were silent. The Gospels find it sufficient simply to tell the story and let it speak for itself. As Dermot McDonald wrote:

> The historical records never betray any attempt to gild the lily. They do not set out to 'prove' His sinlessness. They tell the story without affectation; just as He was among men. The fact is that the Synoptic Gospels made no explicit claim to moral purity on the part of Jesus. But neither do they set out to prove His innocence or to eulogise him. They give an account of his life as he lived it; and that is enough.

> Yet as we follow the record, we note how He stood the tests of intimacy and enmity. His very presence was a rebuke, a cause of shame in others (cf. Matt. 3:14; 27:19; Luke 5:8; 23:47; John 19:6).[35]

Jesus was acutely aware of sin and its impact. He challenged others about it, he released others from it, he grieved over it, and suffered himself as a result of it through the lying, tormenting, hatred and unbelief to which he was subject. Yet, 'with him there was no memory of sin's defeat, no trace of sin's scars, no shame of a bad conscience. He lived all his days without the personal sense of sin's guilt and the personal fear of sin's consequences.'[36] The absence of sin is, as mentioned above, only one side of the two-sided coin of holiness. His lack of doing, thinking or saying anything wrong is only half of the requirement of holiness. The negative has to be replaced by the positive. Full holiness requires the presence of doing good, thinking godly thoughts and speaking gracious truth. These

---

[34] 2 Cor. 5:21; Heb. 4:15; 7:26; 1 Pet. 2:22; cf. 1 John 3:5.

[35] H. D. McDonald, *Jesus – Human and Divine* (London: Pickering and Inglis, 1968), pp. 38–39.

[36] Ibid., p. 39.

he practised in abundance. People reacted to him with astonishment since they had not seen anything like this before. The freedom of his life contrasted with the rule-bound Pharisees; the authority of his words with their bookish arguments; the power of his miracles with their spiritual helplessness; the generosity of his compassion with their calculating approval; and, his sheer goodness with their sanctimonious piety. Watching him, 'People were overwhelmed with amazement. "He has done everything well," they said' (Mark 7:37). In his presence they were 'overwhelmed with wonder' (Mark 9:15). His humanity exuded holiness from every pore in his body. The Gospels do not have to tell us he was sinless for they describe it in his every encounter. He was the one in whom the image of God could most perfectly be seen, the one truly normal man, the one who alone ever exhibited humanity in its unblemished state.

H. R. Mackintosh rightly commented: 'No miracle of Christ equals the miracle of his sinless life. To be holy in thought and feelings; never to fail in duty to others; never to transgress the law of perfect love to God or man; never to exceed or come short – this is a condition outstripping the power of imagination.'[37] Yet Jesus was holy, through and through.

5. Concluding comment

Jesus was holiness personified. No human being has ever demonstrated such perfect holiness before or since. Nor can any fallen human being ever do so. He is the very model of a human being made in the image of God, in whom that image remains unblemished. Holiness is seen in his total consecration to God, which sets him apart from the rest of humanity. Holiness is seen in his faultlessly doing the will of God as he resists temptation and does good; in his powerful acts that defeat evil and display the explosive energy of God's moral purity; in using that power in gracious and compassionate ways; in his perfection as he, alone among human beings, was without sin. There is an integrity in him as these aspects of holiness are seen to be in perfect harmony with each other. He is the complete human who is truly 'the image of the invisible God',[38] 'the radiance of God's glory and the exact representation of his being'.[39]

Writing from within the holiness movement, Lieutenant Colonel

---

[37] Cited in ibid. p. 41.
[38] Col. 1:15.
[39] Heb. 1:3.

Chick Yuill was right in warning, 'All too often our holiness teaching starts in the wrong place. Let us be clear that holiness does not begin at the point of surrender and crisis in the life of a believer . . . [T]his is not the place to begin. It is too man-centred, too self-oriented, too sin-concerned. *The place to begin is with Jesus Christ and his perfect adequacy.*'[40]

---

[40] Cited by Brower, *Holiness in the Gospels*, p. 43. Italics his.

Matthew 5:20, 48; Mark 5:1–43; 7:1–23; Luke 14:1–14
8. Holiness redefined

Jesus embodied holiness. He also redefined it. By the time of Jesus, holiness had come to mean something very specific to the Jews. Holiness was 'understood as separation from everything impure' and Israel's public life was driven by the quest for purity.[1]

Various people handled the quest in various ways. The Essenes took the quest to an extreme and withdrew from society out of fear of contamination. The Zealots saw the presence of the Romans as the biggest threat to holiness, as did others, but they sought to overcome the problem by ridding the land of their presence through violence.

The sect of the Pharisees, the most influential group in Jewish society, sought to put up with the power of Rome but maintain as much internal distance from them as possible by hedging the key institutions of the day around with rules and regulations designed to preserve their purity. The three primary institutions that defined their way of life were the sabbath, the temple and the meal table. They sought to protect the first by taking the great command, 'Remember the Sabbath day by keeping it holy'[2] and breaking it down into minute regulations defining what a person could and could not do on the seventh day of the week. The purity of the temple was maintained by ensuring that nothing unclean entered it, whether that be a Jewish person who had been made unclean through sickness or deformity, or a Gentile who was considered to be unclean by definition. Eating a meal with someone was a sign of friendship and agreement, and therefore it was especially important to maintain separation at the table. Out of the 341 rabbinic regulations that devel-

---

[1] M. Borg, *Conflict, Holiness and Politics in the Teaching of Jesus* (Lewiston, Queenston and Lampeter: Edwin Mellen Press, 1984), p. 51.
[2] Exod. 20:8.

oped from this period, 229 concerned eating with others. For them how one behaved at the meal table was not a matter of etiquette but of holiness.[3] Purity and holiness were intricately related.

Once we understand this, two things become immediately apparent. First, although the language of holiness is rare in the Gospels,[4] set against this background, the concern with holiness is pervasive. When Jesus was discussing the sabbath, healing the sick, challenging the rules about eating and calling into question the role of the temple, he was dealing with the questions of holiness. Secondly, it is immediately apparent that Jesus dissents from the view that holiness has to do with separation and the legalistic maintenance of purity and he redefines it.

The synoptic Gospels sing from the same song sheet as they present us with the new sound of holiness that comes from Jesus. They overlap extensively and have an immense amount in common, yet they bring their own distinctive voice to the performance of the song so that, without distorting their teaching, we can differentiate between them.

1. Matthew: holiness as perfect righteousness

Matthew's word for holiness is *righteousness*, a word that he is the only Gospel writer to use.[5] To Matthew, righteousness means the ethical behaviour one looks for among those who are in the kingdom of God. It focuses on the conduct of the disciples and the 'unique' way in which they are to fulfil the law.[6] Theirs is not to be a slavish obedience to the letter of the law but one that goes to the heart of commandments, not a superficial obedience but one which fulfils the intent of the law. Their primary relationship is, in fact, not to the

---

[3] K. Brower, *Holiness in the Gospels* (Kansas City: Beacon Hill Press, 2005), p. 38, citing, Borg, *Conflict, Holiness and Politics in the Teaching of Jesus*, p. 96. For a thorough study of this area see C. L. Blomberg, *Contagious Holiness: Jesus' meals with sinners*, NSBT (Leicester: Apollos and Downers Grove: IVP, 2005).

[4] Depending on what one includes in the calculation, explicit holiness language occurs forty-two times in the Gospels, out of 191 references in the New Testament as a whole (D. Orsuto, *Holiness* [Sheffield: Continuum, 2006], p. 27). J. D. G. Dunn ('Jesus and Holiness' in S. C. Barton, [ed.], *Holiness: Past and Present* [London: Continuum, 2002], p. 169) identifies 'five "holiness" sayings that are attributed to Jesus' (Matt. 6:9; 23:17, 19; 24:15; Mark 3:9 and parallels) but 'holy' is mainly used as an adjective.

[5] With the exception of Luke 1:75.

[6] D. A. Hagner, 'Holiness and Ecclesiology: The Church in Matthew' in K. E. Brower and A. Johnson (eds.), *Holiness and Ecclesiology in the New Testament* (Grand Rapids: Eerdmans, 2007), pp. 44–55.

law, but to the person of Jesus,[7] whose cross they have embraced. It is his words that they are to obey[8] and his righteousness they are to make a priority that eclipses all other concerns of life.[9]

Among the instructions of Jesus, the teacher,[10] two sayings stand out which relate to holiness. Both sayings occur in the Sermon on the Mount, which in itself is a model discourse calling on the disciples to practise radical holiness. The first calls for a *righteousness* that *surpasses* others (5:20) and the second for a perfection that imitates God himself (5:48).

a. Surpassing righteousness (5:20)

For I tell you that unless your righteousness surpasses that of the Pharisees and the teachers of the law, you will certainly not enter the kingdom of heaven. The righteousness of the Pharisees and the other religious leaders of Jesus' time was concerned, even obsessively concerned, with avoiding impurity. Purity would be maintained, it was thought, if there was an exact obedience of the law, without deviation or hesitation, but also often without ever considering its deeper meaning. Providing one obeyed its surface meaning, as, of course, helpfully spelled out in detail by the rabbis, one could be considered pure.

We find ourselves in a parallel situation in contemporary British culture. The duty of care, for example, is a grand and righteous principle which all those who have responsibility for others, such as employers or teachers, should readily accept as an obligation. In recent days that principle has been translated into a myriad of very particular legal regulations defining how good professional practice or how health and safety is to be maintained, and what processes are to be adopted to demonstrate that those with responsibility have complied with them. But, as with the Pharisees of Jesus' day, it is becoming increasingly obvious that one can comply perfectly with every minute rule and fail to truly exercise care. In fact, the fulfilling of the detailed regulations, during which one ticks all the right boxes, can be used to subvert the fulfilment of the central essence of the law. Righteousness is not avoiding breaking petty rules, which are often tyrannical, but living positively and responsibly before God.

Jesus seeks a righteousness in his disciples that exceeds that of the Pharisees because it does not fall into the legalistic trap. Legalism

---

[7] Matt. 10:37–39.
[8] Matt. 5:22, 28, 32, 34, 39, 44; 24:35 and 28:20.
[9] Matt. 6:33.
[10] Matt. 23:8–10.

is the perennial temptation of those who have a strong desire to be holy and has persistently plagued the evangelical church. But, as is apparent from the context, Jesus does not want his disciples to think they are righteous because they have fulfilled the letter of the law and avoided impurity. So, to be authentically righteous is not only to abstain from murder but hatred also, and to seek to live in a reconciled state with those we have offended (5:21–26). Avoiding adultery is good, but dealing with inner lust is better (5:27–30). Avoiding divorce is right, but true righteousness means remaining genuinely faithful to your marriage partner (5:31–32). Avoiding breaking an oath is important, but being a person of such integrity as to render the swearing of an oath unnecessary is how we should be living (5:33–37). Extracting just and proportional retribution may be what the law permits, but true disciples reject insisting on their rights and replace it with self-giving (5:38–42). True disciples also exchange the selective love which we find natural with the inclusive love which we know to be supernatural (5:43–48), which means, contrary to all conventional Jewish wisdom, even loving the Romans.[11]

In saying this, Jesus is not intensifying the law so much as radicalizing it. If all he intended was the former, he would be laying more burdens on the shoulders of his disciples than the Pharisees had done. His disciples would become even more scrupulous in their observance of inward rules than the rabbis were in their observance of the outward rules. What would be the gain in that?

We can only gain a true understanding of the surpassing righteousness for which Jesus calls if we look to 'the bigger picture', to the 'totality of meaning'.[12] His desire is to be read in the light of Jesus' fulfilment of the law (5:17) and his inauguration of the kingdom (5:20). He is not pointing to an intensified law so much as a new way that is opened up because he has fulfilled the law and vocation of Israel, in his own person, and now invites us to enter into a relationship with God through him. The righteousness which *surpasses that of the Pharisees* is not greater in quantity than theirs but altogether of a different quality because it is a righteousness that stems from the redemptive activity of Jesus. It is a righteousness for the new people of God, brought about through a new covenant, not a new law.[13] The promise of the new covenant[14] has come to

---

[11] Borg, *Conflict, Holiness and Politics in the Teaching of Jesus,* p. 129.

[12] Brower, *Holiness in the Gospels,* p. 117.

[13] This interpretation is dependent on R. A. Guelich, *The Sermon on the Mount* (Waco: Word, 1982), pp. 170–174 and Brower, *Holiness in the Gospels,* pp. 116–123 where fuller justification for this position can be found.

[14] Jer. 31:31–36; Ezek. 36:24–27.

fulfilment in him and with it the law has become an internal matter of the heart rather than an external set of rules.

Robert Guelich summarizes it like this: 'Such "righteousness" connotes a new relationship established by God with his people and among his people, a relationship that issues in conduct that is in keeping with the Father's will set forth in Jesus' teaching and ministry.'[15] So Jesus is not laying on his disciples a life-long duty which, providing they succeed, will admit them to the kingdom of heaven in the end. He is saying, because they belong to the kingdom, this is the lifestyle they will display. It is only living the old way that will keep them out.

b. Modelling perfection (5:48)

If the first saying of Jesus we have examined looked frightening enough, this second saying looks even more frightening! *Be perfect, therefore, as your heavenly Father is perfect.* As Bower comments with commendable honesty, 'This sounds like a requirement that is a worthy but quite unobtainable goal and, hence, an irrelevancy.'[16] And that is how many have treated it.

To understand the command, we need to ask two questions. What is the meaning of *perfect* (*teleios*) and secondly, what does Jesus particularly have in mind when he speaks of *your heavenly Father* as *perfect?*

Teleios does not mean sinless perfection[17] but rather wholeness, completeness, whole-heartedness, and stands for total commitment and being without reservation.[18] It is not possible to build a case for sinless perfection on this verse. John Stott points out that, among other reasons why that is erroneous, Jesus, earlier in the sermon, indicated that hungering and thirsting after righteousness was to be a standing characteristic of his disciples (5:6), and he gives no indication that they will ever become replete. Later in the sermon he instructs his disciples to pray 'forgive us our debts' (6:12). Both these, Stott writes, 'being continuous, are clear indications that Jesus did not expect his followers to be morally perfect in this life'.[19] While he may not expect perfection, he does expect total commitment.

[15] Guelich, *The Sermon on the Mount*, p. 171.

[16] Brower, *Holiness in the Gospels*, p. 103.

[17] The equivalent word is used in Gen. 17:1 where Abraham is said to be 'blameless' but he was clearly not sinless (ibid., p. 123).

[18] A thorough discussion is found in Guelich, *The Sermon on the Mount*, pp. 234–237.

[19] J. R. W. Stott, *The Message of the Sermon on the Mount*, BST (Leicester: IVP, 1978), p. 122.

The immediate context (5:43–48) defines the nature of the whole-heartedness expected and brings into sharp focus the particular aspect of the perfection of God, to which Jesus is alluding. The verses immediately before are about the nature of the love Jesus' disciples were expected to demonstrate. Contrary to all conventional wisdom, then or now, it is not to be limited to loving those who are like us, or to those with whom we feel most comfortable, or to those who are likely to love us in return. It is to be an inclusive love, which not only embraces the stranger but even reaches out to our enemies and persecutors. The Father in heaven is not selective when he sends his rain on the earth but dispenses this good and life-giving gift to deserving and undeserving alike. Like this Father, we are to be indiscriminate in dispensing love. Luke, in his version of this sermon, makes the point explicit. We love, even our enemies, because we bear the family likeness and in this way we 'will be children of the Most High, because he is kind to the ungrateful and wicked. Be merciful, just as your Father is merciful' (Luke 6:35–6).

Matthew views holiness through the prism of a new righteousness. It is not a righteousness that is obtained through a surface obedience to an external law and it is not maintained through ritual purity. It arises from being a member of God's family, a subject in God's kingdom, a beneficiary of God's new covenant, a recipient of God's grace, a disciple of God's son. Through the prism of righteousness, holiness refracts into the colours of a new inner purity, a new depth of character, a new quality of serving, a new way of relating, and, above all, a new kind of loving.

2. Mark: holiness as authentic purity[20]

All the Gospels are concerned with the issue of purity but it comes naturally to the fore in Mark. By both his actions and his teaching Jesus redefines purity. In his kingdom purity is seen in a new light.

a. Jesus' actions: redefined purity demonstrated (5:1–43)

We could go to almost any part of Mark's Gospel to see Jesus battling against the perverted understanding of purity that the Pharisees modelled. His early miracles saw him encountering those declared

---

[20] For another perspective on this subject see K. E. Brower, 'The Holy One of God and his Disciples: Holiness and Ecclesiology in Mark' in Brower and Johnson (eds.), *Holiness and Ecclesiology*, pp 57–75 and Brower, *Holiness in the Gospels*, pp. 83–101.

impure because they suffered from demon possession (1:21–28) or leprosy (1:40). It was not long before the 'teachers of the law' were on his case and when he healed a paralysed man in Capernaum they initiated the criticism which would go on growing until the crucifixion (2:1–12). Undeterred, Jesus further offends his anxiety-riddled critics, by failing to keep the right company (2:13–17); failing to practise fasting (2:18–22); and failing to observe sabbath regulations (2:23 – 3:6).

Three miracles occur in 5:1–43, which demonstrate Jesus' radical approach to purity. First, he heals a demon-possessed man (5:1–18); secondly, a poor, sick woman (5:24–34); and thirdly, he raises a young, dead daughter to life (5:21–24, 35–43). Three common themes regarding purity run through these incidents, although considering them from this perspective far from exhausts the richness of these texts.[21]

(i) In each case Jesus encounters impurity

The impurity of the demon-possessed man seems especially to be emphasized. Living in a Gentile area, where pigs were kept, this man, who we later discover is possessed not by one but by many demons, lives among the tombs, 'a place of uncleanness, [which] has an obvious symbolic appropriateness'.[22] Demon possession alone would have been enough to render him unclean, but his association with death and his self-harming compound his impurity.

The woman in the crowd is reluctant to identify herself because, according to Jewish law, her long-standing *bleeding* made her unclean. We cannot be certain of the exact nature of her illness but laws such as those of Leviticus 15:19–33 would certainly have been applied to her. Furthermore, it was thought that impurity was contagious, so her presence in the crowd would have led to others becoming unclean.

Death was, of course, the ultimate impurity and the law made it very clear that contact with a dead body would make someone ritually impure. The week-long period of uncleanness, as opposed to the usual shorter time, and the elaborate cleansing ritual when a corpse had been touched, testified to the seriousness with which the impurity was viewed.[23] But in none of these cases does Jesus shun

---

[21] They have much to say, for example, about the power of Christ over demons, disease and death.

[22] R. T. France, *The Gospel of Mark*, NIGTC (Grand Rapids: Eerdmans, 2002), p. 227.

[23] Lev. 21:1–4; 22:4–8; Num 19:11–22.

contact or betray any fear of contamination. He does not seek to maintain his holiness by separation from those who were unclean.

(ii) In each case Jesus makes the impure clean

Jesus' way of dealing with the impurity is the reverse of the conventional way. The Pharisees kept their distance from those who were unclean lest they too should become impure. In their view uncleanness was contagious and would pollute purity. Jesus draws the unclean near and banishes their impurity by his divine power (5:6–10, 30). It is not their uncleanness but his own 'purity that can rub off on them and change them for the better. Cleanliness, he believes, is even more "catching" than uncleanness . . .'[24] Holiness, not impurity, is contagious.[25] Jesus settles the problem of impurity not by trying to keep the lid on it but by overcoming it.

'His blatant rejection of the rules covering leprosy, corpses and people with discharges', explains Gordon Wenham, 'was expressive of the new age of redemption he inaugurated. He deliberately touched the unclean and healed their infirmity. The old law was disparaged because the new era of grace had come.'[26] Purity need no longer be protected by the observance of rules for, in the age of the kingdom, grace made the impure pure.

Furthermore, it brought an end to exclusion. Those who formerly were excluded by their impurity could be included in the community again. Jesus' instruction to the healed man to *Go home to your own people* (19), his calling of the healed woman out of the crowd and his telling her, as a *Daughter,* to *Go in peace and be freed from your suffering* (34), and Jesus' delightful touch instructing Jairus' parents to *give her something to eat* (43) are all indications of that. Each resumes their place in the community.

(iii) In each case it is his exchanging places with them that makes them clean

Did this commencement of the new day of grace mean that the old laws were irrelevant and could just be ignored? No, the law is not ignored but fulfilled by Jesus. He exorcizes the demon-possessed, heals the sick and raises the dead not simply because it is in his power to do so but because he puts himself in their place. These

---

[24] Blomberg, *Contagious Holiness,* p. 128.

[25] See further, Brower, 'The Holy One of God and his Disciples,' p. 72.

[26] G. J. Wenham, 'Christ's healing ministry and his attitude to the law' in *Christ the Lord,* ed. by H. Rowdon (Leicester: IVP, 1982), p. 125.

miracles are possible because of the cross, where the one who was clean and altogether pure bears our uncleanness and impurity,[27] to fulfil the law and release those who were on the wrong side of it. Tom Wright is worth quoting about the demon-possessed man:

> At the climax of Mark's story Jesus himself will end up naked, isolated, outside the town among the tombs, shouting incomprehensible things as his flesh is torn apart on the cross by the standard Roman torture, his flesh torn to ribbons by the small stones in the Roman lash. And that, Mark is saying is how demons are dealt with. This is how healing takes place.[28]

Similarly, on the cross he shed his blood, as the unclean woman was doing, and embraces death, as Jairus' daughter had done. Healing takes place because of Calvary and his purity flows from his cross to overcome all our impurities.

b. Jesus' teaching: redefined purity explained (7:1–23)

Mark not only demonstrates this new understanding of how to be holy but records Jesus' teaching on it too. Conflict followed Jesus wherever he went. Earlier in Mark much controversy had been about the sabbath but in chapter 7 it is the issue of the food laws and their associated practices that comes to the fore.

(i) The question he faced (7:1–5)

The food regulations of Leviticus 11 and 17 had come to be central to the Jewish understanding of purity. Holiness required that they were strictly observed and, as happens, a number of customs grew up around them which became as important as the laws themselves. So, Mark explains to his Gentile readers that, before eating, all pious Jews would be punctilious in washing their hands, and indeed, in ensuring that the dishes and utensils had been washed too (3–4). This was not a matter of hygiene but of holiness.[29] When the Jewish leaders spotted that Jesus' disciples did not bother with these regulations they seized on it as another issue of contention.

But they somewhat pulled the rug out from under their own

---

[27] 2 Cor. 5:21 puts it even more startlingly, 'God made him who had no sin to be sin for us . . . .'

[28] Tom Wright, *Mark for Everyone* (London: SPCK, 2001), pp. 56–57.

[29] For fuller background see J. R. Edwards, *The Gospel according to Mark*, Pillar (Grand Rapids: Eerdmans and Leicester: IVP, 2002), pp. 204–208.

feet in the way they put it because they admitted that these ritual washings were *according to the tradition of the elders* (5). The regulations about ceremonial washing could not be found in the written law but were, in fact, oral additions to the law which became the 'received wisdom' of the Pharisees and may not even have been very long-standing.[30] Not all accepted such tradition and some, like the Sadducees, ignored them, refusing to go beyond the written law.

(ii) The critique he mounted (7:6–13)

The question gives Jesus the opportunity to mount a vigorous critique against the understanding of purity these religious leaders held. Quoting Isaiah 29:13 for support, he accuses them of having a worship which is outward but not inward (6–7). On the surface all looks in order but their worship lacked any inner reality and was quite pointless: *They worship me in vain* (7). His second criticism is that their religion is man-made not God-centred (8 and 13). They regard the *human traditions* that have been handed down as more important that the *commands of God*. In fact, they use the one to subvert the other and justify their failure to obey God. This expands into the third criticism (9–12) which demonstrates how their obedience is convenient rather than genuine. They play one law off against another and twist it to their own ends. So, although the law to honour their parents was transparently clear,[31] they played the game of declaring something *Corban*, which meant it was devoted to God and could only be used in the temple.[32] In practice, this was a way of ensuring that they need not support their parents, however needy they were, but could go on using the devoted wealth for themselves. Thus a good law was perverted and used as a convenient device to dishonour rather than honour their parents.

(iii) The principle he taught (7:14–23)

Later, Jesus continued this discussion with the *crowd* (14) and his *disciples* (17) rather than just the Pharisees (14) and explained what lay behind his critique. Once more, in dissenting from the traditional interpretation, he does not abolish the law but radically reinterprets it. He tells them it is not the outside that counts but the inside that matters. The Pharisees were concerned that they would

---

[30] France, *The Gospel of Mark*, p. 283. The oral traditions were codified and written down some two hundred years later.

[31] Exod. 20:12; 21:17; Deut 5:16.

[32] E.g., Lev. 27.

be defiled if they ate forbidden food or if they failed to wash their hands but, as Jesus explains, things that enter the body externally are just passing through it. From God's perspective that is not the issue.[33] The key question is what is a person like on the inside. What is the state of their heart, the centre of their being and source of their behaviour? It is not what goes in but, *What comes out of you is what defiles you* (20). Jesus then pointedly speaks of the *evil thoughts* that lurk within and then find expression without. Those thoughts, he says, by way of illustration, give rise to six ugly actions (*sexual immorality, theft, murder, adultery, greed* and *malice*) and six evil attitudes (*deceit, lewdness, envy, slander, arrogance and folly*).[34] No doubt the list could go on.

Until we know the source of the fire, we are unlikely to put it out successfully. And until we know that the source of our real problem is our deceitful heart,[35] which needs cleansing from within by the healing power of Christ, the trouble will remain.

Mark, then, provides us with a radical reinterpretation of holiness as seen from the perspective of purity. Purity still matters. But the Jewish leaders' way of handling the matter was fundamentally wrong. Purity could not be gained by observing external laws, still less by observing the traditions of the elders. Purity could not be maintained by excluding the impure. Purity was not a matter of separating oneself from external sources of defilement.[36] Purity is a matter of the inside not the outside; the heart, not the rules. In the new era of God's kingdom, Jesus, the pure one, exchanges places with the impure, and thereby restores their wholeness and includes them in the community once again. And he, knowing how dark the human heart is, cleanses people from within and gives them a new heart and a new spirit which delights in pleasing God.[37]

3. Luke: holiness as inclusive compassion

Luke's Gospel frequently portrays Jesus as breaking the contemporary practices with regard to purity. His Gospel endorses the teaching of Mark with regard to purity but presents it with a different voice. The challenge to conventional wisdom remains but is perhaps not as

[33] Dunn, 'Jesus and Holiness' in Barton (ed.), p. 188, says, '. . . purity of heart is reckoned as so much more important that the ritual washing of hands as to render the latter inconsequential.'
[34] Edwards, *The Gospel according to Mark*, p. 213.
[35] Jer. 17:9.
[36] Borg, *Conflict, Holiness and Politics in the Teaching of Jesus*, p. 96.
[37] Ezek. 36:24–27.

sharp. The tone of Luke's more mellow voice is consistently one of compassion. His teaching is as radical and demanding as Matthew's but, again, the voice is more relaxed. The perfect father whom we are called to imitate in Matthew 5:48 has become the merciful father in Luke 6:35–6 who 'is kind to the ungrateful and the wicked'. Throughout his ministry, Jesus demonstrates God's kindness in action as he cares for the poor, the sinners, and 'the great unwashed'.

The overthrowing of conventional ideas about holiness, the essence of which was purity, find their focus in Luke around the meal table. Jesus is constantly presented as eating, and often in the wrong company.[38] The criticisms of his party-going start early as, with Matthew and Mark, Luke speaks of Jesus enjoying 'a banquet' with 'a large crowd of tax collectors and others', following the call of Levi (5:27–32). Jesus does nothing to quell the criticisms and even draws attention to the accusation made against him that he was 'a glutton and a drunkard, a friend of tax collectors and sinners' (7:34). Luke exclusively reports several meals Jesus had and the conversations that took place around the table,[39] the most comprehensive report of which is in Luke 14:1–14, when one sabbath *Jesus went to eat in the house of a prominent Pharisee.*

a. The challenges he faced (14:1–5)

Far from enjoying a relaxed sabbath lunch, it sounds as if Jesus had walked into a trap deliberately planned by his host, for the meal takes a surprising turn and Jesus, we read, *was being carefully watched* (1). Somehow a man with a bloated body approached the table and the gauntlet was thrown down. Would Jesus heal this unclean man on the sabbath or not? The challenge was two-fold. First, the man's illness was considered a punishment for sin[40] and consequently the presence of this man threatened to contaminate the purity of the meal and those who were participating in it. He should have been nowhere near them, leading to the thought that maybe he had been deliberately invited in to see how Jesus would react? Secondly, all this was happening on the sabbath when pious Jews, concerned about their own purity, shunned work of any kind.

---

[38] For an overview see Blomberg, *Contagious Holiness,* pp. 130–163 and M. Thompson, 'Gathered at the Table: Holiness and Ecclesiology in the Gospel of Luke,' in Brower and Johnson (eds.), *Holiness and Ecclesiology in the New Testament,* pp. 76–94.

[39] Material exclusive to Luke on this subject is found in Luke 7:36–50, 11:37–54; 14:1–24; 19:1–10.

[40] J. Green, *The Gospel of Luke,* NICNT, (Grand Rapids: Eerdmans, 1997), p. 546.

Was healing a person work? If so, this poor man's healing would have to wait.

Jesus rises to the challenge and unhesitatingly heals the man, sabbath or no sabbath. He does so by *taking hold of the man* (4), breaking all the taboos and therefore, in the eyes of those around, becoming unclean himself. Compassion overrides the concern for purity. The healing, Luke tells us, was an act of liberation with the man being released (*apelysen*) from his illness and the social exclusion and spiritual denigration that went with it.[41] He then responds to the second part of the unspoken challenge, about healing on the sabbath (5). Even their own interpretation of the law gave them permission to rescue a child or animal if it was in a life-threatening situation. So should not a human being receive healing? Their scribal rules were in danger of missing out on God's intention of saving people. They had misinterpreted the law and needed to be released from their misunderstanding, for 'God's commandments were not about external conformity but about acting with love, justice and mercy.'[42]

b. The observations he made (14:5–11)

While the guests had been watching Jesus closely, he wanted them to know that he had equally been watching them. Honour was a highly prized value in Middle Eastern society and to slight someone's honour was a grave offence. Deciding therefore whether one would accept a dinner invitation depended on who it came from and how one was likely to be treated. Deciding who to invite was a matter of judging whether it would look good and enhance one's social standing. The poor therefore were never given a place, not least because they were not in a position to reciprocate the invitation.

This background explains what Jesus observed and commented on. As the guests arrived, they scrambled for the best seats, *the places of honour*. But the kingdom of God works in the reverse. The proud, the powerful and the rich do not occupy the positions of influence but are humbled.[43] It is the poor, the hungry, and those who are not considered worth inviting to a meal who experience his mercy and are given the best seats. There is no room for self-importance or seeking self-advancement.

People, it should be said, are not encouraged to go for the lowest places as a means to being elevated. Craddock comments that if this is how Jesus is understood, 'the entire message becomes a cartoon

---

[41] Ibid., p. 548.
[42] R. H. Stein, *Luke*, NAC, (Nashville: Broadman Press, 1992), p. 387.
[43] Luke 1:51–53.

if there is a mad, competitive rush for the lowest place, with ears cocked towards the host, waiting for a call to ascend'.[44] Humility has to be a genuine mark of the kingdom living and is essential for both holiness and showing compassion to others.

c. The challenge he issued (14:12–14)

Jesus then turns the screw more tightly. It's not only a question of where you sit but who you invite. Normal custom, then as now, is to invite those you feel comfortable with and those who are likely to return the favour (12). But in Jesus' kingdom the obligation is laid upon us to invite *the poor, the crippled, the lame, [and] the blind* (13). These people were the very ones who were most excluded from having a place among the elect[45] or a seat at God's eschatological banquet.[46] They did not measure up and consequently were never invited to be insiders. But, as Craddock comments, 'Luke's four-fold list of the poor, the maimed, the lame, and the blind (v. 13) is no surprise to the reader; we have known since Mary's song (1:46–55) and Jesus' inaugural sermon (4:16–30) that they were kingdom people.'[47] Once more, holiness is not about the concern to protect one's purity or honour but about imitating the mercy of God who includes the excluded in his kingdom.

Luke gives other insights into Jesus and holiness. His emphasis on the Holy Spirit leads to Jesus being presented as the one truly human being in whom the image of God is perfectly seen.[48] But in the way he behaved at the table we see in the clearest terms the manner in which holiness is being redefined. It is not, and never was, about 'a self-centred piety nor cling-film wrapped purity'.[49] It is about living lives that demonstrate the mercy and compassion of God to the poor and the sinners, about reaching out and touching them, and inviting them into God's kingdom.

4. Concluding comment

To say that there is 'no sustained reflection on the theme of holiness' in the Gospels is somewhat misleading.[50] There is. The theme

---

[44] F. B. Craddock, *Luke*, Int (Louisville: John Knox, 1990), p. 177.
[45] For details see Green, *The Gospel of Luke*, p. 553 and Stein, *Luke*, p. 390.
[46] See the further elaboration of this in Luke 14:15–24.
[47] Craddock, *Luke*, p. 177.
[48] See Brower, *Holiness in the Gospels*, pp. 43–61. See pp. 116–118.
[49] Ibid., p. 54.
[50] Dunn, 'Jesus and Holiness' in Barton (ed.), p. 171. Dunn immediately

is prominent but comes from a different angle than we might have expected. The concern with purity runs through each synoptic Gospel and is the axis around which its teaching about holiness revolves. Matthew emphasizes its ethical dimension and presents holiness as the pursuit of perfect righteousness. Mark emphasizes its inner dimension and presents holiness as a quest for authentic purity. Luke emphasizes the relational dimension and presents holiness as a demonstration of divine compassion.

---

carefully qualifies the statement by saying that, 'However, a narrow focus on the "holiness" is by no means the whole story' and that holiness and purity are closely related.

John 17:6–19
9. Holiness orchestrated

John's is the most intimate of the Gospels and reveals faith in the most personal of terms. With John's Gospel we enter the inner sanctuary of the life of Jesus. He takes us behind the public works and the open-access teaching to the private conversations Jesus has with his disciples and to the innermost thoughts of Jesus as he voices them in prayer to his Father (17:1–26). Understandably deep and complex, in this 'most sacred passage even in the four Gospels', as William Temple described it,[1] he prays first for himself (17:1–5) that he might be glorified; secondly, for his disciples (17:6–19) that they might remain true; and thirdly, for the whole church that they may be united (17:20–26).

His prayer for the disciples focuses on his concern for their holiness.[2] The language of holiness is rare in John's Gospel,[3] as it is in the synoptic Gospels, but, as with them, this does not mean the music of it is absent and John orchestrates it in his own style time and again. In John 14:15–21, for example, several crucial elements of John's understanding are found, all arranged according to typical Johannine themes. Holiness is about the Holy Spirit living within the believer (14:17). It is about the closest of relationships between Jesus and his disciples as, in his words, 'you are in me, and I am in you' (14:20), an intimacy which mirrors the closeness of relationship the Father and the Son themselves enjoy. It is about keeping his commandments (14:21). It is about loving him and equally being

---

[1] W. Temple, *Readings in St John's Gospel* (1940, London: Macmillan, 1968 edn), p. 293.
[2] John uses the verb *hagiazō*, to make holy, or, to withdraw from profane use, which is usually translated 'sanctify'.
[3] Apart from its use in ch. 17, the word group is found in 6:69; 10:36 and as an adjective for the Spirit in 1:33; 14:26; 20:22. D. A. Carson, *The Gospel according to John*, Pillar (Grand Rapids: Eerdmans and Leicester: IVP, 1991), p. 565.

loved by him (14:21). Holiness is more than this but not less. John views it as Spirit-empowered living, expressed in obedience and love, both of which arise from and result in the most intimate relationship with Christ.

This mutual indwelling, it should be said, does not mean that believers are absorbed into Christ in the sense of losing their identity and individuality, any more than Christ is 'contained' in us.[4] That would be to make the wonder of God's creative act, whereby we are all different, redundant, and it would make the incarnation, whereby Christ became a real individual human being, irrelevant. The indwelling Christ brings out to the full the individual personalities and unique lives of each believer, rather than reducing them to a monochrome homogeneity. So, holiness is seen in thousands of different guises, all of which bring glory to God.

The most explicit mention of holiness comes in Jesus' prayer on the last evening of his life. At the heart of the prayer is the request that the Father would *sanctify* the disciples *by the truth* (17:17). But the request is enveloped by two other references to holiness, in verses 11 and 18, which concern the Father and the Son, and mark the essential start and end of the unit.

1. The Holy Father: the root of our holiness (17:11)

Nowhere else is God addressed as *Holy Father*,[5] a title that comes naturally, yet profoundly, from the lips of Jesus. It combines the twin elements of God's transcendence and immanence in a single address and in perfect harmony.[6]

Holy draws attention to God as above us, different from us, awesome to us, sovereign over us and altogether separate from evil. *Father* draws attention to his nearness to us, his involvement with us, his grace towards us, his pleasure in us,[7] and to his nature as Jesus

---

[4] See further K. Brower, *Holiness in the Gospels* (Kansas City: Beacon Hill Press, 2005), p. 76.

[5] The title continues to be rarely used, but was used by P. T. Forsyth as the title for one of his books. See p. 52.

[6] Twentieth-century theology has found it difficult to maintain the balance between transcendence and immanence and has usually emphasized one 'pole' at the expense of the other. See S. J. Grenz and R. E. Olson, *20th Century Theology: God and the World in a Transitional Age* (Downers Grove: IVP and Carlisle: Paternoster, 1992).

[7] Note 17:6. 'Christians often think of Jesus as God's gift to us; we rarely think of ourselves as God's gift to Jesus.' D. A. Carson, *The Farewell Discourse and Final Prayer of Jesus: An exposition of John 14 – 17* (Grand Rapids: Baker, 1980), p. 184.

revealed him to us. High voltage electricity needs to be channelled into our homes through a transformer if it is to be useful to us and not to kill us instantly. So the holiness of God, which was experienced in the Old Testament as a tangible force,[8] needs to be channelled through the 'transformer' of his grace if we are to be made holy rather than merely annihilated by it.

The basis of our holiness lies in God himself. Our holiness is derived from him in two respects. First, holiness is the imitation of his character. When Jesus prays for the sanctification of the disciples (17:11) he is praying in effect the same as saying, 'consecrate yourselves and be holy, because I am holy'.[9] We become holy as we pattern ourselves on God himself.

Our holiness is also derived from God because he is the one who makes us holy in the sense of setting us apart for his exclusive service. We are unable to make ourselves holy. In this respect we are like the priests, sacrifices, furniture and utensils in the tabernacle. They were set apart from the ordinary and were no longer available for everyday use. Once they were 'consecrated' to God they became holy from their close association with God. So we acquire our holiness from our association with him as he sets us apart for his exclusive service. From this perspective, holiness is not about achieving moral perfection but about dedication to God.

2. The consecrated disciples: the nature of our holiness (17:12–17)

The Son makes a number of requests to his Father on behalf of the disciples he is going to leave when he is crucified within the coming twenty-four hours. First, he asks that they may be *protected* (17:11, 12) in or by God's own name.[10] Secondly, he prays that they may be united (17:11) just as the Father and Son are one.[11] Thirdly, he pleads that they may be delighted (17:13) 'despite the formidable foes that will confront them'.[12] Finally, he prayed that they might be dedicated (17:17). The first three petitions are

---

[8] e.g., Lev. 10:1–5; 16:11–17.

[9] Carson, *John*, p. 561, citing Lev. 11:44; 1 Pet. 1:16 and Matt. 5:48.

[10] If *en tō onomati sou* is to be translated '*in* your name' it is a prayer that the disciples will be kept loyal. If it is translated '*by* your name' it is a prayer for their protection by the power of God. See Carson, *John*, p. 562 and G. R. Beasley-Murray, *John* (Waco: Word, 1987), p. 299.

[11] John 10:30.

[12] Bruce Milne, *The Message of John*, BST (Leicester: IVP, 1993) p. 245. The wording of this paragraph follows Milne.

connected to holiness, although it is the fourth petition that gets to the heart of the matter.

a. The prayer for protection (17:11–12)

The first petition (11–12) is a comprehensive plea for protection which they need for several reasons. Since Jesus continues, *While I was with them, I protected them and kept them safe by that name you gave me. None of them has been lost* . . . the protection that is obviously uppermost in Jesus' mind is the need for their loyalty to him to be safeguarded. The hostility they will face in the world would give them plenty of incentives for falling away. The going would be hard. But with God's protection they would remain faithful. Behind that hostility lay the activity of Satan, mentioned in verse 15. He also lay behind the betrayal of Judas Iscariot which is accounted for here by his being *doomed to destruction so that Scripture would be fulfilled* – a reference back to John 13:18 where Jesus quotes Psalm 41:9. But his betrayal can be explained not just by his ingrained evil but also by the activity of Satan.[13] They need protection not simply from their fellow Jews, whom they could see, but from the demonic accuser whom they could not see; protection from his subtle temptations and traps, and from his outright attacks and assaults. Their holiness would be called into question if they failed to keep loyal or if they fell into sin.

b. The prayer for unity (17:11)

The reason Jesus prays for their protection is that *they may be one as we are one.* John has made much of the unity of the Father and Son. Without threatening the distinctiveness of each, the union is so intimate that only the language of being 'in' one another is sufficient to describe it adequately. Jesus longs to see that unity replicated between the disciples and himself and also between the disciples and each other. Unity becomes the major focus of the later part of this prayer when he prays for the wider church (17:21–3). Many forces would seek to separate them from each other including the forces of persecution and hostility, but most of all the forces of their own fallen, self-centred natures.

In the context of John, the unity for which Christ prays is not the superficial unity we might find in a political party that is seeking to win an election, nor the unity of a sports team seeking to rise high in the league. It is altogether more profound. It is not even adequate to

---

[13] Luke 22:3; John 6:70; 13:2.

explain it as a unity that imitates the intimacy of the Trinity: rather, it is unity that participates in the oneness of the Godhead. Jesus does not pray that his disciples' unity may be *like* the Father and the Son but *in* the Father and the Son (17:21). It is not surprising that people have struggled to express this mystery adequately. One image that has long commended itself in Eastern theology and more recently in Western theology is that of a dance.[14] In a dance, partners move around freely but in relation to one another, interweaving, interpenetrating and interdependent, yet maintaining their own identity. The dance is characterized by mutuality, reciprocity, exchange and coherence. Here diversity and unity are both fully expressed. However we seek to express the inexpressible, John insists that our unity is no external convenience but an experience of a deep participation in God – Father, Son and Spirit – himself. From this perspective intimacy with God lies at the very core of holiness.

c. The prayer for joy (17:13)

Strictly speaking, Jesus does not pray for *joy* so much as explain that he is praying for his disciples *so that they may have the full measure of my joy within them* after his departure. Joy, then, is the result of his praying for their protection and unity. It would be all too easy for the disciples to become downcast and discouraged in the face of the opposition they would experience, but joy would drive their fears away. This joy is not a superficial happiness that comes and goes with the circumstances, but a deep joy that persists and shapes character regardless of the situation. The fact that it is Christ's own joy that they are to experience, not in part, but to the full, proves the point. For, as Bruce Milne remarks, 'it is surely remarkable that he can refer to "joy" when he knows that the most appalling suffering is about to engulf him.'[15]

Writing on the life of Joseph, R. T. Kendall made a rather stark comment which I questioned when I first read it. He wrote: 'God wants everyone of us to have pleasure – his pleasure, his joy. God wants us to be happy. It is equally true that God wants us to be holy. But if you are not happy there is good reason to question whether you are holy. Holiness is genuine happiness.'[16] In the light of Jesus' prayer, maybe he has a point!

---

[14] It is often termed the *perichoresis* of the Trinity after the Greek word for dance. See P. S. Fiddes, *Participating in God: A Pastoral Doctrine of the Trinity* (London: DLT, 2000) esp. pp. 71–81.

[15] Milne, *Message of John*, p. 245.

[16] R. T. Kendall, *God Meant it for Good* (Carlisle: Paternoster, 2003), p. 91.

d. The prayer for consecration (17:17)

The climax of Jesus' prayer for his disciples is that God may *Sanctify them by the truth; your word is truth*. Their sanctification does not take place in a vacuum, but within the framework of their partaking of the nature of their *Holy Father* (17:11) and benefiting from his own act of sanctification (17:19). The disciple's sanctification is the outworking of their being in Christ and Christ being in them.

In this context to be made holy means to be set apart and consecrated to God's service, rather than their ethical goodness or their being cleansed from sin. Purification from sin is a precondition of their consecration. 'The disciples have already been purified from sin (13:10; 15:3), though they continue to need ongoing forgiveness (13:10).'[17] To be sanctified here is to be dedicated in the Old Testament sense that people and objects, animals and altars were dedicated to God's service in the tabernacle or temple, and so withdrawn from ordinary use. It is for their unreserved consecration to God's exclusive service for which Jesus prays. He longs that they should willingly, promptly and totally do the will of God.

The surrounding verses elucidate the meaning of this consecrated service.

1. *Location.* The location of their service is in the world (17:15). Disciples do not serve God by withdrawal from the world into a sacred and protected community but by engagement with the world and involvement in its life. That is the sphere in which they discover the protection of God. The protection, unity, joy and consecration for which Jesus prays is with a view to mission. It is so that they might travel safely with the gospel of truth into the alien territory where Satan's lies still hold sway. It is not intended for their own comfort when they are in the safe havens of their own kind. It is so that they may take his water to quench the thirsty, his bread to feed the hungry, his light to shine in the darkness and his life to bring rebirth to those only once-born. So, holiness calls for us to engage with the often-fragile lives of our neighbours, the networks of our communities and the secular and impersonal structures of our powerful institutions.

2. *Value.* The value of our service lies in our difference from them, for though we are in the world we *are not of the world*, says Jesus, *even as I am not of it* (17:16). Though he lived among human beings as a human being, he was not from this world and owed no allegiance to its opinions and authorities but only to the God who

---

[17] R. Bauckham, 'The Holiness of Jesus and his Disciples in the Gospel of John', in Brower and Johnson (eds.), *Holiness and Ecclesiology*, p. 111.

sent him. In like manner, we are human beings called to be involved in our world, but we serve it not by conforming to its attitudes, mindsets and behaviour but by dissenting from them, for they are based on a denial of the truth which we have in Jesus. We must take care that our engagement does not become assimilation and involvement does not become immersion. Our value lies not in our friendship with but our difference from the accepted conventions of our ungodly society.[18]

3. *Nature.* The nature of our service arises from the reason why we are different, as becomes apparent in the third statement explaining our consecration. We differ from the world neither because we wish to be awkward, nor stubborn and opinionated, nor because we are odd and unattractive personalities, nor, even, 'precious' in the wrong sense of that word (although we must confess with shame this is often how Christians have presented themselves to the world). No, we differ from the world because we are sanctified *by the truth; your word is true.* The truth can only be the truth that Jesus taught (17:14), that the disciples had already begun to obey (17:6), and that the Holy Spirit would continue to reveal to them after his departure from the earth.[19] God's Word is the gospel revealed by Jesus and taught subsequently by the Spirit. We are different, therefore, because we are gospel people.

We must even be cautious about the claim to possess the truth, for it can too easily lead to arrogance and intolerance. But if we truly are gospel people we will be set apart for the service of the master who healed a grumpy man at a pool-side, protected an adulterous woman, and washed the feet of his disciples. We shall not therefore be characterized by self-importance but by humility. Being sanctified by the truth means not only knowing it intellectually but living in accordance with it.[20]

Carson summarizes it like this: 'In practical terms, no-one can be "sanctified" or set apart for God's use without learning to think God's thoughts after him, without learning to live in conformity with the "word" he has graciously given.'[21]

The only proper response we can make on hearing Jesus pray for our consecration is to renew our own consecration to him:

Take my life and let it be
Consecrated, Lord, to Thee:

[18] Jas 4:4.
[19] John 16:13.
[20] TNIV mg.
[21] Carson, *John*, p. 566.

141

Take my moments and my days,
Let them flow in ceaseless praise.

Take my hands and let them move
At the impulse of Thy love:
Take my feet and let them be
Swift and beautiful for Thee.

Take my voice and let me sing,
Always, only for my King:
Take my lips and let them be
Filled with messages from Thee.

Take my silver and my gold,
Not a mite would I withhold:
Take my intellect and use
Every power as Thou shalt choose.

Take my will and make it Thine;
It shall be no longer mine;
Take my heart – it is Thine own;
It shall be Thy royal throne.

Take my love; my Lord, I pour
At Thy feet its treasure-store:
Take myself and I will be
Ever, only, all for Thee.[22]

3. The sanctified son: the means of our holiness (17:18)

The consecration of the disciples takes its cue from the consecration of Jesus himself. When Jesus prays, their consecration still lies in the future and concerns the periods after Jesus' departure from the world.[23] By contrast, his consecration has been apparent throughout his life. He has never done other than the will of his Father and never taught anything other than the truth of his

[22] This hymn was written by Frances Ridley Havergal (1836–79) at midnight on 4 February 1874. She was visiting friends at Arley House, Worcester and had prayed for the conversion of all the members of the family. Before she left 'everyone had got a blessing' and she was so happy that the night before her departure she could not sleep and penned this re-consecration hymn.

[23] Bauckham ventures it is something of a commissioning parallel to John 20:21. 'The Holiness of Jesus and his Disciples in the Gospel of John', p. 112.

Father.[24] But his consecration is about to enter a new phase when as soon as 'he had finished praying' (18:1) he goes into the garden of betrayal and so enters upon his passion and execution. There can be no greater consecration than giving oneself voluntarily over to death. Like the sacrifices of old, laying down one's life is the ultimate expression of dedication.

The simplicity of the wording of Jesus' self-consecration means it is easy to miss the double reason he gives for his going to the cross. He says he sanctifies himself *For them,* which is the language of atonement.[25] He dies on their behalf, in their place, as their substitute. He also sanctifies himself so that *they too may be truly sanctified.* The object of his death, in part, is that his disciples might commit themselves to the same mission as he had, of revealing the glory of God, full of grace and truth, to the world.[26]

Bauckham sums up the closure of the circle which these verses feature: '. . .all this Gospel's holiness language coalesces around the consecration of Jesus and the disciples: The Holy Father consecrates Jesus Christ the Holy One, who consecrates himself so that his disciples also may be consecrated, participating in the holiness of Jesus and the Father through the Holy Spirit.'[27]

4. Concluding comment

The orchestration of holiness in John differs from that in the synoptic Gospels, although it does not clash with them. He brings new instruments into play and arranges the theme differently from that of the other Gospel composers. He does not seek to redefine it, as they do, but rather to rehabilitate holiness essentially as separation and consecration. He stands in continuity with the Old Testament's understanding of holiness as that which was dedicated to God, whether persons, animals or things. Dedicated persons and objects were instruments in God's hands to do his will, serve his purposes and accomplish his mission. And yet there is nothing cold, mechanical or merely instrumental about John's understanding of being set apart for God in this way. Rather, holiness is invested with a personal warmth which is unsurpassed in the rest of the New Testament.

Holiness arises from being in the closest of relationships with

[24] E.g., John 5:19–23; 7:16–18.
[25] Carson, *The Gospel According to John,* p. 567, points to similar usage in Mark 14:24; Luke 22:19; John 6:51; 1 Cor. 11:24.
[26] John 1:14.
[27] Bauckham, 'The Holiness of Jesus and his Disciples in the Gospel of John', p. 113.

Jesus who, in turn, is in the closest relationship with his Father. It involves intimacy with the Trinitarian God. It involves knowing God's protection, Christ's joy and the Spirit's guidance. It involves following the example of Christ who sanctified himself for us.

It is out of this relationship with God that the obligations of holiness readily flow. Because we are loved, we love. Because we are united with God we seek to be united with our fellow disciples, by giving and receiving their love. Out of all this flows, too, our mission to the world where we seek to overcome their hostility by modelling and proclaiming the grace of God. 'Keeping the love commandment', writes Kent Brower, 'is the primary way in which the world will know of this mutual indwelling [with God] ... Christian holiness is thus a social, not an individual, phenomenon.'[28] Later he writes, 'In sum, according to John, love is the expression of sanctification.'[29] So it is. But to that end we must give ourselves totally to God and to the doing of his will, just as Jesus did. Anything less than total consecration falls short of the dedication we see in him who sanctified himself that we *too may be truly sanctified* (17:19).

---

[28] Brower, *Holiness in the Gospels*, p. 79.
[29] Ibid., p. 81.

Part 4
The dimensions of holiness

Psalm 51
10. Inner purity

In his modern classic on holiness, J. I. Packer wrote, 'holiness begins with the heart. Holiness starts inside a person . . .'[1] It has to do with the seat of our emotions, motivations and passions before it has to do with our outward actions. More fully, Packer explained:

> Holiness is a matter both of action and motivation, conduct and character, divine grace and human effort, obedience and creativity, submission and initiative, consecration to God and commitment to people, self discipline and self-giving, righteousness and love. It is a matter of Spirit-led law-keeping, a walk, a course of life in the Spirit that displays the fruit of the Spirit (Christlikeness of attitude and disposition). It is a matter of seeking to imitate Jesus' way of behaving, through depending on Jesus for deliverance from carnal self-absorption and for discernment of spiritual needs and possibilities.
>
> It is a matter of patient, persistent uprightness, of taking God's side against sin in our own lives and in the lives of others; of worshiping God in the Spirit as one serves him in the world; of single-minded, wholehearted, free and glad consecration on the business of pleasing God. It is the distinctive form and, so to speak, flavour of a life set apart for God that is now being inwardly renewed by his power.[2]

King David began to understand some of this long before the coming of Christ, but not long after he committed adultery with Bathsheba. His lamentable failure to be holy led him to appreciate the deeper dynamics of sin and sanctification and to acknowledge to God: 'You desire truth in the inward being' (6, NRSV). Long

[1] J. I. Packer, *A Passion for Holiness* (Cambridge: Crossway Books, 1992), p. 22.
[2] Ibid., pp. 31–32.

before Sigmund Freud drew the attention of the modern world to the power of the unconscious, those in touch with God were all too well aware of the inner impulses that drove them, often for ill, and the need for their lives to be cleansed and renewed from the inside out by God. Certainly David was aware of these inner workings, as is evident from Psalm 51.[3] Behind the Psalm, with its intense confession of sin, was one of the darkest of episodes in David's life, his adultery with Bathsheba.

1. David's failure in holiness (2 Samuel 11:1–27)

The account of David's adultery reads like a template for those who wish to give in to temptation. Walter Brueggemann points out, 'The action is quick. The verbs rush as the passion of David rushed.'[4] What are these verbs? They are, he stayed behind, he *saw*, he *sent*, he *slept*, he schemed, and then he slaughtered.

a. He stayed behind (11:1)

In the spring, at the time when kings go off to war . . . David remained in Jerusalem. David had established himself as a victorious and fearsome general before whom enemies fled (1 Samuel 10:17–19), yet at the time when kings were expected to fight, David is found skiving in Jerusalem. 'There is no doubt', Mary Evans writes, 'that the writer is making a specific point in 11:1.' The main function of the king at the time was to be a military ruler but 'perhaps David was a man of huge but fairly short-lived enthusiasms'.[5] Whatever his motivation for staying behind in Jerusalem, he was neglecting his responsibilities and was slacking when he should have been working. As an empty patch of soil easily attracts weeds, so an empty patch of time easily attracts temptation. There's some truth in the old adage, 'The devil makes work for idle hands.'

b. He saw (11:2)

The second step in David's downfall, typically, was as a result of what he saw. The eyes are the gate through which so much

---

[3] See also Paul in Rom. 7:14–25. I am aware that the identification of the 'I' in this passage is much disputed but, regardless of this, many hold the passage to express their own inner struggles with sin.
[4] W. Brueggemann, *First and Second Samuel*, Int (Louisville: John Knox Press, 1990), p. 273.
[5] M. Evans, *The Message of Samuel*, BST (Leicester: IVP, 2004), p. 208.

temptation enters into our minds, especially the male mind. Using an obvious analogy Jesus warned, 'Your eye is the lamp of your body. When your eyes are healthy, your whole body also is full of light. But when they are unhealthy, your body also is full of darkness. See too it, then, that the light within you is not darkness' (Luke 11:34–35). And when John spoke of 'the lust of their eyes' (1 John 2:16) people did not need help in understanding what he meant. David should have averted his eyes but he did not and his failure to do so cost him dear.

It doesn't take much to excite the wrong passions and, in the world in which we live, where we are bombarded by visual stimuli on every hand, much of it of an unhealthy sexual nature, we need to exercise great discipline over the things we look at. The advertisements, magazines and TV programmes which preachers of a former generation condemned remain a source of temptation, but they are now compounded by the almost unlimited access we have to images through the Internet. So, David's predicament is our predicament writ large and David's failure becomes our warning.

c. He sent (11:4)

David need have gone no further than having a tantalising glimpse of a beautiful female form. But he does. He consciously desires her and, without any embarrassment, *sent messengers to get her.* It may have been assumed of course that it was his right as king to summon whatever woman he wanted. He was at the height of his power. Who would refuse him? 'He can have whatever he wants, no restraint, no second thoughts, no reservations, no justification. He takes simply because he can.'[6] Except, of course, she was married, and therefore should have been off limits to him as much as to anyone else. David was very well aware of her married status (3) and should have been equally aware of the penalties prescribed in the law for those who committed adultery.[7] But, like a lot of powerful, public men, he took a great risk with little regard to the effect it would subsequently have on him.

d. He slept (11:4)

To this point, David had been unwise and been toying with sin, but arguably had not yet broken God's written law. Holiness, however, is about being our best for God and even though, strictly

[6] Brueggemann, *First and Second Samuel*, p. 274.
[7] Lev. 20:10.

speaking, no outward transgression might have taken place, he had failed to maintain the standard of holiness that could legitimately be expected from a godly king. In any case, we now know, through Jesus' teaching about the law, that from God's perspective internal passions are as important as external actions and 'anyone who looks at a woman lustfully has already committed adultery with her in his heart'. Hence Jesus' advice, offered with typical Jewish exaggeration, that, 'If your right eye causes you to stumble, gouge it out and throw it away' (Matthew 5:28–29).

We know nothing of Bathsheba's feelings about this. Was she flattered that the king had shown her attention? Was she flagrant in flirting with him? Was she resistant, a mere victim of male power? No matter, the initiative and responsibility lay with David who not only broke the law by having intercourse with her but doubly broke the law by doing so while she was still recovering from her monthly period.[8]

e. He schemed (11:6–13)

Once the predictable result occurred and Bathsheba revealed her pregnancy, David compounds his sin by not confessing it and drawing a line under it immediately. How easily sin sucks us in and we find ourselves going one step further today in order to cover up the evils of yesterday. David sought to devise a plan whereby the pregnancy could be blamed on her husband, Uriah, even though he was on a military campaign and therefore obliged to abstain from sexual relationships. When Uriah didn't jump at the chance his Commander-in-Chief gave him to cut the required corners, David next tried to get him inebriated so he would let his guard down and sleep with his wife regardless. But the Hittite showed greater discernment than the king of Israel and Uriah steered clear of temptation and wisely *he did not go home* (13).

f. He slaughtered (11:14–25)

Having failed to solve an embarrassing situation, or rather a sinful situation, by a cunning and scarcely detectable strategy, David ups the stakes and fixes it for Uriah to be killed as the army besieged the city. This time the result was guaranteed, though David's fingerprints were all over the bow and arrow as if he fired it himself. The king who was usually generous had 'lost all sense of perspective'.[9]

[8] Lev. 15:19–24.
[9] Evans, *Message of Samuel,* p. 210.

David, the great hero, has suddenly fallen and is shown to be like the rest of us, a vulnerable and sinful human being, capable of misusing the opportunities his position gave him. Being a Christian, even a mature Christian, gives us no immunity from failure and those of us who feel secure should 'watch yourselves, or you also may be tempted' (Galatians 6:1). Dale Ralph Davis tells the story of Robert Robinson, a convert of George Whitefield, who wrote the hymn 'Come thou fount of every blessing'. Years later, when travelling on a stage coach, a woman was singing the hymn and he was eventually driven to confess that he no longer had the feelings he had when he composed that hymn and longed for them to return. In the words of his own hymn he was still,

> Prone to wander, Lord, I feel it,
> Prone to leave the God I love.

For David, as for us all, there was a way back to God. The courageous and gracious rebuke of the prophet Nathan (1 Samuel 12) confronted him with the sinfulness of his actions and brought him to his spiritual senses. David knows that he cannot blame his actions on others or justify them in terms of his circumstances. The fault lay within him not outside of him and it was the inner dimension of his life that needed attention. Psalm 51 was composed as a result with its emphasis on the need for inner cleansing and a renewal by the Holy Spirit that penetrates to the depths of his being.[10]

2. David's restoration to holiness (Psalm 51)

As a confession of sin, Psalm 51 is unsurpassed and has been the vehicle by which many burdened sinners have been able to put their failures into words and find relief. It moves through five phases, reaching its apex in the plea for inward renewal in verses 10–12.

a. David's request: the problem of sin (51:1–2)

Two things are noteworthy about the two verses that introduce the psalm. The first is that the psalm does not begin with sin but with God's mercy. Were it not for a firm trust in the grace of God,

---

[10] Some scholars argue that Psalm 51 was composed in exile, or at least that verses 13–19 were added subsequently in exile. For the arguments see J. L. Mays, *Psalms,* Int (Louisville: John Knox Press, 1994), p. 199. But there is no serious reason to doubt the validity of the superscription.

David may well not have ventured further in his forthright confession of sin. But he knows, as we have even more reason to know, that, 'If when we confess our sins, he[11] is faithful and just and will forgive us our sins and purify us from all unrighteousness' (1 John 1:9). David bases his prayer on the covenant faithfulness – *unfailing love* – of God. The only hope he has is that God would *blot out, wash away* and *cleanse* from sin. He does not have the power to deal with it himself.

Secondly, we cannot fail to note how many words David uses for sin. James L. Mays comments that in these verses 'the entire Old Testament vocabulary of sin (transgression, iniquity, sin) is used; and the words appear as plurals as well as in the singular . . .'[12] It is as if David wants to 'cover all bases', ensuring he has missed nothing. He could not emphasize his problem more than he does. Probably little should be made of any distinction between the words although '"transgressions" implies deliberateness'.[13]

b. David's repentance: the seriousness of sin (51:3–6)

David may have used up the vocabulary of Israel in describing his sin but he has not finished unburdening himself about the problem of sin. In seeking God's forgiveness he, firstly, admits his own responsibility for sin and confirms the rightness of God's judgment against him (3–4). Then, secondly, he confesses the ingrained nature of sin and confirms the excellence of God's standards from which he falls so short (5–6).

David shows a rare honesty in his confession. Most of us find it hard to admit our guilt and seek to minimize the horror of sin. C. S. Lewis outlined the strategies we adopt to convince ourselves that sin is not as great a problem as the Bible says it is.[14] To summarize Lewis, he spoke of the way we

i. compare ourselves to others and so feel relatively good.
ii. blame it on the 'iniquitous social system' and admit only to a corporate guilt.
iii. 'have this strange illusion that mere time cancels sin' as it heals

---

[11] 'In the context of 1 John 1:9, 'he' refers to Jesus, the Son. David was praying to his covenant God, but the oneness of God in Trinity means there is no need to see any tension between those to whom confession is made.

[12] Mays, *Psalms*, p. 200.

[13] G. W. Grogan, *Psalms*, Two Horizons (Grand Rapids, MI: Eerdmans: 2008), p. 106.

[14] C. S. Lewis, *The Problem of Pain* (London: Collins, Fontana Books, 1957), pp. 47–54.

pain. But, he says, 'the guilt is washed out not by time but only by repentance and the blood of Christ.'

iv. feel safety in numbers. If all people sin it must be excusable.
v. are more humane than other civilisations and so not as bad as they.
vi. reduce the measure of all virtues to kindness.
vii. protest against excessive emphasis on moral duty because God is more than moral goodness. True, but as a holy God, 'he is not less' than moral goodness, either.
viii. shift the blame to God because sin is a response to 'some inherent necessity in human life', in other words, to the way God made us.

David mounts none of these excuses but freely admits his culpability. He recognizes that sin not only demeans him and harms his neighbour but does harm to God, for it is fundamentally against God and God only that we sin (4). We readily recognize the effect of sin on others, but why does it affect God so much? C. S. Lewis explains, it is because he is a good God. Just as all good people should find sin distasteful, so a good God cannot merely ignore sin but must be opposed to it. Then, in a comment that could have stemmed directly from Psalm 51:4, Lewis writes, 'When we merely say we are bad, the "wrath" of God seems a barbarous doctrine; as soon as we *perceive* our badness, it appears inevitable, a mere corollary for God's goodness.'[15]

David again underlines the depths of his sinfulness by saying that he was sinful by nature from the moment of his conception (5). It is his way of saying that confessing individual sins is too superficial since his whole life has been 'conditioned' by sin from the beginning.[16] He is saying, as we surely acknowledge in our own selves, not I have sinned but I am a sinner. When we comes to terms with that we must admit that from this perspective we are 'a horror to God' and a 'horror to ourselves'.[17]

David was a much loved servant of God, a wise and successful ruler who was God's 'ideal' king over Israel. Yet here we meet him not on the throne but in the 'spiritual gutter', hating his sin and pleading for mercy. It is a place we more naturally share with him as we come to terms with the darkness of our own lives. But that, in itself, is an encouragement. For all the great men and women God has used have been flawed individuals. None of us are exempt, whether prince or

---

[15] Ibid., p. 46.
[16] Mays, *Psalms*, p. 201.
[17] Lewis, *The Problem of Pain*, p. 55.

preacher, whether murderer or mercy-giver. As J. I. Packer puts it: 'We are all invalids in God's hospital. In moral and spiritual terms we are all sick and damaged, diseased and deformed, scarred and sore, lame and lopsided, to a far greater extent than we realised.'[18]

c. David's release: the answer to sin (51:7–9)

Reaching back to the opening verses, David pleads for God to deal with the sin he is incapable of dealing with himself. He uses the same three metaphors as he used then to give flesh to his request for mercy. Coming from different aspects of everyday life, here they occur in a different order with some added insights. Usually, cleansing refers to the process of refinement by which impurities are removed from precious metals in an assayer's workshop. But here, because the instrument of cleansing is said to be *hyssop*, it is specifically linked to the process by which lepers, once healed, were restored to their place in the community.[19] Washing refers to the removal of dirt from clothes to restore their pristine whiteness. Blotting out refers to the expunging of a record of guilt in a court-room. *Hide your face from my sins* is in effect asking the same thing in a different way.

The owners of kitchens in restaurants, hotels and public establishments are required to keep them clean daily. But periodically those kitchens have to be closed to undergo 'a deep clean' which removes the accumulated dirt missed in the daily routine. Taking up the cleansing spoken of in Psalm 51, Hebrews talks of the 'deep clean' that comes from the blood of Christ who cleanses 'our consciences from acts that lead to death' (Hebrews 9:14). One of the many benefits of the cross of Christ is freedom from 'the accusing conscience'.[20]

The main new element here is in verse 8. The psalms recognize that sin takes its toll on one's health and delaying confession of sin can be physically detrimental.[21] David hopes that God's forgiveness would lift the heavy burden of guilt for his failure and that the result of God's mercy would be a restoration of his health once again.

---

[18] Packer, *A Passion for Holiness*, p. 40.

[19] Lev. 14:1–5. Hyssop is also mentioned in the Passover event (Exod.12:22) and at the crucifixion (John 19:29). It is probably going too far to read a reference to the crucifixion as a means of our cleansing in this psalm even though with hindsight it adds an even deeper dimension to the psalm's interpretation than David would have envisaged.

[20] D. Peterson, *Possessed by God: A New Testament Theology of Sanctification and Holiness*, NSBT, (Leicester: Apollos, 1995), p. 39. Peterson helpfully discusses the relationship between the heart and the conscience on pp. 38–39.

[21] Ps. 32:3–4; 77:1–4.

d. David's renewal: the victory over sin (51:10–12)

David goes beyond seeking forgiveness to seek renewal. Having confessed the inwardness of sin, he now seeks to be recreated from the inside out. He does not look for a change of circumstances but a change of himself. The change only of his circumstances might leave him untouched. Many have thought a new home, a new job or even a new church would ease their problems, only to find they themselves are the problem and that nothing really has changed. Even the forgiveness of sins on its own might leave David where he was; joyful at freedom from past guilt but still condemned to be controlled and defeated by sin again. But if he is made a new person, the challenges would still be there but his approach to them different. So, he calls for God to engage in nothing less than an act of re-creation (10) so that he has a new *heart* and a new *spirit*. Spurgeon graphically expressed the prayer as, 'I, in my outward fabric, still exist; but I am empty, desert, void. Come, then, and let thy power be seen in a new creation within my old fallen self.'[22]

In New Testament terms, David is asking for the transformation of his mind (Romans 12:2) and 'a new self, which is being renewed in knowledge in the image of its Creator' (Colossians 3:10).[23] And although he uses his phrase in a different context, that of philosophical arguments, Paul's desire to 'take captive every thought to make it obedient to Christ' (2 Corinthians 10:5) is surely the fulfilment of David's ambition in Psalm 51. Those concerned about holiness will not permit unclean and unworthy thoughts to roam free in their minds but, by the Spirit's daily renewing of the mind, will cage them and give space instead to thoughts that are pure, lovely, admirable, excellent and praiseworthy.[24]

The plea looks back to the first act of creation when men and women were made in the image of God and surely is asking for that unsullied image to be restored.[25] It also looks forward to the prophecies of Isaiah, Jeremiah and Ezekiel, to the time when the external law would be replaced by one written on people's hearts[26] and their hearts of stone would be replaced by a heart of flesh, and a new Spirit put within them enabling them to keep God's decrees.[27]

---

[22] C. H. Spurgeon, *The Treasury of David* (London: Marshall, Morgan and Scott, 1963 edn), p. 405.
[23] See also 2 Cor. 5:17.
[24] Phil. 4:8–9.
[25] Gen. 1:27.
[26] Jer. 31:33.
[27] Ezek. 36:24–27.

Verses 11 and 12, which are cast in the form of a petition, might equally be cast in the form of a consequence. A newly purified and remade heart would lead to a renewal of the personal relationship David had once enjoyed with God but that sin had destroyed, as it always does. Alienation would be overcome and joy restored. The regenerating work of God's spirit would have an impact not only in the removal of offence but in the whole of life, lifting the spirit and reviving the once-burdened body.

Here, in a nutshell, David seeks 'the fullness of justification and sanctification'.[28] He is not content with being put in the right with God (which is justification), great though that is, but seeks something more. He longs to stay in the right with God, increasingly free from sin and enjoying his presence (which is sanctification). Salvation is more than forgiveness; it is a recreation that is both 'radical and constant'[29] as it leads us to wholeness.

e. David's restoration: freedom from sin (51:13–19)

It is typical of the psalms that they do not stop when the psalmist gets what he has been requesting. Coupled with 'the ask' is 'the promise' or 'the vow'.[30] Once healing is given, once forgiveness flows, once regeneration occurs, it leads onto public testimony (13), thanksgiving (14–15) and to the person restored taking up his or her place in public worship again (16–17). The blessings of God are never for private enjoyment but are given for public benefit. The invalid in hospital, to use Packer's metaphor above, is restored so he or she can get back on two feet and fight in the army again. After suffering comes service.

But David comments that he will return to worship as a different person. No longer will worship be the perfunctory offering of ritual sacrifice for his experience has taught him something much deeper. He has discovered that God does not look on the outward ceremonial of sacrifice but that his penetrating eyes perceive what is inside, in the heart.[31] So, when David takes up his place in public worship again, he does not do so as the proud and confident chosen king of Israel but as one who knows his shortcomings and imperfections. He approaches God now, not as of right, but as one who is unworthy, vulnerable and humbled. The *broken and contrite heart* is deeply felt.

---

[28] Mays, *Psalms*, p. 204.

[29] Grogan, *Psalms*, p. 107.

[30] See Psalm 22 for another example.

[31] Verse 16 should not be read as a rejection of sacrifice, only a rejection of sacrifice offered in the wrong way. See Mays, *Psalms*, p. 203.

Yet there is another reality, even more deeply felt and that is that *a broken and contrite heart, you, God, will not despise*. It is not within his nature for God to reject the genuinely repentant for 'The LORD is close to the broken-hearted and saves those who are crushed in spirit' (Psalm 34:18). So for all his failure, he knows that he will be met not with rejection but by the generous mercy and forgiving grace of his covenant God. Isaiah heralded the same good news:

> For this is what the high and exalted One says –
> He who lives for ever, whose name is holy:
> 'I live in a high and holy place,
> but also with those who are contrite and lowly in spirit,
> to revive the spirit of the lowly
> and to revive the heart of the contrite.
> (Isaiah 57:15)

Jesus confirmed the continuing importance of these truths when his first beatitude announced, 'Blessed are the poor in spirit, for theirs is the kingdom of heaven' (Matthew 5:3).

The person who has not experienced the brokenness that comes from knowing how grievous our sin is to God and others, will find it difficult to make progress in holiness. But those who appreciate the darkness of their own hearts will cast themselves, as David does, on the mercy of God and find they are lifted up and renewed from within.

3. Concluding comment

James Packer wrote, 'Important as the outward life of justice, integrity and neighbour-love is, the inner life . . . is held (surely rightly) to be far more important. God calls on his children to give them his hearts.'[32] But there is (surely) no competition between the outward and the inward life. Both are important to God. We cannot choose to specialize in the one at the expense of the other. The call to holiness is a call to integrate the outward and the inward dimensions of our lives so they are at ease with each other. But we may rightly question whether we have understood the Bible's teaching on holiness unless we allow it to address the interior structures of our lives and the darkest depths that we seek to hide from others and even dislike admitting to ourselves. Thank God, he is the God who re-creates us from the inside out.

[32] Packer, *A Passion for Holiness*, p. 98.

Holiness is more than a matter of outward conformity to the laws of God and even more than our determination to obey him. It is about God restoring his image in our fallen lives, about the re-formation of our inner character so that we have a *willing spirit* to sustain us in worship, love, service and obedience. As Richard Foster put it,

> The will has the same deficiency as the law—it can only deal with externals. It is not sufficient to bring about the necessary transformation of the inner spirit.
>
> When we despair of gaining inner transformation through human powers of will and determination, we are open to a wonderful new realization: inner righteousness is a gift from God to be graciously received. The change within us is God's work, not ours. The demand is for an inside job, and only God can work from the inside. We cannot attain or earn this righteousness of the kingdom of God; it is a grace that is given.[33]

[33] R. Foster, *Celebration of Discipline* (London: Hodder and Stoughton, 1980), p. 5.

1 Thessalonians 4:1–12
11. Personal holiness

A simple evangelistic tract that was widely used some years back had as its theme, 'God has a plan for your life.' Indeed, he does. But it is not the plan many are looking for. It is not a career plan, a marriage plan, a financial plan or a retirement plan. It is a plan to make us holy. Paul could not have put it more plainly to the Thessalonians than he did: *It is God's will that you should be sanctified* (3). We may have other priorities but God's priority for our lives is holiness.

In what was probably his earliest letter in the New Testament, a follow-up letter to those recently converted through his ministry, Paul gives a very straightforward call to personal holiness in 1 Thessalonians 4:1–12.[1] His teaching is directed to individual believers, although even here it is difficult to draw the boundaries too tightly for all our behaviour impacts others.

1. Commendation (4:1)

Paul's introduction to the theme of holiness is a model of pastoral wisdom. Although earlier in his letter he had spoken of the Thessalonians as imitating him (1:6)[2] and described himself as being like a mother and father to them (2:7–12), here, still using

[1] Other passages which we could examine regarding this dimension of holiness, like Col. 3:5–17 or Eph. 5:3–20 expand some aspects of the teaching here but the individual and the corporate dimensions are merged more in them.

[2] On imitation, see L. Belville, '"Imitate me, just as I imitate Christ": Discipleship in the Corinthian Correspondence,' in R. N. Longenecker (ed.), *Patterns of Discipleship in the New Testament* (Grand Rapids: Eerdmans, 1996), pp. 120–142 and V. A. Copan, *Saint Paul as Spiritual Director* (Milton Keynes: Paternoster, 2007).

the language of the family, he puts himself now not above them but alongside them as a brother. Few people are motivated to be holy when lectured by a superior. Most are much more inspired when they know that those instructing them in holiness are flesh and blood people who struggle as they do to become what they are in Christ.

A second feature of Paul's approach is the strong encouragement he gives regarding what they are already doing. In fact, Paul's words tend to tumble over themselves in a somewhat complicated way, so eager is he to express the fact that they are already living in the way they should.[3] He does not knock them down in order to build them up, as some do, but encourages them in the progress they have already made. Even so, there is no room for complacency and he wants them to 'abound' and 'overflow' in their new Christ-centred lifestyle. He regards the matter as so important that he writes, *we ask you and urge you in the Lord Jesus to do this more and more.* His use of *ask* (*erōtōmen*) and *urge* (*parakaloumen*) underlines the importance of the matter. His addition of *the Lord Jesus* here, and in the next verse, adds a slight touch of authority to his request and makes it even more emphatic. Encouraging them in this way is possible because of the foundation he laid when he was with them. He is not belatedly introducing them to the small print of the gospel, having hooked them with the bold print of its promises. He is reminding them of what he had already taught. *We instructed you* (TNIV) somewhat disguises Paul's meaning since what he actually says refers here to the 'tradition'[4] into which he had initiated them. It was not Paul's moral opinions or personal ethical ideals he had taught them but the gospel and teaching of Christ as agreed by the founding apostles of the church.[5]

Paul's objective is that they should *please God* which, as Gene Green points out, 'does not mean anything so mundane as "being pleasant" toward him'[6] but serving him by living according to his ethical commands. How to please God is the subject of what follows.

[3] I. H. Marshall, *1 and 2 Thessalonians* NCB (Grand Rapids: Eerdmans and London: Marshall, Morgan and Scott, 1983), p. 104.

[4] *parelabete*, in v. 1, refers to 'receiving' the tradition and *parangelias*, in v. 2, to the authoritative 'instructions' of the apostles. F. F. Bruce, *1 & 2 Thessalonians* WBC 45 (Waco, TX: Word, 182), p. 78–79.

[5] D. Tidball, *Ministry by the Book: New Testament patterns for pastoral leadership* (Nottingham: Apollos, 2008), pp. 131–132.

[6] G. L. Green, *The Letters to the Thessalonians*, Pillar Commentary (Grand Rapids: Eerdmans and Leicester: Apollos, 2002), p. 185.

2. Destination (4:3)

The goal of the Christian life is holiness. Elsewhere Paul can write of sanctification as a status God has already conferred on his people, surprisingly even on the morally-dubious Corinthian believers.[7] But his accent in 1 Thessalonians is not on the status which is theirs but the goal they must pursue. Being holy, in the sense of moral perfection, is something which is still future. In one of those irrepressible prayers which erupt occasionally in Paul's letters, he had prayed for the Thessalonians, 'May he strengthen your hearts so that you will be blameless and holy in the presence of our God and Father when the Lord Jesus comes with all his holy ones' (3:13). Then we shall have reached the goal, but now there is much work still to be done. So, just a few verses later, in saying, *this is God's will for you, your sanctification* (lit. trans.) he puts the emphasis on the process by which they will be made holy.[8] They are on a journey and have not yet reached their destination. The journey began at their conversion and will be completed on their death or at the return of Christ. We are often like impatient children asking their parents, 'Are we there yet?' when the family sets out on an excursion. The answer is plainly 'No!' But the wise parent adds, 'but we are nearer than when we first began'.

What is the holiness towards which we work? Briefly put, in the context of 1 Thessalonians it 'is both to be understood negatively of freedom from sin and positively in terms of love', which are arguably 'two sides of the same coin'.[9]

If we were to expand our understanding we could do no better than use the classic statement of J. C. Ryle that dovetails with the concerns of 1 Thessalonians so well. Practical holiness, he wrote, is not knowledge, profession, doing, respectability, enjoying sermons, nor keeping company with godly people. Aware of the dangers of the exercise lest he should give 'a defective view of holiness', he nonetheless lists a series of characteristics which compose holiness, each backed by biblical references. as follows. Ryle says holiness is

a . . . the habit of being of one mind with God.

b . . . [to] endeavour to shun every known sin, and to keep every known commandment.

---

[7] 1 Cor. 1:2.

[8] The word *hagiasmos* here and elsewhere means the process of sanctification. The present continuous dimension is evident in Rom. 6:19; 2 Thess. 2:13; 1 Tim. 2:15; Heb. 12:14; 1 Pet. 1:2 (Green, *Letters to the Thessalonians*, p. 190).

[9] Marshall, *1 and 2 Thessalonians*, p. 106.

c ... [to] strive to be like our Lord Jesus Christ.
d ... meekness.
e ... temperance and self-denial.
f ... charity and brotherly kindness.
g ... a spirit of mercy and benevolence to others.
h ... purity of heart.[10]
i ... the fear of God.
j ... humility.
k ... faithfulness in all the duties of life.
l ... spiritual mindedness.[11]

In line with the apostle Paul, Ryle adds that this is surely the desire of all true Christians, 'They press towards it, if they do not reach it. They may not attain to it, but they always aim at it.'[12]

3. Motivation (4:2–12)

Our understanding of holiness can easily degenerate into mere moralism and outward legalism. By contrast, when Paul teaches the Thessalonians about holiness, he marinades his instruction in the juice of relationships. Our desire for holiness arises from our relationship with the Trinitarian God and our fellow human beings. It is our being joined to him that motivates us to be like him.

R. T. Kendall claims, 'none of us takes to holiness naturally. We are all congenitally allergic to holiness.'[13] Certainly, we are easily distracted from the pursuit of holiness. Perhaps that is another reason why Paul threads seven reasons why Christians should pursue it with all determination throughout his teaching.

a. Jesus commands it (4:2)

The instructions Paul conveys are given *by the authority of the Lord Jesus*. In using this phrase, Paul is emphasising that the instructions did not originate with him but that he is the messenger on behalf of a higher authority; indeed, the highest authority of all, *the Lord Jesus*. As disciples of Christ they would realize that their place was not to argue about the substance of Paul's teaching but to obey

[10] Ryle adds, 'He knows his own heart is like tinder and will diligently keep clear of the sparks of temptation.'
[11] J. C. Ryle, *Holiness* (Cambridge and London: James Clarke, 1956), pp. 34–38.
[12] Ibid., p. 39.
[13] R. T. Kendall, *Once Saved, Always Saved* (London: Hodder and Stoughton, 1983), p. 103.

their master. Paul's claim not only implies apostolic authority but that the contents of his teaching go back to Jesus himself. It is not difficult to connect Paul's teaching with the words of Jesus, even if the form of the words cannot be traced back to the Gospels. In any case, the instructions may well have been passed on verbally or through the activity of prophets.[14] If this is the point Paul is making, he is stressing that the 'tradition' to which we referred earlier goes back even further than the apostles to Jesus himself. Put simply, if the Thessalonians have made Jesus their Lord, they would do everything in their power to follow his instructions.

b. God desires it (4:3)

To the authority of Christ Paul now adds the will of God the Father. Holiness may not be the only ambition God has for us but it is a major priority and one which encompasses others. Is not his desire that we should know Christ,[15] love one another,[16] walk in the Spirit,[17] or cooperate with him in his mission?[18] Certainly. But these cannot be undertaken apart from holiness. Holiness is both a cause and a consequence of those other desires. For Paul, holiness is 'the essence of a life of Christian discipleship'.[19]

The therapeutic gospel, the prosperity gospel, and the postmodern gospel which so many contemporary Western Christians have bought into, gives the impression that God's will for us is our comfort, ease or satisfaction. But God's real desire is to reconstruct our lives, removing the rubble of wrongdoing and evil desires, and building lives where integrity, purity, honour and sheer goodness are evident.

c. Love requires it (4:6)

The next motivation Paul mentions is an example of how holiness is an all-encompassing quality. It has implications not only for our relationship with God but our relationships with our brothers and sisters. Failures in holiness take their toll of relationships and not infrequently mean, as mentioned here, that we *wrong or*

---

[14] See a similar reference in 1 Cor. 14:36–37.
[15] 1 Cor. 1:9; Phil. 3:10.
[16] John 13:34; 1 John 3:23; 4:11.
[17] Gal. 5:25; Eph. 5:18.
[18] Matt. 28:19–20; Acts 1:8.
[19] J. A. D. Weima, '"How you must walk to please God": Holiness and Discipleship in 1 Thessalonians,' in Longenecker (ed.), *Patterns of Discipleship in the New Testament*, p. 107.

take advantage of a brother or sister. Taking advantage of a fellow Christian is commercial language, the language of defrauding or cheating, but the focus is still firmly on someone enriching himself sexually, not financially, at the expense of another member of the church.[20] Holiness leads to respect not disrespect; to thoughtfulness, not a lack of consideration; to courtesy, not rudeness; to harmony, not conflict; to building up the community, not destroying it. Love compels us to live a holy life.

d. Judgment underlines it (4:6)

A further incentive to holiness lies in the thought of the coming judgment. The reality of judgment is introduced by Paul as a warning. Perhaps, however, it should not be read as the dire warning of a hell-fire preacher. The early Christians lived constantly in the light of the future, much more than we do. The very next topic to which Paul is going to turn in this letter is that of the coming again of Christ (4:13 – 5:11). Paul's whole ministry was framed by his belief in the future God was planning.[21] He constantly shows an acute awareness that we are accountable for the way we live our lives. [22] 'We must all appear before the judgment seat of Christ, that everyone may receive what is due to them for the things done while in the body, whether good or bad' (2 Corinthians 5:10). It was such a fundamental part of early Christian teaching that it would have been surprising if Paul had not mentioned it. Living in the light of the future, of one day meeting our master, is a powerful reason for being serious about holiness.

e. Conversion entails it (4:7–8)

Holiness is implicit in our calling as Christians. Just as the vocation of the doctor is to heal, and the vocation of the teacher is to educate, and the vocation of a soldier is to fight, so the vocation of the Christian is to be holy. The seed planted in us at conversion springs to life in holiness until it reaches full bloom on the day of Christ. This is the point Peter makes in 1 Peter 1:2, as we saw in chapter 2. The Greek stresses this calling comes from God;[23] not from an inspirational preacher, motivational guru, military or

---

[20] Weima, ibid., p. 109, Abraham J. Malherbe, *The Letters to the Thessalonians,* AB (Doubleday: New York, 2000), p. 232.

[21] E.g., 1 Cor. 9:24–27; 1 Thess. 2:17–19; 2 Tim. 4:8. Tidball, *Ministry by the Book,* pp. 111–113.

[22] Rom. 14:12.

[23] Marshall, *1 and 2 Thessalonians,* p. 113.

political authority but from the highest authority of all, from God himself. To reject this calling then is not to *reject a human being but God.*

f. The Spirit enables it (4:8)

The calling is, of course, matched by God's enabling of us. We are not left to struggle alone for, as Paul immediately and emphatically adds, *God . . . gives you his Holy Spirit.*[24] The Spirit of God himself, the Spirit who is constantly described as 'Holy', is given as an indwelling agent of change, just as the prophets foretold as they looked forward to the messianic age.[25] This has become a reality for Gentiles as well as Jews.

Divine energy is channelled into our lives to produce the desired fruit.[26] Holiness is not only our work but his. With him we can achieve what we could not achieve alone and though effort is still required on our part, and the struggle can sometimes be intense, yet the path to holiness is not as impossible an upwards climb as it would be if the Holy Spirit were not assisting us. Furthermore, the gift of the Spirit is a sign not only of God's empowering but of his commitment. We need not despair about our progress, or lack of it, because with Paul our confidence lies not in ourselves but in 'the one who calls you [who] is faithful, and [who] will do it' (1 Thessalonians 5:24). Unlike us fickle human beings, he does not commence a job he will not complete, so we can be sure that 'he who began a good work in [us] will carry it on to completion until the day of Christ Jesus' (Philippians 1:6).

g. Witness compels it (4:12)

If asked why we should be holy, many Christians would respond first by saying that our witness to others is made or marred by it. The point is right but what is the first reason many of us give is the last reason to which Paul comes. Paul is much more God-conscious and God-centred in his thinking than we are. Even our quest for holiness, like much of the practice of our Christian faith, can be very focused on people – ourselves and others – rather than on him. Paul's starting point has been the Trinitarian God and his call on our

[24] The Greek places the emphasis on God, 'the God who indeed gives you his Spirit'.
[25] Ezek. 36:26; 37:14. See further Weima, in Longenecker (ed.), *Patterns of Discipleship in the New Testament*, pp. 110–112 and Malherbe, *The Letters to the Thessalonians*, p. 235.
[26] Gal. 5:22–23.

lives. Only after that does Paul write that his readers are to live holy lives *so that your daily life may win the respect of outsiders.*

The point need not be pressed. The newspapers broadcast the failure of Christians, especially their leaders, enough for us not to need reminding that major lapses in holiness cause believers to be ridiculed and the name of Jesus Christ to be denigrated. We must be careful, however, not to allow this reason for holiness to turn us into anxious legalists. Mark Twain talked of people who were 'good in the worst sense of the word'. The respect of outsiders is not earned by Christians leading inhibited lives that are imprisoned in rules and regulations and so 'precious' as to be ignorant of and insulated from the surrounding culture. Respect is won by warm, positive, wholesome and responsible lives, as will be explained further in the next chapter.

4. Application

Paul has a very specific and practical agenda in view as he addresses the need for holiness. His discussion of its incentives is no theoretical exercise but plaited with practical application as tightly as a girl's pigtails. He is writing to Gentiles who live in a culture sated with sexual liberty and whose men have been schooled to take certain sexual rights for granted. Furthermore, he is writing in a context where a change of religious belief did not necessarily entail a change in ethical behaviour. But conversion to Christ involves a total change. In Christ, the Gentiles who have been incorporated into the new Israel are expected to live according to the moral standards that applied to Israel.

a. Sexual purity (4:3–8)

The frequent cry is heard: 'Why is the church obsessed with sex?' Many would regard it as typical that Paul immediately applies his early teaching on holiness to the sexual life, both here and in 1 Corinthians.[27] There are, I think, several answers as to why the church is legitimately concerned about sexual issues. Arguably, the media is obsessed with sex and the culture in which we live so fixated by it that it makes it very difficult for the church to avoid discussing it. The moral boundaries have shifted so fast (or been removed so rapidly) in recent years that the church has had to rearticulate its position on sexual ethics. What is more, the church

[27] 1 Cor. 5:1–13; 6:12–20.

has had plenty of other agendas in recent years, like the abolition of poverty, but its campaigns and good works in those areas are ignored by the press who often only seem interested in the church when it speaks about sex.

But there are deeper issues that make it appropriate too. The sexual dimension of our lives is very significant to our created identity as human beings[28] and many find the sexual drive very powerful. Sexual practice has to do with who we are as people and reaches deep into our personalities. So, Paul explained to the Corinthians that while sexual sin is not more serious than other sins, it is of a different kind. 'All other sins people commit', he writes, 'are outside their bodies, but those who sin sexually sin against their own bodies' (1 Corinthians 6:19).[29] Sexual expression and identity are intimately connected and affect the whole person. And since our identity is now determined by our being joined to Christ and being temples of the Holy Spirit, we cannot sleep around, joining our bodies to anyone other than our marriage partner. Moreover, the implications of various sexual practices for the shape and health of families and communities is immense. What sort of a gospel would it be, then, than did not address such a fundamental human issue?

Whether culturally, morally or religiously, Thessalonica took a very lax view about all kinds of sexual practices, whether heterosexual or homosexual. Innkeepers and shopkeepers kept slave girls to provide sexual entertainment for their customers.[30] The worship of Aphrodite, Dionysius and other gods would have involved sexual activity. The cult of Cabirus which had a pronounced sexual character was especially popular in Thessalonica.[31] Cicero described those who thought youths should not have affairs as 'eminently austere'.[32] Adultery was common. And so on.[33]

Gentile converts might not have understood the connection between their conversion and their conduct and may have continued to live according to old standards. So, Paul addresses the issue

---

[28] Gen. 1:27; 2:19–25.

[29] The interpretation of the verse is complex. See A. Thiselton, *The First Epistle to the Corinthians* NIGNT (Grand Rapids: Eerdmans and Carlisle: Paternoster, 2000), pp. 470–474. Thiselton concludes, p. 474, that 'far from *devaluing* sex, *the very opposite comes about,*' as a result of Paul's argument. 'In this area Paul was far ahead of first-century cultural assumptions in perceiving the sexual act as one of intimacy and *self-commitment which involved the whole person;* not the mere "peripheral" function of the whole body.'

[30] Weima, in Longenecker (ed.), *Patterns of Discipleship in the New Testament*, p. 105.

[31] Ibid.

[32] Cited by Malherbe, *The Letters to the Thessalonians*, pp. 235–236.

[33] For details of Thessalonica see, Green, *Letters to the Thessalonians*, p. 187.

with some straight talking. His instructions are first negative and then positive.

(i) Negatively: 'avoid sexual immorality' (4:3)

The general command to *avoid sexual immorality* avoids mentioning specific sexual sins and so provides no one with a tick-box approach to sexual ethics: the 'I haven't fallen into that particular sin, so I'm alright!' type of argument. Avoiding sexual immorality (*porneia*) means abstaining from all sexual intercourse outside of marriage. The call, as Howard Marshall points out, is for total abstention not moderation, as it necessarily is whenever Christians are tempted to evil.[34] The command applies to all, not just those like the young or the unmarried who face particularly fierce battles in this area. Everyone is caught in its net, young or old, married or single.

The call also goes to the heart of holiness as separation. Christians are to separate themselves from the commonly accepted sexual practices of their pagan culture because they are separated to God. As with Israel, under the new covenant, believers have a distinctive lifestyle.

(ii) Positively: 'learn to control your own body' (4:4–5)

Turning from the negative to the positive Paul instructs them to *learn to control* their own bodies or to gain mastery over them. The very terminology recognizes that holiness is not necessarily going to be achieved easily but through a process of experiential learning, which might well involve setbacks and failures, as well as success and progress. The problem arises because of the strength of *passionate lust* (5) to which we are subject. Malherbe says this is the language of the Stoics who saw emotions and passions as opposed to reason, 'as an irrational and unnatural movement of the soul, as an impulse in excess'.[35] Consequently, as we would submit our bodies to a disciplined regime of training if we wished to achieve some sporting success, so our emotions need to be approached in the same way under the coaching of the Holy Spirit.

[34] Marshall, *1 and 2 Thessalonians*, p. 107.
[35] Malherbe, *The Letters to the Thessalonians,* p. 229. Malherbe advocates the view that Paul's moral teaching reflects the Greek philosophical schools of his day, although he qualifies it in recognising that Paul is different in that his exhortations are steeped in theological language (p. 238). Others see this as unnecessary and argue that Paul's ethics are sufficiently explained by his understanding of the Old Testament. See also, M. Elliott, *Faithful Feelings: Emotion in the New Testament* (Leicester: IVP, 2005), pp. 13–79.

So much is clear. But Paul's choice of vocabulary has caused debate for it is possible to translate his words not as 'to take control over his own body in holiness and honour'[36] but as 'to take a wife for himself in holiness and honour'[37]– the key words *skeuos katasthai* are ambiguous. If Paul meant the latter, it would seem that he is specifically addressing the unmarried and saying to them, as he did to the Corinthians, that 'if they cannot control themselves, they should marry, for it is better to marry than to burn with passion' (1 Corinthians 7:9). In other words, if one cannot control oneself, one should find a legitimate outlet for one's sexual drive. This seems to denigrate marriage and Green is surely right in pointing out, it is the more general sense of controlling one's body that is in line with the persistent teaching of the New Testament and therefore to be preferred.[38] It is, then, not only a question of refraining from genital sexual activity except within marriage, but developing wholesome self-discipline in all areas of our emotional life. If any passions, emotions or addictions master us, rather than us mastering them, we lack the holiness Paul advocates to the Thessalonians. In this regard I find it helpful to reflect on four questions given to Jerry Bridges by a friend to help him distinguish right from wrong.[39]

    i. Is it helpful – physically, spiritually and mentally?
    ii. Does it bring me under its power?
    iii. Does it hurt others?
    iv. Does it glorify God?

b. Social responsibility (4:9–12)

Although it is commonly accepted that Paul applies his teaching to the sexual life (4:3–8), it is less commonly seen that he goes beyond that and applies it to our social responsibility as well (4:9–12). *Now* in verse 9 suggests that Paul is introducing another topic whereas, in fact, he is introducing another application of the same topic, namely, holiness. Verse 10 repeats the encouragement of verse 3. Verse 11 encourages them not to be busybodies.[40] Jeffrey Weima captures

---

[36] The preferred translation of NEB, JB, NIV, NRSV, TNIV. For arguments in favour see Green, *The Letters to the Thessalonians*, pp. 192–194.

[37] The preferred translation of RSV, NAB. For the arguments in favour see Malherbe's extensive discussion in *Letters to the Thessalonians*, pp. 226–228.

[38] Green, *Letters to the Thessalonians*, pp. 193–194. He refers to Acts 15:20, 29; 21:25; 1 Cor. 6:12–20; Eph. 5:3; Col. 3:5; 2 Tim. 2:21–22.

[39] J. Bridges, *The Pursuit of Holiness* (London: Authentic Media, 2004), p. 62. The questions are based on 1 Cor. 6:12; 8:13; 10:31.

[40] 2 Thess. 3:11.

Paul's advice when he translates it as, 'Make it your ambition to have no ambition'.[41] The *quiet life* to which he alludes is captured in a phrase widely used of those who had withdrawn from political and public life, but this is not Paul's meaning here. In fact, his argument is essentially the reverse of that. He may be concerned that they love each other in the church so much that they are failing in their wider social responsibilities. Some churches are wonderfully warm cosy fellowships who show intense concern for those who belong but total indifference to the concerns of those outside. But such introverted fellowships do not honour God.

Paul's advice that they should lead a *quiet life* is to be understood in the light of what follows in verses 11 and 12. He is not proposing that Christians should withdraw into a contemplative life and have nothing to do with wider society. Rather his concern is with those who have ceased to engage responsibly in the wider community because they no longer earn their own keep but spend their time interfering in other people's business. The reason they have given up work is not because they cannot get it (which is not an issue Paul addresses) but either because they think the second coming is so imminent that it's not worth pursuing such a mundane thing, or that they have become such enthusiastic converts that they see manual labour as second best to preaching. Typically Jewish, Paul values manual labour for its own sake. But he is also concerned about the ridicule these people provoke among *outsiders*. Later on he refers to these people as 'idle and disruptive' (5:14). And he is forced to return to the matter once more in his second letter to the Thessalonians where he bluntly says, 'Anyone who is unwilling to work shall not eat' (3:10) and commands them to 'earn the bread they eat' (3:12). If they do not they are spongers, even thieves,[42] and meddlers who are mistaken in their belief that they are doing the will of God. His will is that they should accept their responsibility to care financially for themselves and their own families[43] and to contribute to the communities to which they belong.

Holiness affects the whole of life. For the Thessalonians, possibly because of reports he has received about them, Paul applies his teaching to their sexual practices and their social obligations, but he could have applied it to other matters as well. Pleasing God entails what goes on in the bedroom and the market place, the office and the factory, and not just what goes on in the church.

---

[41] Weima, in Longenecker (ed.), *Patterns of Discipleship in the New Testament*, p. 117.

[42] Eph. 4:28.

[43] Similar strong instructions are found in 1 Tim. 5:4, 8.

5. Concluding comment

The Thessalonians had begun to reconstruct their personal lives according to God's ambition for them to be holy but the reconstruction was far from complete. Perhaps some of them had not even grasped the extent to which the calling of holiness was going to reshape them. There was, though, no need to despair because the apostle would instruct them and the Trinitarian God would continue his work in them until the task was complete. They had every reason to join John Newton in saying:

> I am not what I ought to be – ah, how imperfect and deficient! I am not what I wish to be – I abhor what is evil, and I would cleave to what is good! I am not what I hope to be – soon, soon shall I put off mortality, and with mortality all sin and imperfection. Yet, though I am not what I ought to be, nor what I wish to be, nor what I hope to be, I can truly say, I am not what I once was; a slave to sin and Satan; and I can heartily join with the apostle, and acknowledge, 'By the grace of God I am what I am.'[44]

---

[44] As quoted in *The Christian Pioneer* (1856), edited by Joseph Foulkes Winks, p. 84.

1 Peter 2:4–10; Ephesians 4:17 – 5:20
12. Corporate holiness

Truth to tell, I was already in the ministry before I came to understand the importance of the church in God's eyes. My faith had been
nurtured in contexts that stressed the need for a 'personal' spiritual
experience but which I understood to mean an 'individual' spiritual
experience. Whenever I read a command or a promise addressed
to 'you', I foolishly took it to be addressed to 'me', individually.
The lenses of modern Western individualism through which I read
the Bible, prevented me from seeing what was obvious, that often
these things were addressed to the church corporately. The responsibilities, promises, identity and destiny of which it spoke, were
frequently shared obligations and privileges. I knew, theoretically,
that God had called Abraham to be the father of a new people[1] but it
was 'me' rather than 'us' that I took to be his primary focus. Michael
Griffiths wonderfully captured my position when he wrote, 'It is as
though most Christians expect to fly solo to heaven with only just a
little bit of formation flying from time to time!'[2]

What relief there was, as well as new challenges, when I discovered God's intention was for the church to fly in formation towards
its destiny of being 'confident and unashamed before him at his
coming' (1 John 2:28). Twice Paul uses imagery related to marriage
to describe this goal for the church. In 2 Corinthians 11:2 he speaks
of the church as a virgin bride, needing to be kept pure for her
groom. In Ephesians 5:27 he speaks of the church as a beautiful bride
on her wedding day and says that Christ will 'present her to himself
as a radiant church, without stain or wrinkle or any other blemish,
but holy and blameless'. So, although we rejoice in the truth that
Christ 'loved *me* and gave himself for *me*' (Galatians 2:20), it must

[1] Gen. 12:1–3.
[2] M. Griffiths, *Cinderella with Amnesia* (London: IVP, 1975), p. 23.

be balanced with the truth that 'Christ loved *the church* and gave himself up for *her*' (Ephesians 5:25).

The church is far from incidental to my personal desire to be holy. The church is the instrument God will use, in part, to rebuild my life and reconstruct his image in me. Its worship and preaching, relationships, love and even its irritations will shape and mould me to be more Christ-like. God has arranged it so I cannot make progress in holiness without it. But to see the church's connection with holiness only from that perspective is still to be imprisoned in the mindset of individualism. It is asking what the church can do for *me*. To equate holiness with personal purity alone, as many evangelicals do, is to fall short of the biblical teaching on holiness because the church collectively has a calling to be holy. There is a 'goal of congregational development and progress' that many of us overlook. This means that we 'have tremendous responsibilities to the congregation, because all of us are supposed to be developing and progressing together as a wonderful new community of God's people'.[3]

The New Testament presents this message from two complementary viewpoints: the privilege and the practice of holiness.

1. The privilege of corporate holiness (1 Peter 2:4–10)

When God revealed himself to Moses on Mount Sinai, he had promised Israel that if she kept his covenant stipulations, she would be more than a mere descendant of Jacob,[4] and would become his 'treasured possession', 'a kingdom of priests and a holy nation' (Exodus 19:5–6). Among all the people God had created they would become 'the "crown jewel" of a large collection, the masterwork, the one-of-a-kind piece', as John Durham terms it.[5] With their status as a 'treasured possession' would go their responsibility to be the go-betweens between God and his world. As priests they would enjoy free access into his presence while serving as intercessors on behalf of others. In like manner, as 'a holy nation' they would have a unique role in the world of being God's showcase and displaying God's glory among the nations.

For all their stated commitment, however, Israel soon, and thereafter frequently, proved an unreliable people. In erecting a golden calf so shortly after God offered them their special status,[6] Israel

---

[3] Griffiths, *Cinderella*, p. 31.
[4] J. Durham, *Exodus*, WBC (Waco: Word, 1987), p. 262.
[5] Ibid.
[6] Exod. 32.

failed to remain true to God and so the privilege of each of them being priests 'became vested in the tribe of Levi and the family of Aaron'.[7] Their continuing failure to keep the covenant meant they failed, too, in their role as a showcase to the world of the difference being in covenant with God can make, and eventually they ceased to be a nation in any real sense as God first sentenced them to exile and then to be scattered around the world.

God's vision, however, for a new people who would embody these expectations to be created was never exhausted and came to be inherited by those who became obedient to Jesus Christ.[8] In continuity with Israel, the church came to be the new Israel, and to receive the privileges and calling of Israel. In contrast to Israel who stumbled *because they disobey the message*, Peter explained, you (the church) *are a chosen people, a royal priesthood, a holy nation, God's special possessions, that you may declare the praises of him who called you out of darkness into his wonderful light* (2:8–9). Each phrase has deep resonances with what is said of Israel in the Old Testament[9] but equally has sharp implications for the people of God today.

a. A chosen people

Isaiah spoke of Israel as *chosen* to be the servant of God in the world (Isaiah 44:1) and empowered to 'bring justice to the nations' (Isaiah 42:1). Especially protected (Isaiah 49:2), the outworking of international events would serve their ends (Isaiah 45:4) so that the world could see his splendour manifest in them. Although these things had patchily come true in Israel, they had been fully fulfilled in the life of Jesus, the Servant *par excellence,* as Peter is aware. He may have been rejected by human beings but was *chosen by God and precious to him* (2:4). So when Peter says to Christians that they are *a chosen people* he is quite consciously connecting them with Jesus. They are chosen because he was chosen and they have become united to him. They are precious because he was precious and they have been joined to him. To use a Pauline term, it is because they are 'in Christ' that they experience the status and responsibilities of being God's elect servants in the world.

But his claim is even more extraordinary. He is writing to people who have no natural reason to belong to each other.[10] They are

---

[7] A. Motyer, *The Message of Exodus,* BST (Leicester: IVP, 2005), p. 199.

[8] 1 Peter 1:2.

[9] The first and last phrases come from the references in Isaiah to Israel as a servant and to Isa. 43:20–21. The central phrases come from Exod. 19:5–6.

[10] 1 Pet. 1:1.

scattered exiles, dispersed around God's world. But as they have been drawn to Christ, so they have been drawn to each other and from this disparate group of unrelated persons a new 'clan' has been formed and a new body of bonded people has come into existence.[11] He has not elected a few individuals so much as created a new 'third race'.[12]

b. A royal priesthood

The privilege of priesthood equally stems from the believer's relationship with Jesus Christ. Priests offer sacrifices and the whole church now composes a priesthood *offering spiritual sacrifices acceptable to God through Jesus Christ* (2:5).

God's original intention, which had been frustrated by Israel, has now in Christ become a reality. There is no longer a special class of persons who are priests within the church, rather the whole church is a priesthood and each member of it a priest. The church collectively has direct access to God to offer worship and intercession without the need for another human intermediary apart from Jesus Christ, the high priest.[13] The point here is 'not on the priestly role of each believer but on the priestly identity of God's people'.[14] So, although the doctrine of the priesthood of believers is a true New Testament doctrine, to build the doctrine on the foundation of these verses is to miss Peter's meaning. Collectively, the church has a role in offering sacrifices to God. The sacrifices they offer are 'spiritual sacrifices' which must include praise, love and holiness of life.[15] The priests are *royal* because they are priests who belong to the king and exclusively serve him.

c. A holy nation

Our real interest in the passage lies in the designation of the church as *a holy nation.* Some argue this is nothing to do with their moral achievements,[16] whereas others, while recognizing that it means they are a distinct people who belong to God in a way no others do, say that, above all, the term, 'lays on them the obligation to be

[11] J. B. Green, *1 Peter,* Two Horizons New Testament Commentary (Grand Rapids: Eerdmans, 2007), pp. 61–62.

[12] The term 'third race' was a term of abuse hurled against the early Christians, referred to by Tertullian. The first two races were, of course, Jews and Gentiles.

[13] Heb. 4:14–16;10:19–39.

[14] Green, *1 Peter,* p. 61.

[15] Heb. 13:15; 1 Peter 1:15, 22.

[16] P. H. Davids, *The First Epistle of Peter,* NICNT (Grand Rapids: Eerdmans, 1990), p. 92.

holy'.[17] In reality the distance between them is paper-thin. Being a holy nation is 'a community identity',[18] a status conferred on them by God. They are his special envoys in the world, in a separate class from other people and marked out as different from others. But this very difference necessarily manifests itself in their living differently. They are to be 'recognizably, visibly, and substantively different, as the people belonging uniquely to Yahweh and therefore representing his character and his ways . . .'[19]

That visible difference, however, is to grow out of a recognition of their identity as people designated holy to God. Our standing is not affected by how far we succeed in living a holy life in practice, for our standing has been determined by God alone and is the result of his grace. Though unrighteous, we have been declared righteous by God and his own power has made us holy.[20] But this is no legal fiction, no mere superficial change of status. The civilian who accepts the Commander-in-Chief's commission to serve as a soldier cannot continue to live as a civilian. The status brings with it a new way of life, new privileges and new challenges. Above all, soldiers do not spend time contemplating what authority they will recognize, whose orders they will accept or on which side they will fight. The new status involves many changes. So, implicit in our status as *a holy nation* is the call to free ourselves from attachments to other authorities and to live the sort of ethical life that pleases the one who has bestowed on us the honour of being his special envoys in the world.

d. God's special possession

Peter's readers have become a *precious* people because they have been liberated from alien, usurping authorities who once ruled their lives, 'with the precious blood of Christ' (1 Peter 1:19). Such is the cost of their redemption and the value God places on their lives, a value that far exceeds 'silver and gold' (1:18). So those redeemed by Christ become 'the apple of his eye',[21] 'the jewel in his crown'.

Again, the accent falls on their status. From the conventional social, economic and political viewpoint, this bunch of *foreigners*

---

[17] I. H. Marshall, *I Peter*, IVPNTC (Downers Grove: IVP and Leicester: IVP, 1991), p. 75.

[18] J. B. Wells, *God's Holy People: A Theme in Biblical Theology* (Sheffield: Sheffield Academic Press, 2000), p. 229.

[19] Chris Wright, quoted by J. Green in 'Living as Exiles: The Church in the Diaspora in 1 Peter', in K. E. Brower and A. Johnson (eds.), *Holiness and Ecclesiology in the New Testament* (Grand Rapids: Eerdmans: 2007), p. 322.

[20] 1 Cor. 1:30.

[21] Ps. 17:8.

and exiles who had become believers in Jesus Christ were nobodies. But the status conferred on them because of the death and resurrection of Christ meant that they were now *the people of God.* If they were rejected or ignored by everyone else, the Lord God of the Universe, the one who ultimately mattered, delighted in them and, even more than longing just to be associated with them, took care of them and bestowed significance on them.

The accent might also, according to Ramsey Michaels, fall on their future destiny. He argues the phrase has a future thrust that is usually ignored and that it is best translated, 'a people destined for vindication',[22] which would certainly make sense in the context.

My wife and I had visited Romania during the dark days of Ceausescu's tyrannical Communist regime and met with scattered believers who were harassed by the authorities and treated as dirt. It was then my privilege to return in October 1990, some time after the revolution, for the founding of the Evangelical Alliance of Romania. How wonderful it was to see 4,000 Romanian Christians sitting in the Parliamentary auditorium, where Ceausescu used to harangue his party about staying loyal to Marxism, praising God and listening to his Word. Ceausescu and his party were now nowhere. But the people who had been nobodies were now somebodies. The accused had been vindicated. The outsiders were now on the inside and their ongoing significance to God was beginning to be seen by the wider world. This is exactly what Peter was teaching the early Christians about their status in God's eyes.

Yet the status is never separated from the obligation, as Peter makes clear. They are *God's special possession* in order *that you may declare the praises of him who called you out of darkness into his wonderful light.* They step into the shoes of Israel and at the same time take up the calling of Israel to be a light to the nations, testifying to the God of mercy and grace, so that news of his salvation 'may reach to the ends of the earth'.[23]

2. The practice of corporate holiness (Ephesians 4:17 – 5:20)

If this is the theory, what of the practice? How is the church to develop and display this corporate holiness?

Peter is not without answers. A deep love for one another is necessary (1 Peter 1:22). This love recognizes even failing brothers

[22] J. R. Michaels, *1 Peter,* WBC (Waco: Word, 1988), p. 109.
[23] Isa. 49:6.

and sisters in Christ as God's special possession, already sanctified, and so leads believers to forgive one another, be patient with one another and restore those who fall. Personal purity and integrity are necessary (2:1), so that individual members do not infect the body with spiritual poison. The living of a 'good' life, supported by actively doing 'good deeds' (2:12), which can be observed by pagan neighbours, is also an indispensable item on the agenda.[24]

We might, however, gain a fuller understanding of the practice of corporate holiness by examining Paul's exposition of it in Ephesians 4. The emphasis on the church is evident throughout his letter. With Peter, he sees it as a primary and vital agent in the mission of God (Ephesians 3:10), not the secondary and incidental instrument we sometimes are apt to consider it to be. Concern for the unity (4:1–13), progress (4:11–16) and the eventual maturity (4:16) of the church comes into focus in chapter 4. And it is with the church in mind that Paul now tells them how they are to live differently from the Gentiles. His language is urgent. Here is not advice that they may take or leave but something that he *insists on . . . in the Lord* (4:17).

a. The principle of difference (4:17–24)

Paul roots his practical teaching in good theology. The *Therefore* of 4:25 indicates that he is moving on to application, but it is very much working out the implication of what has been said up to this point in his letter rather than starting a new and unconnected topic. In fact, his reluctance to hurry to application too quickly is underlined by his discussion of the principles of difference first, in 4:17–24. He wants to avoid being misinterpreted. The Christian life is not a new set of rules, a new legalism. It is the outworking of a new life and unless that is understood the Christian faith quickly degenerates into a new and crippling moralism.

As often in Paul's teaching, he sets out his argument negatively and then positively.

(i) Negatively (4:17–19)

They *must no longer live as the Gentiles do*. Their whole way of thinking is futile and leads to them being controlled by *sensuality* and *greed*. This is not purely a matter of lifestyle choice, as people would have it today, but a fundamentally different way of living

---

[24] Michaels, *1 Peter*, p. 119, comments that Peter 'dissolves the metaphor, "Let your light so shine" (Matt 5:16a; cf. vv 14–15) into a straightforward reference to "good conduct" – this despite his own phrase, "marvellous light," in 2:9'.

which arises from their spiritual stance. Paul forensically dissects the reason for their chosen lifestyle. Their minds are befuddled and their lives alienated from God, their maker, because of their ignorance about him. This is not an intellectual ignorance; it is a moral and spiritual ignorance which stems from their choice to harden their hearts against God, to shut him out of their lives. The *thinking* ('minds', NRSV) that has become darkened and is ignorant here is not just the reasoning and intellectual aspect of a person, although that is included, but the 'understanding, conscience and affections' together with its emotional capabilities.[25] In other words, it is the entire personality. Such a life is empty, futile. As Martyn Lloyd-Jones concluded when preaching on these verses, 'Life without Christ is always empty, it is always vain, it takes from you, it takes out of you, and it leaves you at the end the empty husk. It leaves you exhausted, with nothing to lean on, nothing to be proud of, and nothing whatsoever to look forward to.'[26]

(ii) Positively (4:20–24)

What a difference being taught about Christ makes. Uniquely, Paul does not speak here of just learning about Christ but that they 'learned Christ' (NRSV). The truth is personal and the metaphor of teaching/learning is no more restricted to the intellectual dimension of life than the reference to minds and *thinking* was in the preceding verses. To be *taught in him* is to grasp the message, to have one's eyes opened and to see the truth. It is to understand the gospel as opposed to believing and living a lie. It is, in Peter O'Brien's words, 'welcoming him as a living person and being shaped by his teaching. This involves submitting to his righteousness and responding to his summons to standards and values completely different from what they have known.'[27] The learning cuts deep.

What composed the syllabus? Paul reminds them it was *to put off your old self, which is being corrupted by its deceitful desires; to be made new in the attitude of your minds; and to put on the new self, created to be like God in true righteousness and holiness.* The old self was the term for life before Christ. It refers to the whole person, not just a dimension of our beings.[28] Its engine was the

[25] D. M. Lloyd-Jones, *Darkness and Light An exposition of Ephesians 4:17 – 5:17* (Edinburgh: Banner of Truth, 1982), p. 33. This volume is probably the best classic exposition of this passage.
[26] Ibid., p. 37.
[27] P. T. O'Brien, *The Letter to the Ephesians*, Pillar (Grand Rapids: Eerdmans and Apollos: Leicester, 1999), p. 324.
[28] The word translated 'self' in Eph. 4:22–24 (and in Rom. 6:6 and Col. 3:9–11) is

deceitful desires spoken of in verse 22. They are *deceitful* because although they promise much they fail to satisfy and indeed rather than leading to a healthy life, they corrupt it and put it on the path to decay and ruin. The pleasures of sin we find so tempting are, in reality, not even an illusion. They are more than that. They are a great big lie. In Christ a radical transformation takes place that enables us to put on *the new self*. Consciously alluding to Genesis 1:26, Paul says, the new self recreates us in the image of God and restores the masterpiece we have corrupted to its original state of *righteousness and holiness*.

But it is important we do not skip over how this happens. The new life is *put* on and this restoration of the image of God takes place because we are *made new in the attitude of [our] minds.*[29] If the blame for our living like Gentiles was located in the mind, the mind must also be the realm where the renewal takes place so we can start living with and for him. The renewed mind doesn't alter our IQs but it does change our orientation in life, our attitudes, ambitions, motivations and worldview.

b. The practice of difference (4:25 – 5:20)

In continuity with what Paul has been teaching he now illustrates what needs to be put off and what needs to be put on as far as Christian behaviour is concerned. The image comes, of course, from initiation ceremonies in the ancient world, and particularly from the practice of baptism, where converts to be admitted to the Christian fellowship would be clothed in new clothes as part of the initiation ritual.

The double action of *putting off* and *putting on* is to be noted. Michael Griffiths insightfully remarks on the way in which much teaching about Christian holiness majors on the putting-off aspect of the call. It's all about not doing certain things. 'There is', he

---

anthrōpos, that is, 'person'. Some translate it old/new 'nature' but this can be misleading as implying only part of the picture, while 'self' is too individualistic. The word denotes the whole person and whether he or she is in a relation with Adam (the old person) or Jesus Christ (the new person). See D. Dockery, 'New Nature, Old Nature', *DPL,* pp. 628–629.

[29] See the parallel verse in Col. 3:10 where Paul writes, 'the new self, which is being renewed in knowledge in the image of its Creator'. NRSV and others translate verse 23 as 'to be renewed in the spirit of your minds'. This leads to a common interpretation that the mind is renewed by the Holy Spirit. But this is not Paul's point here. For discussion see O'Brien, *The Letter to the Ephesians,* p. 330. See also discussion of renewal in D. Peterson, *Possessed by God: A New Testament Theology of Sanctification and Holiness,* NSBT (Leicester: Apollos, 1995), pp. 126–136.

writes, 'a kind of Christian negative holiness which rejoices in discarding various forms of worldliness, but which leaves the individual stark naked. True Christian holiness demands also the putting on of positive virtues like a suit of beautiful new clothes.'[30] Paul gives the negative, what we are to stop doing, but he follows it with the positive, what we are to put in its place, and often justifies it with a reason.

Verse 29, for example, is typical. Negatively, we are to put off *unwholesome talk*. But we are not therefore reduced to silence. Where destructive, critical, negative, crude, suggestive and sordid words once would have come out of our mouths, we now put on words that are *helpful for building others up*. In Christ, our language becomes constructive, truthful, encouraging, gracious and clean. And here is the reason: *that it may benefit those who listen*. The simple test, 'Is my conversation beneficial?' would soon lead many of us to transform our speech. It would do this not only for the person who engages in smut but for other Christians who pride themselves on speaking the truth and constantly correcting others but, truth to tell, often wound people and display arrogance, rather than understanding, by their words.

Although the ethical ideals he sets out appear to be addressed to individuals and concern personal holiness rather than corporate holiness, that is only partially true. Paul's concern in Ephesians is a corporate one, the creation of 'one new humanity' (2:15). 'But this new humanity also comes to expression individually.'[31] It is hard to separate the two dimensions in reality for although Paul may appear to be addressing individuals the ethical issues he raises particularly relate to the body of the church as a whole. The New Testament knows nothing of solitary Christians. To be a Christian was to belong to a body and the behaviour of its individual members either strengthens or undermines the church. It either helps the church make progress in holiness or impedes it. Paul makes this connection explicit in 4:25 where he gives his reason for banning lies and encouraging truth: *for we are all members of one body*. To lie is to impact the body for ill. To speak truth is to impact the body for good. Holiness is more than personal; it is inevitably corporate. The church needs to be a body that practises truthfulness and integrity throughout.

The topics Paul mentions are illustrative rather than exhaustive but have the touch of raw life about them. They cover:

---

[30] Griffiths, *Cinderella with Amnesia*, p. 78.
[31] A. Lincoln, *Ephesians*, WBC (Dallas: Word, 1990), p. 286.

(i) Our speech (4:25, 29; 5:4, 6, 19–20)

Introduced in 4:25, this issue is re-expressed in one way or another, weaving its way through the ethical instructions Paul gives until reaching its climax in 5:19–20. The purpose of our faculty of speech as an instrument of truthfulness (4:25; 5:6) is not only to build others up (4:29), but that we can be thankful (5:4) and, above all, express praise to God (5:19–20).

(ii) Our emotions (4:26, 31 – 5:2)

The emotions we *put off* are those of *anger* (4:26, 31), *bitterness, rage,* and *malice,* which give rise to *brawling and slander* (4:31). The designer wardrobe with which we replace such emotions consists of kindness, compassion, forgiveness and love (4:32 – 5:2). Paul is saying, in effect, we're going to wear something, but the choice of the wardrobe is in one respect up to us. We are going to be emotional people because God has wired emotions into our very beings. The question is whether we choose to spend our emotional energies on passions that will destroy the fellowship and damage other people or strengthen the fellowship and build others up.[32]

(iii) Our work (4:28)

The double action of putting off and putting on is transparent in Paul's instructions about stealing and work even though the words are not used. Christians were converted from all sorts of backgrounds, and, praise God, still are. God loves people, just as they are. But, as the saying goes, he loves them too much to leave them just as they are. So those who bring a criminal background to their Christian life have to abandon it and learn a new way of living. Having known a number of criminals converted, I know this is not always a simple matter, since their whole way of life and network of relationships predisposes some of them to think in such terms. It will often require them to move out of the subculture in which they have been schooled into a new, but initially very alien, Christian subculture, and the battles may be fierce. That's why I wrote 'and *learn* a new way of living'. It may be a tough process.

But Paul's point is clear.[33] To give up making your living by stealing is one thing. To earn your living honestly by working is another.

---

[32] For an understanding of emotions from a the New Testament perspective, see M. Elliott, *Faithful Feelings: Emotion in the New Testament* (Leicester: IVP, 2005).

[33] This overlaps with Paul's teaching in 1 Thess. 4:11–12 and 2 Thess. 3:11–13, but is developed differently.

Putting off bad habits is only half the battle, and may be quite a victory but adopting new habits is necessary for the war to be won and process of transformation to be complete. Christians are called not only to stop doing wrong but start doing good. They are to play their part as active and responsible citizens, not only earning their own keep, but having enough to *share with those in need* as well. The thief takes from others; the Christian gives to others. The one robs while the other contributes. The one grasps while the other is generous. The one plays an irresponsible part in society while the other plays a responsible part in fostering its economic and moral health.

(iv) Our relationships (4:32 – 5:2, 6–7)

What we say, do and feel inevitably impinge on our relationships. The garments that Paul has told the Ephesians to strip off destroy relationships, while the designer clothes we are invited to wear build them. Lying gives birth to mistrust, dishonesty spawns suspicion, bitterness breeds resentment, anger generates retaliation. Each of these causes people to distance themselves from each other. By contrast, integrity, kindness, compassion, forgiveness, and love draw people to each other and create strong and lasting bonds between them. This means that the unity that God purposed to create in the 'one new humanity' is winsomely displayed to a watching world (2:15).

While Paul's concern in 4:25 – 5:20 focuses on individual character traits that might destroy or build peace in the church, earlier in writing of this new humanity, in 2:11–22, his concern had been with social, ethnic and cultural differences that divided Jew from Gentile. It must be borne in mind that Christians need to be conscious of and put off racial prejudice, social bigotry, class intolerance, national chauvinism and gender discrimination that undermine holiness, as much as the ugly personal traits mentioned at this point in Ephesians. Christians who keep themselves unblemished sexually but who are racially or socially prejudiced have some way to go before they reach the standards of holiness set out by the apostles for whom, in Christ, there was 'neither Jew nor Gentile, neither slave nor free, neither male nor female' (Galatians 3:28).[34] Such discriminatory attitudes are a stumbling block to the church's corporate holiness. Relational ethics are as important a component of holiness as are personal ethics.

---

[34] Col. 3:11 makes exactly the same point about the diverse and unprejudiced nature of the new community in the explicit context of putting 'on the new self, which is being renewed in knowledge in the image of its Creator'.

(v) Our spiritual life (4:27, 30; 5:18)

Paul does not obviously use the image of putting off and putting on in this passage about our spiritual lives. Elsewhere he talks about clothing ourselves with Christ[35] but here, we are encouraged to follow the example of Christ (5:1), inherit his kingdom (5:5), walk in his light (5:9), and do his will (5:10, 17). The idea of putting off the old self and putting on the new is implicit, however, in Paul's two references to the Holy Spirit, who provides the dynamic of our Christian lives. In 4:30 we are instructed not to grieve him, which we will do unless we put off the unwholesome speech that comes out of our mouths (4:29). In 5:18 we are told to be filled with him in specific contrast to getting drunk with all that follows when we are in a state of inebriation (5:17). In other words, we are to put off behaviour where we are controlled by a substance that makes us less than human in order that we might put on the Spirit who makes us truly human.

(vi) Our sex life (5:3–14)

Much of the central portion of this passage concerns our sexual lives where we are encouraged to put off *even a hint of sexual immorality, or of any kind of impurity* and put on behaviour of which we would not be ashamed in the full light of day (5:11–13). The parallel passage in Colossians 3 spells out the issues, if anything, even more with its reference to putting to death 'your earthly nature' which is defined as 'sexual immorality, impurity, lust, evil desires and greed, which is idolatry' (Colossians 3:5).

The connection of sexual immorality with idolatry (3:5) strikes the modern reader as somewhat odd. But there is a logical connection that may escape us. Peter O'Brien explains that not only do sexual licence and idolatry come together in pagan worship but that in the Jewish mind 'fornication and sexual lust were linked with idolatry' because 'sexual lust is an idolatrous obsession [since] it places self-gratification or another person at the centre of one's existence, and thus the worship of the creature rather than the Creator (Rom. 1:25)'.[36] We are to shed the rags of lust and idolatry, whatever form they take, and replace them with the new outfit of purity, respect for others and the worship of the Creator God alone.

The wearing of the new wardrobe that Paul encourages and illustrates here is like the donning of a uniform. It means that Christians

---

[35] Rom. 13:14.
[36] O'Brien, *Ephesians*, p. 363.

will be readily identifiable by others outside the church, just as we can pick out a policeman or paramedic in a crowd. It also means that we will be identified with one another. For just as we expect those wearing uniforms in ordinary life to have a common identity, to adopt certain standards, enjoy certain privileges, relate to each other in a special way, and be trained to undertake certain responsibilities and exercise certain skills, so people can expect the church to do the same in relation to God. Holiness is corporate as well as personal.

3. Concluding comment

Central to God's plan is the creation of a new humanity who will be the royal priesthood and holy nation Israel had failed to be. They were holy by virtue of being set apart for him as his special possession. It was a status conferred upon them not in virtue of their own saintliness but by the virtues of Christ who became their sanctification. The people were not just a collection of odd individuals but a collective body who belonged to each other and functioned together, through whom God was at work coherently and corporately in his world. There is all the difference in the world, Michael Griffiths observes, between a body and a pile of mincemeat![37] And the church is called to be a holy body, not a pile of similar but unrelated (and dead!) individuals' strands of holiness.

The call to holiness is in practice both a negative and a positive call. It calls people who are members of that body to refrain from behaviour that would destroy it but replace that with behaviour that is winsome, warm, personable, attractive and constructive. Some Christian teaching has been so concerned about avoiding certain behaviour and remaining clinically clean that it has failed to teach a full biblical doctrine of holiness which is wonderfully positive. The holiness advocated by some reminds me of stainless steel sinks. They are efficient, easy to keep clean, and hard to stain, but they are cold and unattractive. Biblical holiness is anything but that. To return to Paul's metaphor, the church as a whole is told:

You've done with that old life. It's like a filthy set of ill-fitting clothes you've stripped off and put in the fire. Now you're dressed in a new wardrobe. Every item of your new way of life is custom-made by the Creator, with his label on it. All the old fashions are now obsolete. . . . So, chosen by God for this new life of love, dress in the wardrobe God picked out for you: compassion,

---

[37] Griffiths, *Cinderella with Amnesia*, p. 54.

kindness, humility, quiet strength, discipline. Be even-tempered, content with second place, quick to forgive an offence. Forgive as quickly and completely as the Master forgave you. And regardless of what else you put on, wear love. It's your basic, all-purpose garment. Never be without it.[38]

Micah 6:1–8
13. Social Holiness

The agenda of younger evangelicals looks different from that of their parents and grandparents. By common consent major changes have taken place within evangelicalism that make it hard for some more traditional evangelicals to recognize their younger friends as members of the same family. The changes affect virtually every aspect of the practice of their faith, from their way of doing church, to their approach to the Bible, worship, culture, spiritual formation and to their understanding of holiness.[1]

Whereas an older generation sought to foster holiness by withdrawing from the world, the contemporary generation passionately believe in the need to be a transforming presence in the world. Holiness consists not in insulating themselves against corruption but in being salt and light in the world, and viewing 'the church as the "embodied presence" of Jesus Christ' among the people he loved.[2] Whereas a former generation was concerned about issues of family and personal ethics, this generation is concerned about social issues. Concern over abortion, pornography, alcohol, drugs, marriage and divorce, while not altogether absent, has been replaced by a concern for the poor, the abused, contemporary slavery and the environment. More important than personal purity, they argue, is social responsibility. Salvation is not about the interests of individual salvation so much as the recreation of community and the restoration of a fallen creation, in which individuals have a part to play. The goal is not so much personal sanctification as discipleship in the world. The issue is not about keeping the rules of the evangelical

---

[1] The most accessible and comprehensive documentation of the changes is found in R. E. Webber, *The Younger Evangelicals: Facing the Challenges of the New World* (Grand Rapids: Baker, 2002).

[2] Webber, *The Younger Evangelicals*, p. 230.

subculture as becoming an authentic human being, living freely and sacramentally among broken communities.[3]

Do they believe in separation from the world? Yes. But the separation is not a social separation by which Christians withdraw into their spiritual ghettos but a separation from the ideologies of the world, oriented as they are around individualism, success, comfort and materialism. The rejection is often a rejection of the middle-class values that have deeply infected the church (and these trends are most evident among the children of middle-class Christian parents). The church, they say, is in danger of substituting a middle-class lifestyle for the more radical lifestyle of the original disciples, and of confusing being British or American with being Christian.

The rediscovery of social holiness is a rediscovery of a seam of biblical teaching about holiness, although it should not be at the expense of the inward, personal and corporate seams of holiness discussed in the previous chapters. Our approach should be one of 'both . . . and' rather than 'either . . . or'.

1. The biblical mandate for social holiness: Micah 6:1–8

Micah's God is an awesome God whose intervention in the affairs of Judah makes mountains melt and valleys split open.[4] As Isaiah had a vision of God's holiness in the temple, so Micah hears the voice of God 'from his holy temple' (Micah 1:2). The same God, who is holiness through and through, speaks through Micah to condemn his people's lack of holiness. This lack was most evident in the social and political arena of life. The leadership was corrupt, their economy fraudulent and their justice bogus, yet they felt secure because they falsely presumed on the Lord's presence among them (Micah 3:1–12).

Micah and his contemporaries were called to puncture their spiritual complacency and bring the nation to a point of self-awareness and renewal before it was too late. Micah used the device, common among the prophets, of picturing Israel on trial in a divine court: *For the* LORD *has a case against his people; he is lodging a charge against Israel* (6:2). So momentous was the accusation that the age-old mountains and very foundations of planet Earth were called to witness the trial (6:1–2). The trial leads to the profound summary statement of the judge who sets out in memorable and unmistakable terms what a holy God requires of his holy people. But what leads up to the pronouncement is just as significant.

[3] Ibid, pp. 173–186.
[4] Mic. 1:4.

a. The accusation of the complainant (6:3–5)

The relationship between God and his people has broken down because the people had chosen to fundamentally misinterpret their God.

(i) They felt that God had become a burden to them (6:3)

The other nations provoked the scorn of the prophets, and rightly so, for manufacturing idols from wood, stone and metal and then parading them around on their shoulders.[5] They were literally, as well as spiritually, dead weights. The God of Israel, by contrast, was the living Saviour who relieved people of their burdens and daily bore their burdens for them (Psalm 68:19). But Judah couldn't see it. To them, religion was a dead weight, the temple sacrifices a drag, and the law an albatross around their necks. It prevented them from getting on with the important stuff in life, which was making money, and denied them the freedom to make that money in the most 'efficient' and 'economical' of ways, by corruption and abuse of power where necessary. From where they stood, the living God of liberation might just as well have been an idol, indistinguishable from the rest of the religious objects people in other nations venerated.

(ii) They forgot that God had removed the burdens from them (6:4–5)

They could, of course, only come to this conclusion because they had very short memories. A moment's thought would remind them that God had not imposed burdens on them but rather had removed burdens from them. Even if they recalled this, they did so merely by superficially recalling the past rather than truly remembering. True remembrance allows the past to impact the present, rather than merely recalling facts as a fleeting mental image.

The prosecutor accuses them of forgetting the exodus when they were *brought . . . up out of Egypt.* As Leslie Allen comments, the form of words are as if God was saying to them, 'I have not let you down – on the contrary, I brought you up.'[6] And where was the wilderness journey in their thinking, when they experienced God guiding them as he *sent Moses to lead* them, and protecting them against their enemies, as in the story of Balak and Balaam?[7] As if that

[5] E.g., Isa. 46:1–13; Jer. 10:1–16.
[6] L. C. Allen, *The Books of Joel, Obadiah, Jonah and Micah,* NICOT (Grand Rapids: Eerdmans, 1976), p. 366.
[7] Num. 22 – 24.

was not enough, what about the entry into the Promised Land when they moved *from Shittim* (the last point before crossing the Jordan) *to Gilgal* (the frontier of the Promised Land)[8] and eventually took possession of it against all odds? Were their memories so short? How could they accuse their God of being a burden to them?

b. The defence of the accused (6:6–7)

People often expose their stupidity when defending the indefensible. Those accused of failing to have the necessary TV licence in the UK have been known to excuse themselves on the basis that only their pets watched the TV, or they only watched Australian programmes on TV and so did not think a licence was needed! The defence Israel makes is barely more believable. They say:

(i) Their religious practice was conscientious

The language they use is heavy with religious freight: they *come before the LORD*, they *bow down before the exalted God*, they *come before him with . . . offerings*. It sounds good. It is the language of lowly submission, deep reverence and conscientious observance. But the language disguises the true state of their hearts. Outwardly they may be bowing down but they are not submitting to God's law. Physically they may be 'coming before' but their minds are at their bank and building sites. Ritually they may be offering sacrifices but inwardly they are calculating the cost (and no doubt putting it down as a tax-deductible gift, or whatever the ancient equivalent was).

(ii) Their religious practice was costly

An inspection of their outward religious behaviour would demonstrate, they argued, that their religion was no cheap option for them. They offered *calves a year old,* sacrifices that were costly because they were in the prime of life. They offered *thousands of rams with ten thousand rivers* (rivers, note, not trickling streams) *of oil.* Their sacrifices were abundant, not the bare minimum, just as we, today, often offer God the endless singing of worship songs as if he measures our spirituality by the length or quantity of rituals we undertake. Furthermore, they were prepared to go beyond all this and asked if God wanted them to offer their firstborn as a means of expunging their sin? The offering of the firstborn was everywhere forbidden in

[8] Josh. 4:19–24.

their law,[9] but they were prepared to go further than the law required if it would help. They were prepared to pay the costs involved. But this betrayed their true attitude. For, truth to tell:

(iii) Their religious practice was consumerist

They were seeking to purchase forgiveness from God. They were trying to establish the current rate for purchasing the favour of God. So, as Peter Craigie explained, 'The whole sacrificial system and worship of the temple has been debased into a kind of national insurance policy: we can sin as we wish, the leaders thought, so long as we are up-to-date with our insurance premiums at the temple.'[10] It has the effect of downgrading their covenant with God, in which a total and personal commitment was made to each other, into a contract, which involved the provision of a limited service by God (forgiveness) in exchange for the agreed negotiated fee. Religion had become commodified, forgiveness packaged and the market had taken over in the temple.[11]

c. The judgment of the court (6:8)

The accused are undoubtedly guilty and the verdict and sentence will follow (6:9–16). But the interest of the court is to establish understanding of the essence of the law rather than rush to pronounce guilt. The great principle around which the case revolved needed enunciating with clarity so that there could be no possible excuse for people[12] to subsequently plead ignorance of his law. Their behaviour was already inexcusable, for God had made his will plain in a multitude of ways, over a multitude of years. As Micah says, *He has shown all you people what is good.* Nothing here was new, and nothing should have taken Israel by surprise. From their earliest days they had been taught to love

---

[9] The firstborn belonged, of right, to God and was at his disposal alone (Exod. 22:29) which usually meant the firstborn were 'redeemed' with a monetary substitute (Exod. 34:19–20). Israel was forbidden to offer its children as a sacrifice (Lev. 18:21; 20:2–5). When God commanded Abraham to offer up Isaac (Gen. 22), it must be remembered that God stepped in before the sacrifice was complete and Isaac was not killed.

[10] P. C. Craigie, *The Twelve Prophets*, Vol. 2, Daily Study Bible (Edinburgh: St Andrew Press and Philadelphia: The Westminster Press, 1985), p. 46.

[11] See D. Prior, *The Message of Joel, Micah & Habakkuk*, BST (Leicester: IVP, 1998), pp. 175–176.

[12] The word for 'people' in 6:8 is *'ādām*, stressing their collective humanity and also their creatureliness and, therefore, their need to know their place before their creator God.

their neighbour as themselves (Leviticus 19:18). From the exodus onwards they had been instructed to keep the memory of their suffering alive by constantly retelling the story[13] so that they would be sensitized to the suffering of others, avoid the perils of power, and be reminded that their God was in the business of relieving suffering, not inflicting it.[14]

Nonetheless, no one would ever now be able to ask, 'What does God want?' and claim they did not know, for the answer was straightforward, yet demanding. *And what does the LORD require of you? To act justly and to love mercy and to walk humbly with your God.*

(i) To act justly

If we were to play a game of word association we are likely to link 'justice' with 'law' or 'the law courts'. *To act justly* certainly has implications for what goes on in a court of law, but its implications are much wider than that. To 'do *mišpāṭ*' is to live in a socially responsible way in every arena of life. It is the term for the obligation we have to our neighbours and especially stresses the obligations we have towards weaker members of our society. 'It insists on the rights of others' and rules out behaviour like oppression, perjury, bribery and taking advantage of the vulnerable.[15] It turns its back on living according to our own advantage, comfort or desire.[16]

To act justly is to make a personal and practical contribution to the creation of a society that reflects the way God desires us to live in community, with respect, integrity and love. It is to 'do to others what you would have them do to you' (Matthew 7:12). It is also to make a positive and political contribution to the creation of such a society, wherever we have the freedom to do so. Some apply these verses to their personal relationships but see no application beyond that. But these verses are addressed to the people of Israel as a community about their social obligations to one another. Political and social arrangements have changed since the days of Micah, not least because of the growth in population and the resulting complexity of society. Not all live in societies where they have the freedom

---

[13] Deut. 6:21–25.

[14] For a discussion of this as 'The Biblical Metanarrative' see, J. R. Middleton and B. J. Walsh, *Truth is stranger than it used to be* (London: SPCK, 1995), pp. 87–107.

[15] Allen, *The Books of Joel, Obadiah, Jonah and Micah*, p. 373.

[16] E. Achtemeier, *Nahum-Malachi*, Int (Atlanta: John Knox Press, 1986), p. 352.

to influence the wider culture and government, but where such freedom exists this stirring call obliges God's people to use their freedom to ensure that their communities and societies act in a just way, as set out above, towards all. To limit the command to act justly to the sphere of personal relationships and to neglect to apply it in the political and social sphere is seriously to fall short of what God wants.

(ii) To love mercy

The translation, *to love mercy* does scant justice to the prophet's plea. In using the word *ḥesed* (covenant love) it goes far beyond the idea of mercy (a legitimate translation and necessary component of it) and calls for people to be loyal to all the covenant obligations. The covenant bound people to God and in doing so equally bound people to one another. Human beings gained their identity not as individual 'Is' but as part of the 'we', enmeshed in a bond of relationships where they both gave and received.[17] People were all created in the image of God and were bound together in a community of love, as confirmed by the covenant. As Elizabeth Achtemeier explains, such loving solidarity exists,

> so that community is established between poor and rich, weak and strong, female and male, slave and free, alien and Israelite (cf. Gal. 3:28), and all care for one another in mutual respect and protection and sharing. *Ḥesed* binds people together as one in the bundle of life, so that God is not worshiped and obeyed apart from concern for one's fellow human being (cf. Matt. 5:23–24; Gal. 5:14; 6:2).[18]

Ḥesed is the very opposite of the absence of love which was evident in the Judah of Micah's day, where the individualism of the day determined ethical questions on the basis of 'what's in it for me?' It is the very opposite of the calculating love that only acted when it was reasonable to do so, and when those who received love were deserving of it. It gave freely, when there was no hope of reward and recognition. It is a love that remains loyal because fellow humans, male and female, are made in the image of God, however marred that image may be. Consequently, as Archbishop Ndungane of Cape Town has written, it means 'to grant them the same dignity,

---

[17] On the biblical understanding of personal identity see J. Sacks, *The Politics of Hope* (London: Jonathan Cape, 1997), pp. 60–62.
[18] Achtemeier, *Nahum-Malachi*, p. 353.

the same respect, the same opportunities that we enjoy in this life, as well as in the life to come'.[19]

Hesed is more than the daily oiling of the wheels of society, helping it to run smoothly and without conflict.[20] It not only lubricates; it enhances. It changes those practices in society where injustice remains and people are treated as objects, impersonal resources or units of production, consumption or income generation. It personalizes the political issues of our time and puts economic justice, land ownership and environmental issues on our agendas as God's holy people.

(iii) To walk humbly

The third requirement God has of his people is that they *walk humbly* with him. Without this it might be possible to read the first two requirements as purely a humanistic or political agenda. But this clause prevents us from making that mistake. Those clauses are not about some socialist dream; they are an expression of the character and will of God. It is not only that our motivation for acting justly and loving mercy comes from him. It is that we are incapable of acting justly and loving mercy in its fullest sense unless we are walking humbly with God.

The word *humbly* is a pointed word in Micah's context. The land speculators, asset strippers, property developers and get-rich-quick merchants of his day were anything but humble. They showed not only breath-taking arrogance in relation to their fellow human beings but in relation to God and his laws as well. They were prepared not only to ignore him but to argue with him and point out the errors of his ways. In contrast, God desires a humility which means they are attentive to his word, keep their eyes on pleasing him, never letting him out of their sight, and not following their own paths and desires. It is the attitude servants display, according to Psalm 123:2, of never taking their eyes off their master or mistress so that they might be ready to serve their every wish.

Their social obligation is not different from their religious obligation. They are two sides of the same coin. The God who speaks 'from his holy temple' (1:2) is not a God who can be confined to his temple but a God who moves out 'from his dwelling-place' (1:3) and inspects how his people are caring for his world. Holiness is not

---

[19] N. Ndungane, 'Loving Mercy, Restoring Personhood, Restoring Society' in M. Hoek and J. Thacker (eds.), *Micah's Challenge* (Milton Keynes: Paternoster, 2008), p. 13.

[20] Ibid., p. 15.

restricted by a religious straightjacket. It escapes into the world of politics and economics, of social ethics and human justice. The holy God requires his people to demonstrate a social holiness.

2. The New Testament perspective on social holiness

Some will ask, 'Is this not an Old Testament agenda?. Where is the New Testament evidence that Christians today are called to social holiness? Does not the New Testament display a concern primarily for those within the church as an alternative community and show little interest in the wider world as such?' Keith Warrington, for example, writing as a New Testament scholar, says,

> Social transformation is the conversion of society. It is not clear, however, that this was a priority for the early believers . . . little explicit indication is given (in the New Testament) that the early believers thought the church would or even should transform the wider world. It appears that the early church saw its chief role as being to model an alternative society, which others would be attracted to join. Any change in social norms and practices over and above this is assumed to be coincidental, or a bonus.[21]

Does this mean that 'the genie of social holiness' can be put back in the bottle and no longer be of concern to New Testament Christians? Can Christians withdraw from the public square, like the Essene Community at Qumran, and be content to foster their own holiness with a view to being an inert display case of holiness in the world rather than an active participant in its transformation? To these questions Christians who enjoy political freedom must answer an emphatic 'No!'[22]

a. The implicit mandate

Alan Kreider has said, 'God wants us to experience the fullness of holiness. In calling us to be holy, he is calling us to realign ourselves with the story of Jesus.'[23] If we do that we align ourselves with the

---

[21] K. Warrington, 'Social transformation in the Missions of Jesus and Paul: Priority or Bonus?' in *Movement for Change: Evangelical Perspectives on Social Transformation* ed. D. Hilborn (Carlisle: Paternoster, 2004), pp. 38–39.

[22] For fuller expositions of the biblical and theological basis of this theme see, T. Chester, *Good News to the Poor* (Leicester: IVP, 2004), and D. Hughes and J. Grant (eds.), *Transforming the World?* (Nottingham: Apollos, 2009).

[23] A. Kreider, *Journey towards Holiness: A way of living for God's nation* (London: Marshall Pickering, 1986), p. 212.

in-breaking of the kingdom of God with all its implications for personal and social transformation. It is to be 'salt and light' in the world, for salt is useless if left in the salt cellar and light is pointless if placed under a bucket (Matthew 5:13–16). It is to align ourselves with the Nazareth manifesto of Luke 4:16–21, with its concern 'to proclaim good news to the poor . . . freedom for the prisoners . . . recovery of sight to the blind [and] to set the oppressed free'. It is to align ourselves with the 'poor', the no-hopers and socially unacceptable, as Jesus did, time and again (e.g., Luke 14:1–23). It is to take seriously John's version of the great commission when Jesus told his disciples, 'As the Father has sent me, I am sending you' (John 20:21). They were being sent into a hostile world (see John 17:15–17) not only to preach, as Jesus had, but do good works that brought about practical transformation in the lives of others, as he also had done. We cannot align ourselves with the mission of Jesus unless we practice holiness outside the church as well as within.

b. The political limitation

So, why did the early church not espouse a more explicit policy of social transformation? Why did their priorities seem to lie elsewhere?[24] The primary answer must lie in the political context in which the early church was born. It is difficult for those of us who enjoy the privileges of democracy to envisage what it is like to live in a society where the people have no political rights, no freedom of expression, and where the merest hint of revolution or opposition is violently crushed. Given our freedoms it may be easy for us to blame the early Christians for their apparent inactivity regarding social transformation, but it is arrogant and unfeeling to do so. They did not enjoy the choices which are ours.

The ancient historian E. A. Judge has investigated the question of the social impact of early Christianity on classical society on a number of occasions. In one essay he explores Paul's vision of 'one new man' in Ephesians 2 as a key concept that could have led to radical social change. But, he concludes, it is 'not clear to me how Paul expected this to work out in practice'.[25] Conceiving of such an open society would have made no sense in the context of the Roman Empire, no more sense, indeed, than one of the many tribal

---

[24] Warrington reviews a number of answers to this question, some of which are more convincing that others. Hilborn, *Movement for Change*, pp. 39–41.

[25] E. A. Judge, 'The Impact of Paul's Gospel on ancient society,' in P. Bolt and M. Thompson (eds.), *The Gospel to the Nations: Perspectives on Paul's Ministry* (Downers Grove: IVP and Leicester: Apollos, 2000), p. 298.

languages of Uganda might make to one who speaks no language but English. Yet, the vision was fulfilled eventually and the gospel had the most profound social impact, which affected family life and led to the abolition of slavery, even if that impact was, in Judge's words, 'long delayed'.[26]

c. The explicit hints

Although no social policy or explicit strategy of social transformation can be detected in the New Testament, the building blocks for them are strewn throughout the New Testament.

In Romans 13, Paul emphasizes our civic obligations in view of government being established by God to defend the righteous and punish the wicked. In 1 Corinthians 11:17–34, Paul's ethic of the Lord's table stands conventional social etiquette on its head. In Galatians 3:28, the great divides of the ancient world on the lines of race, 'class' and gender are neutralized in Christ. In Ephesians 2:14, Paul proclaims the demolition of 'the dividing wall of hostility' between Jew and Gentile by Christ and the creation of one new reconciled community. In Philippians, the gospel of the Jesus before whom 'every knee should bow' is brought right into the heart of the empire (2:9–10 and 1:13). Throughout Colossians the powers and authorities that made people cower in fear are exposed as empty by the sovereign authority and liberating work of Christ. Most of all, perhaps, in Philemon we see the effect of the gospel in undermining existing social structures and their being displaced by a new, more egalitarian, social arrangement.

The same raw materials are evident in the writings of others. James's letter not only brings the old social structures crashing to the ground in 2:1–13 but, in his denunciation of the wealthy (5:1–6), who were self-indulgently indifferent to the needs of others, James breathed out as hot a fire as any Old Testament prophet.

Peter calls on his readers to 'Live such good lives among the pagans that, though they accuse you of doing wrong, they may see your good deeds and glorify God on the day he visits us' (1 Peter 2:12). He calls for proper respect to be shown to all and, although his call to honour the king and to endure suffering seem unlikely to inspire Christians to challenge injustice or be anything other than socially conservative, the letter is shot through with calls to enhance society by their good living and, consequently, to transform it. Peter is aware of the precarious nature of the church's existence at the time of his writing. He writes from 'Babylon' (1 Peter 5:13) and knows

---

[26] Ibid., p. 308.

that, humanly speaking, opposition could easily snuff out the feeble flame of faith. So, his writing is adapted to the situation and appropriate for the need of the hour.

John, surely one of the most mystical and spiritual of writers in the New Testament, nonetheless puts forward a thoroughly practical ethic in his first letter. Love needs to find itself expressed in very down-to-earth terms. 'If any one of you has material possessions and sees a brother or sister in need but has no pity on them, how can the love of God be in you?' (1 John 3:17). While the brother or sister refers to those within the Christian fellowship, behind them stand other human beings made in the image of Christ.

The application of social holiness may be changed by the context. The New Testament church was neither a state nor a theocracy, but a tiny fledgling movement in a totalitarian society. But the flame of social holiness had not been extinguished. It went on quietly burning away until the day came when it could flare into greater life once more. The obligation to live in the world and transform it for good, to the limits of one's ability and to the limits of the opportunities provided, remained at the heart of what a holy God wants his people to do.

d. The ultimate vision

All this is true before we take into account the ultimate vision of the transformed society and renewed creation which is set before us in Revelation. Here is the society in which justice and righteousness reigns, covenant loyalty is practised and people walk humbly with God. Here we get a glimpse of the society the prophets advocated in their preaching but could only dream of in practice. Their vision – God's vision – at last will become a reality. What has this to do with us, now? To adapt a metaphor of Bishop Tom Wright, if Revelation 'is the music God has written for all his creatures (eventually) to sing, . . . we are called to learn it and practise it now so as to be ready when the conductor brings down his baton.'[27] So, welcome to choir practice.

3. Concluding comment

The younger evangelicals, as Webber terms them, are surely right. The biblical vision of holiness is not restricted to inner cleanliness, personal morality or to community purity but extends to a way of

[27] T. Wright, *Surprised by Hope* (London: SPCK, 2007), p. 301.

living in the world that recognizes: (a) that this earth is God's earth and is therefore deserving of care; (b) that all people are made in his image and therefore deserving of mercy; (c) that all power corrupts and therefore requires to be challenged; and (d) that God requires his people to work for justice and not to argue with him, but to walk humbly before him.

Holiness does not require withdrawal from the world but engagement with it. We are called to be 'in the world but not of it' whereas some holiness teaching has called us to be 'of the world but not in it'. We must be world-renouncing when it comes to attitudes and lifestyles that are contrary to God's claims on our lives, but world-engaging, to the extent that we can, in our participation as citizens and members of communities. In this respect we are called to 'a holy worldliness'.[28] The difficulty, as John Stott has pointed out, is to secure the right balance in our 'double identity'. It is easy to emphasize 'holiness' at the expense of 'worldliness' and just as easy to emphasize 'worldliness' at the expense of 'holiness'. 'The effectiveness of the church depends', John Stott writes, 'on its combination of "holiness" and "worldliness"',[29] and of getting the right balance between them.

Bill Clinton was much criticized, and rightly so, for his sexual behaviour when in the White House. A number of Christians sought to distance themselves from this 'born again' President because of his lack of personal morality. But as Tony Campolo pointed out, Clinton had done more to build homes for the homeless and care for the poor than many of his predecessors. While the one does not excuse the other it raises for us the stark question of how we measure holiness. To do so in terms of personal ethics alone is to diminish the biblical vision of holiness, perhaps to make it fit the individualistic culture of our time. But what God wants remains plain, if demanding. As biblical Christians we cannot let holiness evacuate the public square and retreat to the safe confines of the church. We must open the doors and let holiness invade the social and public sphere, just as surely as Micah saw God move out from his holy temple into his hurting world to bring about the reform and renewal it so desperately needed.

[28] A. Vidler, quoted in J, R. W. Stott, *Issues Facing Christians Today* (London: Marshall Morgan and Scott, 1984), p. 24.
[29] Ibid.

Part 5
Pathways to holiness

Galatians 5:13 – 6:10
14. The Spirit of God

The charismatic winds that swept through the church in the second half of the twentieth century expressed the longing of many Christians to experience power to overcome their ineffectiveness in witnessing, and to discover intimacy to overcome their distance from God. Any biblical understanding of the Holy Spirit would have added the quest for holiness to overcome our failure to conquer sin and daily to live the new life which our union with the risen Christ makes possible.[1] According to the New Testament, one of the primary tasks of the Holy Spirit is that of making believers holy in practice so that they live up to the status of holiness which Christ has conferred on them. Our salvation is made more complete 'through the sanctifying work of the Spirit' (2 Thessalonians 2:13), who has been given to us by God as the agent of change in our lives. He works within us, providing us with motivations, energies, desires and resources that do not come naturally to us and he perseveres with us until Christ is formed in us.[2]

1. Galatians and the Holy Spirit

No letter in the New Testament is more charismatic than the letter to the Galatians. Although usually (and rightly) associated with the doctrine of justification by faith, the letter is laced with teaching about the Holy Spirit that covers all the major aspects of the Christian life.[3] The first mention of the Holy Spirit comes in 3:1–4

---

[1] Rom. 6:1–4.
[2] Gal. 4:19.
[3] There are some seventeen references to the Holy Spirit in Galatians. Gal: 3:2, 3, 5, 14; 4:6, 29; 5:5, 16, 17 (x2), 18, 22, 25 (x2); 6:1, 8 (x2). For a full exposition

and refers to his work at the beginning of the Christian life. Putting one's faith in Christ led to receiving the Spirit (3:2, 3). Believing in Christ and receiving the Spirit were synonymous in Paul's view, as Romans 8:9–10 confirms. This reception of the Spirit was something conscious, dynamic and tangible since it led to the working of miracles (3:5). As Lesslie Newbigin commented about Acts 19,

> The apostle asked the converts of Apollos one question: 'Did ye receive the Holy Spirit when ye believed?' and got a plain answer. His modern successors are more inclined to ask either 'Did you believe exactly what we teach?' or 'Were the hands that were laid on you our hands?' and – if the answer is satisfactory – to assure the converts that they have received the Holy Spirit even if they don't know it. There is a world of difference between these two attitudes.[4]

The unmistakable reception of the Holy Spirit as a real and indwelling presence marked the beginning of the Christian life.

The second work of the Holy Spirit is that of giving believers assurance that they are genuine and much-loved children of God (4:6), not insecure slaves, who need to feel uncertain about their relationship with their master. The indwelling Spirit provides us with assurance. He makes himself know not just in spectacular ways, as in the miracles mentioned earlier, but in providing us with the regular, inward sense of confidence which makes us cry out from deep within that God is our '*Abba*, Father'. He leads us to be at home with God. Elsewhere we read of the way in which we can grieve,[5] quench[6] and resist[7] the Spirit's work in our lives, so that we no longer feel at ease in our Father's presence. But in spite of those warnings, there is a very real sense in which believers can relax, secure in the relationship God has cemented through Christ.

The third reference to the Holy Spirit in Galatians that concerns us, addresses our impatience and the need for perseverance in the Christian life. Rather than having every whim satisfied now, as the Galatians sought to do by obeying the law, 'we who live by the Spirit eagerly wait to receive by faith the righteousness God has

---

see, F. F. Bruce, 'The Spirit in the Letter to the Galatians' in P. Elbert (ed.), *Essays on Apostolic Themes* (Peabody: Hendrickson, 1985), pp. 36–48 and G. Fee, *God's Empowering Presence* (Peabody: Hendrickson, 1994), pp. 367–471.

[4] Lesslie Newbigin, *The Household of God* (London: SCM, 1953), p. 95.

[5] Eph. 4:30.

[6] 1 Thess. 5:19.

[7] Acts 7:51.

promised to us' (5:5).[8] The Christian life may be a marathon, rather than a sprint, but the Spirit provides us with the encouragement and the energy to keep going to the finishing tape, which we will not reach until the day of Christ. He also provides us with direction to keep on the course, rather than allowing us to stray off it, attracted by other so-called gospels. For us, the finishing tape is to be like Christ, to know perfect holiness.[9] Hence, Tom Smail commented, 'When the Holy Spirit moves, the destination is always more important than the emotion, what we feel matters less than where we're going . . . The Spirit moves us towards Christ.'[10]

Having already 'opened the windows to give a rather full-orbed picture of the life of the Spirit' that covers the beginning (our conversion), carrying on (assurance) and conclusion (perseverance) of our Christian lives,[11] Paul expounds more fully the Holy Spirit's role in making us holy in the last part of his letter. As Fee explains, Paul's essential point is that the Holy Spirit can do what the law sought to do, but failed to achieve. The Spirit can bring about the righteousness that the law demands. 'Whereas [law] was unable effectively to deal with the "passions and desires of the flesh," the Spirit does that very thing.'[12]

His teaching is shaped by the phrases *live by the Spirit, the fruit of the Spirit,* and *keep in step with the Spirit.*[13]

2. Living by the Spirit: a privilege to realize (5:16–26)

a. The principles (5:16–17)

Paul uses the phrase *live by the Spirit* twice, once as a command (5:16) and once as a statement (5:25). One of the significant features of Paul's teaching in this section (5:16–26) is that the indicative outweighs the imperative, that is, his description of what the Spirit does in our lives is more prominent than his telling us what we should do. Nonetheless, Paul begins with the command that we are to *live by the Spirit,* not as a one-off experience but as a continuous practice. The point is made clearer once we realize that the Greek

[8] New Living Translation.
[9] Gal. 4:19.
[10] T. Smail, *Reflected Glory* (London: Hodder and Stoughton, 1975), pp. 11–12.
[11] Fee, *God's Empowering Presence*, p. 469.
[12] Ibid, p. 371.
[13] Paul also speaks, in 6:8, about sowing and reaping – 'those who sow to please the Spirit' who will 'from the Spirit reap eternal life'– but space does not permit a discussion of this further phrase.

word he uses is *peripateite,* and means 'walking', which we cannot claim to be doing if we only take one step! Paul frequently talks in this way about how Christians should behave. His use of the metaphor of walking is natural because its roots go back deep into the Jewish understanding that to walk in the ways of God was to live ethically, as well as the fact that it was used elsewhere in the classical world.[14]

The command is followed by a promise, *and you will not gratify the desires of the sinful nature,* rather than a warning about the consequences if we do not. He wants us to see the positive possibilities of transformation that living in the realm of the Spirit brings. Soaking up the atmosphere of the Holy Spirit, living in his presence and walking in his company inevitably brings about the demise of *the desires of the sinful nature.* The *sinful nature* (*sarki*) which is often translated, as in the NRSV, by the term *flesh,* is not meant to suggest that we destroy the body and become a disembodied spirit. Far from it. The *sinful nature,* or *flesh,* is Paul's main description of 'life before and outside of Christ'.[15] It refers to the old way of life when, before our conversion, we permitted our lives to be led by our desires, however selfish, inconsiderate and destructive those desires may have been. As we shall see, living by the Spirit very much affects the way we live in our physical bodies on earth, so no denial of our humanity is intended. Rather, as Tom Smail engagingly expressed it, 'The Holy Spirit is the spirit of Jesus and he comes clothed in Christ's humanity, not to make us super-spiritual saints, or ascetic anchorites, or miracle mongering super-naturalists, or chandelier-swinging fanatics but quite simply to make us [human].'[16]

The desires to which we once gave expression cannot co-exist with the Spirit in our lives. To be filled with him[17] is inevitably to expel those desires from our lives, just as light expels darkness and just as filling a bottle with liquid expels the air that previously had occupied it. Because we are all different temperaments and subject to different strengths and weaknesses, some may be able to discipline themselves to restrain some expressions of the old nature more than others, but all of us need the Holy Spirit to rid ourselves of *all* that is unworthy. Thomas Chalmers once said that when autumn comes some dead leaves fall off the tree naturally but some cling

---

[14] Fee, *God's Empowering Presence,* p. 429. Timothy George notes that 'the students of Aristotle were known as *Peripatetics* because of their habit of following the philosopher around from place to place as he dispensed his teaching', *Galatians,* NAC (Nashville: Broadman and Holman, 1994), p. 386.

[15] Fee, *God's Empowering Presence,* p. 384.

[16] Smail, *Reflected Glory* p. 65. My substitution is for 'men'.

[17] Eph. 5:18.

tenaciously to the branch throughout the winter and only finally drop to the ground when the power of the tree's new life expels them. We, too, need, the powerful life of the Holy Spirit within to expel those sinful desires that cling tightly to us.

The secret of holy living, then, is to give free rein to the Spirit in our lives, or, reverting to Paul's metaphor, consciously to walk closely with him. The moment we drift from him, as I know in my own life, we begin to give way to the old nature which, while defeated by Christ, still exists and which, though having no rights over us, still longs to pretend it has a claim upon us.

b. The purpose (5:18)

Paul urges the Galatians to understand that if they are living by the Spirit neither the old way of living nor the law has any continuing power over them. They belong to the past age and in Christ a new age has dawned. Their 'essential power has been crippled by Christ's death and resurrection'.[18] We are now empowered by his Spirit to live his resurrection life and to exceed anything that the law would have required by way of a righteous life. Consequently, we *are not under law* (5:18) – it is an irrelevance from this viewpoint. The promise of the new covenant, anticipated by Jeremiah,[19] has come into being through Christ, and people need no longer live according to an external law, since the Spirit is within them to write that law on their hearts.

c. The practice (5:19–21)

Going beyond the statement of principles and purpose, Paul clothes his teaching with flesh (if you will forgive the pun) and illustrates the sort of behaviour which does not fit if someone is living by or being *led by the Spirit*. In a style that would have been familiar to his readers,[20] he lists fifteen vices which fall into four categories. First, there are the sexual sins of promiscuity (*immorality*), dirty-mindedness (*impurity*) and sexual excess (*debauchery*). Secondly, there were sins which have to do with corrupt worship: namely, the setting up of alternative altars and gods at which to offer worship (*idolatry*) and sorcery (*witchcraft*), which had always been

---

[18] Fee, *God's Empowering Presence*, p. 422.
[19] Jer. 31: 31–34.
[20] R. Longenecker, *Galatians*, WBC (Dallas: Word, 1990), pp. 249–252. Similar lists appear, for example, in Rom 1:29–31; 1 Cor. 6:9–10; Eph. 5:3–5; Col. 3:5–8; 2 Tim 3:2–4 and 1 Pet. 4:3.

forbidden in Israel. Thirdly, there were sins that related to the emotions including *hatred*, strife (*discord*), *jealousy, fits of rage, selfish ambition, dissensions, factions and envy*. These, as has often been pointed out, are not only a catalogue of ugly personal characteristics that describe thoroughly unpleasant people, but a list of characteristics that destroy relationships and make fellowship in the church impossible.[21] Finally, Paul lists *drunkenness* and *orgies*.

Having named specific examples of the pre-Christ lifestyle he had in mind, it is easy to see why Paul should think them incompatible with living by the Spirit.

3. The Fruit of the Spirit: a character to cultivate (5:22–23)

From the everyday metaphor of walking, Paul now turns to an agricultural image to make his next point. Having painted the portrait of a person who is not being led by the Spirit, he now paints the portrait of someone who is. To do so he speaks of how the *fruit of the Spirit* is manifest.

a. The image Paul uses

The image of fruit is richly evocative. Fruit grows as a result of the inner life of the fruit tree and it grows according to its kind. Attaching apples to an apple tree by some external means fools no one. Fruit also develops from whatever kind of life is within. Oranges being taped to a plum tree, or bananas being tied to an apple tree, equally fools no one. An orange tree produces oranges; a plum tree, plums; and an apple tree, apples, each according to their kind. Furthermore, the fruit takes time to grow, even if the tree is mature. We do not plant a tree one day and expect it to produce fruit the next. A tree needs to rest during the autumn and winter before bursting into life in the spring and producing its crop in the summer. In some cases, several years pass before the tree is established enough to produce decent fruit. We also know that trees need to be pruned.

There are obvious parallels with the process involved in our producing the fruit of holiness. Holiness does not consist in our seeking to reform our lives by our striving to observe external rules. We cannot produce it by our own efforts. It is a gift from God and an

---

[21] Fee points out that some characteristics that appear elsewhere, such as greed, lust and covetousness are absent here because he judges the emphasis is not on the kind of sins that are 'associated with warfare within the human breast' but on those that cause a breakdown in relationships, *God's Empowering Presence*, p. 442.

expression of the life of Christ's Spirit within us, without which it is impossible to produce a Christ-like life. In this respect, the Christian may be somewhat passive (though see below) and it may be significant that the picture of fruit is deliberately chosen to contrast with *the acts* (or works) *of the sinful nature,* mentioned in verse 19.[22] It is God's work, not ours, that gives birth to the fruit. Paul is saying that what is within will express itself to others and if our inner life is still driven by our *sinful nature* it is our sinful natures that others will encounter. The mature fruit we long to produce is likely to take time to grow and unlikely to develop overnight. Consequently, we need patience with ourselves and with others to allow the crop to ripen. We also need to accept that God's pruning, alluded to in verse 24, may be necessary if we are to produce good fruit.[23]

The odd thing about Paul's use of this image, or so it appears to us, is that he speaks of a single fruit of the Spirit and yet lists nine different forms the fruit takes. It would be anachronistic to think that Paul had in mind something like the blended fruit juices containing nine different flavours we now enjoy, as if that was the single juice of the Spirit-led life that refreshes others, nice though the thought might be. In fact, Paul would have used the word fruit as a collective singular, as we do when we describe a variety of fruits in the fruit bowl merely as 'fruit'.[24] Even so, this fruit salad is one. We are not able, as it were, to choose to be apple people as opposed to orange people, but rather should allow the Spirit to bring out the variety of his produce in our lives, each one bringing out the full flavour of the others.

b. The characteristics Paul names[25]

The fifteen ugly illustrations of the *acts of the sinful nature* are more than balanced by the nine attractive characteristics that comprise the fruit of the Spirit. Timothy George describes the way they are listed, in three triads, as a 'beautiful harmony, balanced and symmetrical, corresponding to the purposeful design and equilibrium of a life

---

[22] F. F. Bruce, *Commentary on Galatians,* NIGTC (Carlisle: Paternoster: 1982), p. 251, Longenecker, *Galatians,* p. 259.

[23] See chapter 15.

[24] Fee, *God's Empowering Presence,* p. 444.

[25] Each of the virtues mentioned here is rich in resonances with other parts of Scripture, and, with the exception of *self-control,* was applied to God himself. Space does not permit a full exposition but the works of Bruce, Fee and Longenecker are especially worth referring to, as is Ronald Fung, *The Epistle to the Galatians,* NICNT (Grand Rapids: Eerdmans, 1988) and S. F. Winward, *Fruit of the Spirit* (Grand Rapids: Eerdmans, 1981).

filled with the Spirit and lived out in the beauty of holiness'.[26] It would be wrong to speculate too much on the arrangement of these groups but John Stott's suggestion that the first three (*love, joy* and *peace*) 'seem to portray the Christian's attitude to God'; the second three (*patience, kindness, goodness*) to other people, and the third three (*faithfulness, gentleness and self-control*) relate to oneself, may have some merit.[27]

Love is the over-arching quality of the Spirit[28] of which Martin Luther said, 'It would have sufficed to list only love, for this expands into all the fruit of the Spirit.'[29] It has been described as 'the white light which enters a prism: the other virtues are a rainbow and together they make up love'.[30] *Agapē* is the primary and all-encompassing quality which calls for the exercise of selfless sacrifice and is at the same time immensely practical about the ordinary relationships of life, as set out in 1 Corinthians 13. Love cannot exist without it being expressed to others.

Joy speaks of the pleasure we derive once our lives are focused on our gracious God. Happiness happens as a result of our circumstances but joy endures in spite of our circumstances and is fuelled by the hope we have in Christ. Joy does not imply that all Christians should have extrovert characters, for God has made us all differently and joy may be deeply felt rather than loudly expressed. But the marks of a deep contentment and thankful spirit will be evident somehow in the lives of those in whom the Spirit is at work. Dour sobriety honours God no more than inconsiderate revelry, both of which may be symptoms of being self-centred rather than God-centred and both of which may lack consideration for others.

God's *šālôm*, a major concern of the Old Testament, is here a fruit of the Spirit. *Peace* (*eirēnē*) was used in the ancient world to describe a city which enjoyed tranquillity because it was governed well. Being under the rule of Christ enables Christians to enjoy such serenity. Like love, it is a primarily a social quality, not an individual emotion. Here and elsewhere, such as in Colossians 3:15, it describes the way Christians relate to each other. Although it may not be possible for us to be at peace with others unless we know

---

[26] George, *Galatians,* p. 399, contrasts this with the 'disorderly, chaotic and incomplete' listing of the acts of the sinful nature which corresponds 'to the random and compulsive character of sin itself'. I have argued that there is a sense of order in Paul's list of the sinful acts.

[27] J. R. W. Stott, *The Message of Galatians,* BST (London: IVP, 1968), p. 148.

[28] See Col. 3:14.

[29] Cited by George, *Galatians,* p. 400, n. 96.

[30] R. Warner, *Rediscovering the Spirit* (London: Hodder and Stoughton, 1986), p. 98.

peace within ourselves, biblically speaking the reverse is even more true. No Christian can truly be at peace in their individual emotions unless they are at peace with the other members of their church.

The next triad of graces brings out the social dimension of the fruit of the Spirit even more obviously. *Patience* means we do not give in to anger or give up on each other. Like other qualities, patience is ascribed to God himself in Romans 2:4.

Kindness and *goodness* belong together. The former is the disposition of grace which cannot but express itself as we serve others. The latter, if there is a difference, is a more active quality and has a nuance of generosity, but it is difficult to distinguish between them. Together these virtues are the mirror opposite of the vices mentioned in verses 20 and 21.

The final group emphasizes personal qualities, but, as is immediately apparent, they are qualities that would attract others to be friends with those who possess them. *Faithfulness* is not so much faithfulness to the truth as trustworthiness in general, and reliability in all relationships and commitments, just as God is faithful.[31]

The word *gentleness* easily becomes confused with spinelessness. The older translation of *praütēs* was meekness, which, being a less common word, raised questions as to its meaning. In the ancient world it was used for the breaking in of a horse so that the animal's passions were tamed, its strength disciplined, and its energies directed to constructive ends. The 'horse power' continued but was now channelled into service. So, here, the fruit which the Spirit grows in our lives does not reduce us to weak and feeble personalities but refines and controls our passions and strengths so that they become submissive to God and serviceable to others. *Gentleness*, like humility, makes us teachable and considerate.

The last virtue is that of *self-control*, which is an unusual word and, alone of these graces, is not applied to God. It means that the Spirit works within us so that we master our passions, our unbridled self-expression and our pampered self-indulgences, rather than letting them master us. Instead of excusing ourselves when we commit the *acts of the sinful nature* by saying, 'We cannot help ourselves,' we say instead, 'Sin shall not reign over us.'[32] We may say, 'We cannot help ourselves,' but we quickly add, 'But the Holy Spirit can help me.' Described like this, holiness is attractive. The Spirit develops warm and winsome people, not grouchy, inhibited, holier-than-thou Pharisees. This beautiful character is the product of the Spirit at work over a lifetime. En route there may be many failures,

[31] Rom. 3:3; 1 Cor. 1:3; 1 Thess. 5:24.
[32] In Rom. 6:12 this is an exhortation.

211

but, as Helder Camara remarked, 'Being holy means getting up immediately every time you fall, with humility and joy. It doesn't mean never falling into sin. It means being able to say, "Yes, Lord, I have fallen one thousand times. But thanks to you I've got up a thousand and one times."'[33]

4. Marching in step with the Spirit: a rhythm to keep (5:25 – 6:6)

Paul's imagery changes once more. Having used the metaphors of walking and fruit-bearing he now turns to a military metaphor: *Since we live by the Spirit, let us keep in step with the Spirit.* The Holy Spirit is now seen as the Regimental Sergeant Major, drilling a platoon of soldiers, of which we are one. Holiness not only concerns our individual walk with the Spirit but our marching in step with others, under his command. Note that the imperative *live* (or walk) *by the Spirit*, in 5:16, has now been turned into an indicative, *since we live by the Spirit*, in 5:25. The basis of our being able to march together as a holy community is that we are walking individually with the Spirit in our personal lives. Given that, it is the Spirit's task to keep us in line.

Paul develops his metaphor by telling us first how we can get out of step (5:26) and then what it means to march in step (6:1–6).

a. How to get out of step (5:26)

Three dispositions put us out of step with the Holy Spirit, and with each other in the church. There is the superiority complex whereby we become *conceited* and believe ourselves to be better than others, whether because of our knowledge, experience or our social standing. This puts us ahead of the rest of the army who find it difficult to keep up with us. We look down on the 'poor things' with whom we share the church. Secondly, there is the competitive complex in which we enjoy *provoking each other* and delight in tripping our fellow marchers up. Paul uses a word from athletics where one competitor has to outdo another. Such one-upmanship often arises from deep-seated anxiety or insecurity. But there is no room for it in the church where we are all equally valued and gifted by God. Thirdly, he speaks of the inferiority complex, which manifests itself in our *envying each other*. With this disposition, we lag behind, complaining we're no good and having nothing to

---

[33] Quoted in Warner, *Rediscovering the Spirit*, p. 102.

contribute, which is, of course, to contradict what God has said of us.[34]

b. How to keep in step (6:1–6)

Speaking positively, Paul now illustrates the sort of ways in which we can *keep in step with the Spirit* and so with each other. It means, verse 1, we will *restore* the person who *is caught in a sin . . . gently.* We will not gossip about them, criticize them, write them off, or even merely pray for them, but *restore* them. It means, verse 2, we will relieve the burdened by off-loading them in practical ways and shouldering part of their load ourselves, as Christ's law expects. It means, verse 3–5, that we will accept responsibility for our own lives without interfering in the lives of others. If we act with humility and take our share of carrying the church's kit, we will having nothing to fear. We should never compare ourselves with others because God has made us all unique and able to carry different capacities. Comparisons either lead us to superiority, as we think ourselves better, or depression, as we think ourselves useless in comparison with others. Only one measurement matters, and that is how we measure up to being the people God has made us to be. Lastly, to be in step, means, verse 6, we will also recompense those who provide us with spiritual instruction rather than glibly assuming that their reward will be in heaven.

5. But how?

Paul's concern is to stress that God has given us the Holy Spirit in order that our lives may be transformed so we become like Christ. In Galatians he does not directly answer the question that has preoccupied so many Christians in recent years, namely, 'How can we be fuller of the Holy Spirit than we are?'

It is axiomatic to Paul, as we have seen, that the believer in Christ has the Holy Spirit, yet he can still urge Christians to 'be filled with the Spirit' (Eph. 5:18).

It is also axiomatic that he sees our growth in holiness as a progressive experience rather than a sudden achievement through some particular encounter with the Holy Spirit. His command to walk continuously in the Spirit, his image of bearing fruit, and his encouragement to *keep in step with the Spirit*, all speak of continuous and progressive experience. It is teaching us that 'the Christian's total

[34] See 1 Cor. 12:4–31.

213

self is progressively renewed and restored throughout the sanctifying process – refocused on God, reintegrated with God at the centre, reconstructed in character, habits and reaction patterns, sensitized to God's values, redirected into God-glorifying purposes, and made more alert to others' needs and miseries'.[35]

Is a crisis experience of the Spirit, that some have called 'baptism in the Spirit', needed or does his progressive work in us rule that out? There may be many reasons why God meets us on occasions in out-of-the ordinary ways and gives us an exceptional experience of the Holy Spirit in our lives. It may be used to overcome resistance, to kick-start our thirst for God, to prepare us for new ministries, to exercise new gifts, or to face new challenges. But such experiences are never advocated in the New Testament as the key to lifting us onto a higher plane of holiness. The clue to that is much more rooted in our daily walk with the Spirit in the ordinariness of life.

It is also clear that Paul does not expect us to attain sinless perfection now, and for it to be uninterrupted from now on. Our expectations need to be real. We are currently 'those who sow to please the Spirit' and must not grow weary of the waiting, 'for at the proper time we will reap a harvest if we do not give up' (6:8–9). The harvest is still future. Any exceptional experience of the Holy Spirit, however valuable, is not going to make us immune from temptation and incapable of falling.

Accepting these cautions, how can we come more under the influence of the Holy Spirit so that we may be filled with him? For most of us it starts with our desiring to be so. Many of us are not filled with the Spirit because we show little real commitment to being so. We dance to other tunes and are content to play around in the shallows of holiness than to wade out more deeply. If the appetite is there, it will lead us to confession of our sin, consecration of our lives, urgency in our prayer, faith in God's provision and obedience in our daily lives.[36] There are no shortcuts to sanctification. The key is consecration, 'an act, done in studied deliberateness, in full awareness of the implications, and without reservation'.[37] It 'remains superficial if it does not reach the jugular of the self nature'.[38] The clue is found earlier in Galatians when Paul writes, not as a matter of

[35] J. I. Packer, *A Passion for Holiness* (Cambridge: Crossway Books, 1992), p. 111.

[36] A. W. Tozer listed surrender, Rom. 12:1–2; asking, Luke 11:13; obeying, Acts 5:32 and believing, Gal. 3:2. Cited in R. Taylor, *Exploring Christian Holiness*, Vol 3, *The Theological Formulation* (Kansas City: Beacon Hill, 1985), p. 167.

[37] Harold Ockenga, cited in ibid., p. 171.

[38] Ockenga cited in ibid., p. 172.

theory but of experience, 'I have been crucified with Christ and I no longer live, but Christ lives in me. The life I now live in the body, I live by faith in the Son of God, who loved me and gave himself for me' (2:20). To be filled with the Spirit is to be crucified with Christ.

2 Timothy 3:14–17
15. The Word of God

Bishop J. C. Ryle claimed,

> . . . [T]he Bible has worked moral miracles by thousands. It has made drunkards become sober, – unchaste people become pure, – thieves become honest, – violent-tempered people become meek. It has wholly altered the course of men's lives. It has caused old things to pass away and made their ways new. It has taught worldly people to seek first the kingdom of God. It has taught lovers of pleasure to become lovers of God. It has taught the stream of men's affections to run upwards instead of running downwards. It has made men think of heaven, instead of always thinking of earth, and live by faith, instead of living by sight. All this it has done in every part of the world. All this it is doing still.[1]

Bishop Ryle's words make a grand assertion about the transforming power of the Bible and the ability it has to turn unholy people into those who have a heart for God. He goes so far as to claim that, 'The Bible applied to the heart by the Holy Ghost, is *the chief means by which men are built up and stablished in the faith,* after their conversion.'[2] In advancing the claim he perhaps overstates his case since God uses many and varied means to build people up, but certainly the Bible is among the most important. To neglect it is to sentence oneself to struggle more than necessary in the battle for holiness and to live an anaemic spiritual life. Scripture claims as much for itself and countless men and women could testify to its power. For example, Dr John White, the late psychiatrist and Christian author, wrote,

[1] J. C. Ryle, *Practical Religion* (London: James Clarke, 1959 edn), pp. 80–81.
[2] Ibid., p. 81. Italics his.

Bible study has torn my life apart and remade it. That is to say that God, through his Word, has done so. . . . If I could write poetry about it I would. If I could sing through paper, I would flood your soul with the glorious melodies that express what I have found. I cannot exaggerate for there are no expressions majestic enough to tell of the glory I have seen, or of the wonder of finding that I, a neurotic, unstable, middle-aged man have my feet firmly planted in eternity and breathe the air of heaven. All this has come to me through a careful study of Scripture.[3]

1. The Bible's role in sanctification: the wide view

Throughout the Bible there is an awareness that God's written Word has an important part to play in enabling people to overcome the effects of the fall and live in ways which are more pleasing to God. It would be anachronistic, of course, to say that the Bible claims this of the complete canon of Scripture as we now have it, but the logic of Scripture relentlessly pushes us in that direction, as we shall see. We select just four examples, one from the Old and three from the New, before looking in detail at a key passage. These are not proof texts but representative of a stream that forms a consistent picture of God's Word as dynamic and life-changing.

a. The Old Testament (Psalm 119)

Our Old Testament witness is Psalm 119, which shows a deep affection for the words God has spoken and an excitement about their role in helping people to live a blameless life. Elsewhere, I have identified six aspects to the Psalm's role.[4]

1. God's Word provides guidance as to how to live wisely and distinguish right from wrong, *How can those who are young keep their way pure? By living according to your word* (9). Similarly, verse 105 speaks of God's Word as *a lamp to my feet and a light for my path.*

2. Imbibing God's Word deeply provides strength against temptation: *I have hidden your word in my heart that I might not sin against you* (11).

3. It protects the weary and those who are attacked or who

[3] J. White, *The Fight: A Practical Handbook for Christian Living* (Downers Grove, Illinois: IVP, 1976), pp. 54–55.
[4] D. Tidball, 'The Bible in Evangelical Spirituality' in P. Ballard and S. Holmes (eds.), *The Bible in Pastoral Practice* (London: Darton, Longman and Todd, 2005), pp. 258–274.

might get worn down in their discipleship, as in verses 28, 50, 116 and 156.

4. Obedience to God's Word liberates people and releases them to live the full life God intended. In verse 32 the psalmist shows an enthusiasm for God's commands because they set the heart free. Similar positive emotions are expressed in verses 35 and 45.

5. Living according to God's Word causes one to get right priorities in life, to shun the worship of worthless things (37), and to enjoy both the living Creator and his creation to the full (73, 90–93 and 134).

6. God's law stands over against us, pointing out our sin, leading us to change direction, correcting our course, turning us to God and becoming a catalyst for holiness, as verses 5–6, 25–26 and 36 illustrate.

b. The New Testament

(i) John 17:17

Our first witness from the New Testament is Jesus himself. Praying for his disciples before his crucifixion he asks the 'Holy Father' (John 17:11) to protect them from the evil one and to preserve their unity while they mingle in the world. Then he prays, *sanctify them by the truth; your word is truth.* Christ's longing is that they should be set apart for the sacred duty of serving God in the world. The agent that will cause them to be set apart initially and the preservative that will maintain their on-going distinctiveness is *the truth* which, Christ explains, is God's *word.* In the context, this must mean the reliable revelation that the disciples have received about Christ, who is the Word incarnate,[5] which the Holy Spirit is going to remind them of and explain further as the need arises.[6] Don Carson points out that this revelation is now to be found in the pages of John's Gospel, and, by extension, in the whole of the Bible. 'In practical terms', Carson writes, 'no one can be "sanctified" or set apart for the Lord's use without thinking God's thoughts after him, without learning to live in conformity with the "word" he has graciously given.'[7]

---

[5] John 1:1, 14.
[6] John 14:26; 16:13.
[7] D. A. Carson, *The Gospel According to John,* Pillar Commentary (Leicester: IVP and Grand Rapids: Eerdmans, 1991), p. 566.

(ii) 2 Thessalonians 2:13

A similar emphasis is found in 2 Thessalonians 2:13, which speaks of our being sanctified by the Holy Spirit *and through [our] belief in the truth.* The Spirit and the Word are partners in the enterprise of holiness.[8] The truth refers to the gospel they had preached to them which Paul had just mentioned in the previous verses.[9] But one should not think that this means merely an introductory evangelistic message, for it is evident from Paul's earlier letter to the Thessalonians that his exposition of the gospel was much fuller than we might have expected and included, among other topics, teaching about ethics and the second coming of Christ.[10] All this they accepted 'not as a human word, but as it actually is, the word of God' (1 Thessalonians 2:13). This is the word, then, that plays an on-going part in making the converts holy.

(iii) James 1:21

In his teaching about holiness, James instructs his readers to *get rid of all moral filth and the evil that is so prevalent, and humbly accept the word planted in you, which can save you.* The implanted word, again, is the word of the gospel in its fuller, rather than streamlined, sense. From the context this word contains a great deal of ethical teaching and, submitting to it, rather than ignoring it or fighting against it, is the antidote to unholy living. This is James's way of saying what Paul says when he instructs Christians to put off the old way of living and put on the new.[11]

In putting it his way, James uses the interesting image of the implanted word. Implicit in the metaphor is the word as a living, dynamic and growing organism, which is affirmed elsewhere.[12] The power of a tiny seed to develop into a small plant, to break through tough ground, and grow into a strong and healthy flower inspires awe in the natural world. James is surely suggesting that God's Word, similarly, is a life-giving power which produces spiritually mature Christians. The seed of the gospel had been planted so now, as James Adamson advises, 'the soil of the heart must be

---

[8] Cf. 2 Tim. 1:13–14.

[9] Cf. 1 Peter 1:25. 'That word is the good news that was announced to you' (NRSV).

[10] 1 Thess. 4:1 – 5:11.

[11] Eph. 4:22, 25; Col. 3:5–14.

[12] Cf. Heb. 4:12–13. In 1 Pet. 1:23 Peter uses the image of a seed: 'You have been born again, not of perishable seed, but of imperishable, through the living and enduring word of God.'

hospitable, if the seed of the Word is to grow'.[13] And that means giving up impure living and letting the seed flourish 'in the soil of obedience'.[14]

These sayings and other teaching within the New Testament[15] provide evidence that God intends to use the truth Christians believe, in partnership with the Spirit, as an instrument of growth in holiness. Having gained a wider perspective, we turn to look close up at one passage that speaks directly to the issue.

2. The Bible's role in sanctification: the close up view (2 Timothy 3:14–17)

Paul's last letter betrays not a little anxiety on his part about the future of the church and therefore is crowded with instructions to Timothy about how he is to conduct his leadership in it. While holiness is not a major theme it is never far below the surface and breaks through the surface on a couple of occasions. First, Paul reminds Timothy that our calling as Christians is to 'a holy life' (2 Timothy 1:9), that is, to a life of moral purity and high ethical standards. Later, in 2:20–21, he mentions that in any household there are noble vessels set apart for use on special occasions and others that are in ordinary use and have to do with disposing of the refuse. Although the picture is one that could be drawn from any number of sources, his particular language suggests he has the sacrificial instruments of the tabernacle or temple in mind. There, some instruments would have been 'unclean' and concerned with the disposal of ashes but others were holy and reserved for special use. Without applying the picture, Paul implies, as the following verse suggests, that Timothy should take care to cleanse himself from sin and be set apart ('made holy') and become 'useful to the Master and prepared to do any good work'.

a. The nature of the Bible (2 Timothy 3:14–15)

The third use of the word 'holy' in the TNIV and NIV is different. It refers not to persons but to the Scriptures and is not the normal word, *hagios*, but *hieros*, meaning sacred.[16] Perhaps we should not

---

[13] J. Adamson, *The Epistle of James*, NICNT (Grand Rapids: Eerdmans, 1976), p. 81.

[14] Ibid., p. 82.

[15] E.g., Col. 3:16; Heb. 4:12–13; 1 Pet.1:23 and the exegetically complex 2 Pet. 1:21.

[16] NRSV translates it as 'the sacred writings'.

make too much of Paul's use of this particular word for in Romans 1:2 he had used the more usual word for holy to describe them. Both words indicate that these writings are set apart from the ordinary and have a special status in relation to God and a special role in relation to his people.

The sacred writings Paul has in mind are, of course, the writings of the Old Testament, and the phase he uses is apparently virtually a technical term for them.[17] Given that the documents of the New Testament were only just being written, or at least collected and acknowledged, he does not have them in mind. But given (1) that Peter refers to Paul's letters on a par with 'the other scriptures' (2 Peter 3:16), and (2) that much of the New Testament contains the teaching of Jesus, and (3) that the collective wisdom of the church under the guidance of the Holy Spirit decided before long that the documents we now have in the New Testament canon were the inspired ones and of universal value, it is reasonable to extend Paul's teaching here to embrace the full Bible.

Paul urges Timothy to continue on the path he has started in relation to the Scriptures and then pauses to look backwards and then forwards on that path. As he looks back he sees the way in which he was taught the Scriptures from his earliest years by his mother and his grandmother (1:5). Their teaching immersed him in the Old Testament writings and his faith stands in continuity with them. The lives his 'teachers' had led provided plenty of evidence of the value and trustworthiness of those Scriptures.

As he looks forward he sees the destination to which those Scriptures lead. They would make him *wise for salvation through faith in Jesus Christ.* Several aspects of this densely packed phrase are worthy of note. The Scriptures are seen to have an educative role in making people *wise,* very much as the law, the stories, the wise sayings and the prophecies of the Old Testament were seen to function.[18] The wisdom gained through their study is *for salvation.* But surely, Timothy was already saved through God's grace, according to what Paul had written in 1:9? Why does Paul now speak of it as if it is future. It is true that Timothy was saved and could be sure of his salvation, but the salvation he had already experienced was merely the first instalment and there is a much fuller experience of it for him to enter yet, if he remained steadfast. This salvation is *through faith in Jesus Christ,* who is the focal point of all the Scriptures, with everything in the Old Testament leading up to him and then

[17] P. H. Towner, *The Letters of Timothy and Titus,* NICNT (Grand Rapids: Eerdmans, 2006), p. 582.
[18] Ps. 19:7.

everything in the New leading on from him. The Jewish leaders made the mistake of searching the Scriptures but failing to recognize the Christ of whom they spoke (John 5:39). Studying the Scriptures had become an end in itself, thus they missed their whole point. The Bible must always take us to Christ.

In one of his earlier writings John Stott used a telling parable which is worth quoting in full to make the point clear:

> To suppose that salvation lies in a book is as foolish as supposing that health lies in a prescription. When we are ill and the doctor prescribes some medicine for us, does he intend that we should go home with the prescription, read it, study it and learn it by heart? Or that we should frame it and hang it on our bedroom wall? Or that we should tear it into fragments and eat the pieces three times a day after meals? The absurdity of these possibilities is obvious. The prescription itself will not cure us. The whole purpose of a prescription is to get us to go to the chemist, obtain the medicine prescribed and drink it. Now the Bible contains the divine prescription for sin-sick souls. It is the only medicine which can save us from perishing. In brief, it tells us of Jesus Christ who died for us and rose again. But we do not worship the Bible as if it could save us; we go to Christ. For the overwhelming purpose of the Bible is to send us to Christ and to persuade us to drink the water of life which he offers.[19]

b. The inspiration of the Bible (2 Timothy 3:16)

The reason the Scriptures are able to achieve these goals in our lives is because, although written by human authors, they are at the same time divinely 'inspired' (NRSV), or *God-breathed* (TNIV). Some argue that this verse is ambiguous and the text might either read *All Scripture is God-breathed and is useful,* or, 'all inspired scripture is also useful'. But since the reference to the *Holy Scriptures* in verse 15 was all-inclusive and treated Scripture as a coherent whole, there can be no serious doubt that Paul intends us to understand *all* in the sense of every part of *Scripture is God-breathed.*[20]

Paul describes Scripture as *theopneustos,* a word which is not found elsewhere in the Bible, and means God blowing into or

---

[19] J. R. W. Stott, *Christ the Controversialist: A Study of the Essentials of Evangelical Christianity* (London: Tyndale Press, 1970), pp. 101–102.

[20] For the arguments see Towner, *The Letters of Timothy and Titus,* p. 585–587, W. Mounce, *Pastoral Epistles,* WBC, (Nashville: Thomas Nelson, 2000), p. 566.

breathing on the writings and thus imparting his own life and authority to them. Paul is unconcerned about the relationship between God's inspiration and the human authorship of Scripture. The mechanisms by which the authority of God and the freedom of the authors (and editors) are both maintained with integrity is not of interest to him.[21] His only concern is to underline that the Scriptures are trustworthy and are marked by the very stamp of the living God who cannot lie.[22] Through inspiration, God has caused what he wished to be communicated as revealed truth to men and women to be written as a living and life-giving Word.[23] As William Mounce concludes after a detailed examination of this text, the usefulness 'of Scripture flows out of its inspiration. The entirety of Scripture comes from the mouth of God. To read it is to hear him speak. It is therefore true, and it can therefore be trusted.'[24]

c. The usefulness of the Bible (2 Timothy 3:16)

Although evangelicals have often used these verses to stress the authority of the Bible, the thrust of Paul's teaching here is that the Bible is useful, rather than authoritative (which it is!). Its practical value lies in the way in which it impacts our lives and thoroughly equips us for every good work. It does this by *teaching, rebuking, correcting and training [us] in righteousness.*

The four functions Paul identifies display a beautiful symmetry. They begin and end positively, *teaching* and *training*. These serve as the envelope of two negative functions, *rebuking* and *correcting*, that are placed in the middle. It is attractive to relate the first two words to the positive and negative aspects of what Christians believe and the second couple to how Christians behave.[25] There is ample evidence from the emphasis on teaching elsewhere in the Pastoral Letters to think that Paul may be referring to the contents of Christian belief. *Rebuking* would then involve pointing out heresy and rebuking people for holding the wrong beliefs. If this interpretation is right, *correcting* involves pointing out wrong behaviour

---

[21] The idea that God dictated the Scriptures must be rejected as failing to give sufficient weight to the human authors. The answer may well lie in the idea of 'concursive action' in which human action and the work of the Holy Spirit coincide without detriment to either party, as J. I. Packer suggested in *'Fundamentalism' and the Word of God* (London: IVP, 1958), pp. 81–82.

[22] Num. 23:19; Titus 1:2.

[23] Packer, *'Fundamentalism' and the Word of God*, p. 77.

[24] Mounce, *Pastoral Epistles*, p. 570.

[25] Mounce, *Pastoral Epistles*, p. 570. Cf. I. H. Marshall, *The Pastoral Epistles*, ICC (Edinburgh: T & T Clark, 1999), p. 795.

with a view to amending it and *training* to educating a person in right living. But this is probably a little too neat and reads more into the arrangement of the words than Paul may have intended. His purpose throughout is practical and the accent therefore is more likely to fall on the side of adopting a right lifestyle than adopting right beliefs at this point in his letter.

As to the words themselves:[26] *teaching* is about instructing the ignorant or uneducated. *Rebuking* is to make someone aware of sin, hoping that the censure will lead them to amend their behaviour and make it unnecessary to take matters further. *Correcting* aims to put the wrong situation right and at restoring the one who has fallen. *Training* is a more general word and was widely used among the Greeks to speak of instructing young people to become virtuous and often included 'a strong element of discipline and correction'.[27] Here the goal of the education is to enable a person to live an upright life before God, which will be marked by the qualities Paul listed in 2:22, namely, righteousness, faith, love, peace and a pure heart. Reading the Bible often brings about a conviction of sin as the Holy Spirit brings a particular passage or verse to our minds which rebukes us for wrongdoing. Reading its stories and learning about the consequences of sin can serve as severe warnings that encourage us to avoid evil. More positively, reading Scripture informs us of the will of God for our lives and the blessings of obedience. It does this both through direct instruction and through the stories and examples of others. A regular exposure to God's Word has the effect of increasing our spiritual appetite and creating a hunger within us to live God's way. It also helps to reshape our thinking and remould our attitudes. We need not only to expose ourselves to the Bible but digest it. We need to get into the Bible in order that the Bible may get into us.[28]

d. The purpose of the Bible (2 Timothy 3:17)

While Paul's comments may first and foremost be directed to Timothy himself it is evident that his teaching about the power of the Bible is by no means limited to Timothy. God uses the Bible as

---

[26] Towner, *The Letters of Timothy and Titus*, pp. 590–592.

[27] Marshall, *The Pastoral Epistles*, p. 796.

[28] L. Eims, *Be the Leader You Were Meant to Be* (Wheaton: Victor Books, 1975), p. 19, wrote, 'We must get into the Word and the Word must get into us. We get into it by hearing it preached, reading it, studying it, and memorizing it. We get the Word into us through meditation. By meditating on it we assimilate the Word of God into our spiritual lives. Like physical food, it is not what we take in that affects us but what we digest and assimilate. That's meditation.'

an instrument by which to equip all his people for whatever good or charitable works they may be required to undertake. The Bible is not given to us in order that we may argue over passages that are obscure, dogmatize on secondary issues where its voices are ambiguous, speculate about questions left unanswered or anathematize fellow believers who do not believe exactly what we believe. It is given to us to make us godly. It is neither a work of fiction for us to enjoy but not believe, nor a map book to direct us every time we come to tiny junctions in our lives, nor a systematic textbook to answer our every intellectual curiosity. It is a training manual which prepares us to live a God-centred, Christ-honouring and Spirit-filled life.

Paul's language is hardly reticent at this point. Through the Scriptures, he says, God intends his people to *be thoroughly equipped for every good work*. We are not partially equipped for some good works but kitted out with everything we will ever need to meet whatever demands we face. Students frequently complain about what they were not taught in college. But such a complaint can never be mounted against God, for his Word gives us a more than sufficient tool to prepare us to live godly lives, even if, like Timothy, we live them in challenging times.

3. Concluding comment

We end this chapter, as we began, with a quotation from Bishop J. C. Ryle. 'For another thing,' he wrote,

> read the Bible in a spirit of obedience and self-application. Sit down to study it with a daily determination that you will live by its rules, rest on its statements, and act on its commands. Consider, as you travel through every chapter, 'How does this affect my position and course of conduct? What does this teach me? It is poor work to read the Bible from mere curiosity, and for speculative purposes, in order to fill your head and store your mind with opinions, while you do not allow the book to influence your heart and life. The Bible is best read which is practised most.[29]

---

[29] Ryle, *Practical Religion*, p. 95.

Hebrews 12:1–17
16. The discipline of God

I have travelled with some extraordinary people. Some travel very lightly, while others manage to pack everything, so that whatever eventuality we face on the journey they can fish in their baggage and produce the answer. Like the proverbial Boy Scout, they live by the motto, 'Be prepared.' The writer to Hebrews tells us that there is a good deal of baggage we should shed on our journey[1] to 'the city of the living God, the heavenly Jerusalem'[2] because it would hinder our progress, but one item is indispensable: holiness. *Make every effort to live in peace with everyone and be holy; without holiness no-one will see the Lord* (12:14). If Christ is our passport, as it were, holiness is the visa we are required to have to accompany it.

Throughout Hebrews, holiness is a gift that God bestows on his people. In continuity with the sacrificial understanding of the Old Testament, God 'makes people holy' (2:11) through the offering of the perfect sacrifice of his Son, who in perfect obedience to his Father had led a sinless life. He consecrates people to God through his death.[3] Yet, while believers are never called to make themselves holy, they are called to care for the gift they have received and display it to the best advantage in the present world. To use the metaphor a friend mentioned to me,[4] we have inherited the gift of the family silver. We neither earned it, nor purchased it. It became ours through someone dying. But now it is ours, we must polish it and prevent it from being tarnished, using it for the benefit of others and displaying it to the best advantage.

---

[1] Heb. 12:1.
[2] Heb. 12:22.
[3] W. Lane, *Hebrews 9 – 13* WBC (Waco: Word, 1991), p. 450 and D. Peterson, *Possessed by God: A New Testament Theology of Sanctification and Holiness*, NSBT (Leicester: Apollos, 1995), p. 75.
[4] Tim Fergusson, Minister of Aylestone Baptist Church, Leicester.

The encouragement not to leave holiness behind as we're packing for heaven is not a free-standing exhortation cast adrift from its surroundings, although it is often used that way.[5] It is anchored to the argument that the writer has been developing throughout the chapter. Telling us to *make every effort . . . to be holy*, is the summary exhortation that follows an explanation of how God helps us to *share in his holiness* (12:10). To resort to the two metaphors above, the earlier part of the chapter tells us about the polish that will keep the family silver bright, and how to obtain the visa that needs to accompany the passport. The answer is an uncomfortable one. It is by submitting to God's discipline.

Contemporary society may be ambiguous about discipline. While, on the one hand, it admires the discipline of the sportsmen and women who undertake rigorous training for years in order to win a medal at an important competition, it is less sure about the moral disciplining of children, who many believe should be left to find their own way of life. In the ancient world it was commonly accepted that the task of the parent was to discipline their child so that they would grow into a responsible adult. Discipline was understood to combine 'the nuances of training, instruction, and firm guidance with those of reproof, correction, and punishment'.[6] And all these nuances are evident in Hebrews. The practical expression of holiness comes about as a result of the training, sometimes, tough training, and the chastening of God our Father. But before the writer focuses fully on the training his readers are undergoing, he inspires them with the experience of Jesus, who endured a more difficult training course than they are on and emerged triumphant from it.

1. The model of discipline (12:1–3)

Jesus was never anything but morally perfect, and yet Hebrews speaks of him like this: 'Son though he was, he learned obedience from what he suffered and, once made perfect, he became the source of eternal salvation for all those who obey him . . .' (5:8–9).[7] Does his learning obedience through suffering suggest 'that Jesus had

[5] D. Peterson, *Possessed by God*, p. 71, points out that J. C. Ryle uses it in this way in his classic work, *Holiness*, p. 34.

[6] Lane, *Hebrews 9 – 13*, p. 420. Paul Ellingworth points out that the word 'discipline' (*paideia*) is also used in Eph. 6:4 and 2 Tim. 3:16, and 'has a range of meaning which runs from training and education to corporal punishment', *The Epistle to the Hebrews*, Epworth Commentaries (London: Epworth Press, 1991), p. 122.

[7] See also Heb. 2:10.

some disobedience that needed to be knocked out of him?', Gordon Thomas asks, before supplying his own answer. 'Definitely not! But morally and spiritually the implication is that baby Jesus was not the finished article. If he was fully human, then like all of us he had to grow and learn in order to reach maturity (cf. Luke 2:52).'[8] Jesus underwent a developmental process in which at each stage he revealed his perfect obedience to the will of his Father, up to his enduring of the cross (12:3). Being the perfect Son of God did not mean that he would float through life, free from conflict, opposition and pain. It was, in fact, those very antagonistic experiences that trained him by testing his obedience and deepening his submission to his Father. This ensured that he was the unblemished sacrifice for sin.

Hebrews invites its readers to fix their eyes on Jesus and in doing so to learn from his example of single-mindedness and perseverance. He set aside every hindrance to achieving his goal. He demonstrated stamina and perseverance in running the race. He refused to give up and ran through the excruciating pain barrier of the cross to secure the victory of sitting *down at the right hand of the throne of God* (12:2).

The readers of Hebrews were in danger of giving up, so the author explains to them that they are running the same race that Jesus did. Their experience is neither unique nor questionable. They may face 'physical suffering, social ostracism and abuse from their opponents', but so did he.[9] He is to serve as their model, a model not only of perseverance but, more significantly, also of the benefits and rewards of enduring and not giving up the training.

2. The need for discipline (12:4)

The reason that these early Christians needed to endure, Hebrews says, was because, *In your struggle against sin, you have not yet resisted to the point of shedding your blood.* From the more gentle sporting imagery of the Christian life as a running race, the author now turns to the more brutal imagery of it as something more akin to a boxing match.[10] They cannot give up, not because it would have been a dishonourable thing to throw in the towel – that is beside the point; they cannot do so because the battle is not yet over, the bell

---

[8] G. J. Thomas, 'The Perfection of Christ and the Perfecting of Believers in Hebrews' in K. E. Brower and A. Johnson (eds.), *Holiness and Ecclesiology in the New Testament* (Grand Rapids: Eerdmans: 2007), pp. 296–297.

[9] Peterson, *Possessed by God,* p. 71.

[10] Lane, *Hebrews 9 – 13*, p. 417, points out that Paul makes a similar switch in 1 Cor. 9:24, 26.

has not been rung at the end of the contest and they have not yet achieved the victory. There are a few more rounds to go yet.

They are offered no soft comfort for their weariness. They are not told to take a holiday, enjoy sabbatical leave, or take it easy for a while, for their struggle is endless. Rather the author, like a school-master egging on weary children in a cross-country race, gives them robust encouragement to keep going because they were not dead yet, and no blood had been shed! There was to be no let-up in the fight as they had not resisted to the point of martyrdom.

The contest in which they were engaged is a contest against *sin*. The nature of the sin is unspecified but, in view of their expressed tiredness, may well have been the sin of giving into discouragement, which is sometimes a thin disguise for unbelief, and the resulting sin of compromising their faith rather than standing firm for Christ.[11] It is, perhaps, wise that the sin is left undefined here. Had it been specific we might have excused ourselves on the grounds that we never encountered that particular sin as an opponent. Being less specific, we can list the sins against which we particularly battle and against which we have not yet fought for the last time. The final bell of the contest will not be rung until the day of Christ and we remain in training until then.

3. The explanation of discipline (12:5–8)

The Hebrews may have been among the first to ask why the Christian life was so difficult, but they were certainly not the last. Why was suffering experienced? Was it necessary? How could it be squared with their being loved by God and set apart as his special people? Surely, if they were so special, God would offer them pro-tection and exempt them from hardship. But to argue in this way was is to misunderstand the nature of love, as the writer explains.

Quoting from Proverbs 3:11–12, he reminds them that discipline is not the obverse of love but rather an expression of genuine love. Children are not chastised because their father[12] does not love them but precisely because he does. The father who did not love would not care what his child would become, would lay down no boundaries, would instil no wisdom, and would exercise no discipline. Life would be indulgent, easy, and the child would grow up flabby, ill-trained

---

[11] Ibid., p. 409.
[12] The choice of 'father' as opposed to parent or 'father and mother' is deliber-ate in view of the fact that it was considered the father's responsibility to train his children in the ancient world.

for the adult world. But the father who loves would want the child to grow to its full and best potential and realize that that child would benefit from being stretched, corrected and disciplined. And if this is how our imperfect, yet loving, human parents related to us, how much more should we expect our perfect and loving God to do so.

Verse 9 underlines the point. The hardships that God permits are not a sign of his indifference or cruelty towards us, but a sign that we are genuinely his children and not illegitimate offspring, for whom a father may not care.

4. The experience of discipline (12:7)

The explanation puts the Hebrews' suffering in context and explains its purpose. It serves to provide the trainees with an incentive to keep going. But it does not make the suffering they undergo any less painful, anymore than the recruit who is desperate to win the coveted Red Beret of the Commandos thereby finds the selection process a gentle walk in the countryside. To the Hebrews, their suffering meant divisions within their families, as some converted to Christ and some said it was a betrayal of the Jewish faith; it meant being cold-shouldered by friends and excluded from old networks and business partners; and it may have meant being denounced as traitors in the synagogues where once they worshipped. Some had already been imprisoned.[13] Martyrdom was a real, if rare, possibility, although, on the evidence of verse 4 they had not yet encountered it. What they endured was as hurtful as the suffering undergone in recent years by many a convert to Christianity from Islam.

God's discipline comes in many forms, not just suffering for being a Christian. To some it might mean a period of sickness, which is what Paul alludes to in 1 Corinthians 11:30 when he explains that some in that church had become ill because they behaved towards their fellow believers at the Lord's Table in an unacceptable manner. Time out, perhaps due to illness, often provides us with the space to examine ourselves and confront spiritual issues that in the normal hurly-burly of life we can easily ignore or even repress, justifying our doing so to our own satisfaction.

Sometimes God's chastening comes through a direct encounter with God himself, as we pray, or as his Spirit invades our minds, perhaps when we are alone at night, or as he pricks our consciences in the day. Jacob's wrestling with God at Peniel is one such example.[14]

---

[13] Heb. 13:3.
[14] Gen. 32:22–32.

The struggle went on all night and left Jacob with a permanent limp. But it resulted in a refined, matured and humbled Jacob who was no longer quite so incapable of trusting anyone, including God, as he had been before. The new man was marked by the new name that God gave him. From now on, he was to be called Israel.

God's discipline equally comes through the rebuke of trusted Christian friends, through a prophetic insight given to someone we do not know, through the reading of Scripture, or through frustration of our plans and dreams. It may come through our losing what we love, or life suddenly taking an unexpected twist.

Sometimes God's discipline is needed to express his displeasure at sin in our lives, especially if we are becoming careless about sin, and to move us to repentance. John Bunyan, who spent years in prison for his faith, understood this well when he wrote in his *Seasonable Counsel* or *Advice to Sufferers,*

> We are apt to overshoot, in the days that are calm, and to think ourselves far higher, and more strong than we be, when a trying day is upon us. . . . We could not live without such turnings of the hand of God upon us. We should be overgrown with flesh, if we had not seasonable winters. It is said in some countries that trees will grow, but will bear no fruit, because there is no winter there.[15]

Suffering is often a spiritual wake-up call when we have drifted into sin and become less attentive to God's voice than we should be. It is often God's only way of getting through the layers of complacency we clothe ourselves with. In C. S. Lewis's well-known words it is because, 'God whispers to us in our pleasures, speaks in our conscience, but shouts in our pains: it is his megaphone to rouse a deaf world .'[16]

But God's discipline is not always provoked by our wrongdoing, by any means. Rather than always being punitive, we will often experience discipline as God's way of training us so that we make progress in our Christian lives rather than being content with the level of spirituality or maturity which we have already reached. In this light, however tough the experience, we can view it as a positive experience that we are privileged to receive as a mark of his love for us.

In the Bible, no one illustrates these two reasons for God's discipline more clearly than Joseph. It is evident that Joseph began life as something of a spoiled brat whose arrogance needed to be overcome. His dreams came from God, but the know-it-all teenager

---

[15] Quoted in J. Piper, *Tested by Fire* (Leicester: IVP, 2001), p. 72.
[16] C. S. Lewis, *The Problem of Pain* (London: Collins, 1957), p. 81.

was not yet mature enough to know how to handle them. This partly explains why God chastened him by allowing his brothers to sell him into slavery in Egypt.[17]

By the time Joseph had served in Potiphar's house, however, he seems to have made rapid spiritual progress and was a refined character, distinguishing himself as a trustworthy young man with leadership qualities.[18] Yet, God still let him be the victim of false accusation and languish in prison for many years before his dream came true. There is no evidence that this was punishment for any sin on Joseph's part. Indeed, he seems to have behaved blamelessly. So what was God doing in Joseph's life all this time? How can it be that we can read 'the Lord was with Joseph' during those heartache years in jail?[19] R. T. Kendall helpfully explains that Joseph 'was being severely chastened – but not because of any particular sin, for chastening is not God getting even but only his way of refining us'.[20] God's training programme for Joseph was tough in the extreme but designed to prepare him for the enormous task ahead. Earlier, Kendall had explained more generally,

> God's chastening is not God's way of getting even: God got even on the cross . . . the chastening isn't God getting even; it is preparing that person for something better, more valuable and worthwhile. God chastens us 'for our profit, that we may be partakers of his holiness' (Heb. 12:10). Often God chastens the very one who, as far as anyone could tell, didn't apparently need it or deserve it.[21]

Joseph's story teaches us how serious God is about our training. We do not know how long Joseph was in prison. But we do know it was 'two full years' after a glimmer of hope first shone in his prison cell, that the cupbearer, whose dream he had interpreted, remembered him and mentioned him to Pharaoh, leading to Joseph's release and elevation.[22] It was thirteen years in all since Joseph went to Egypt before God fulfilled his promise.[23] That's a long training programme! But God does his work thoroughly and patiently, always

[17] Gen. 37:1–36. The other essential element in why God arranged this was to ensure that Joseph got to Egypt and was in the right place when his dream was to be fulfilled.
[18] Gen. 39:1–6.
[19] Gen. 39:21–23.
[20] R. T. Kendall, *God Meant it for Good* (Carlisle: Paternoster, 2003), p. 68.
[21] Ibid., pp. 46–47.
[22] Gen. 41:1.
[23] Gen. 41:46.

stretching us to achieve new goals of Christ-likeness and never going beyond what is necessary.

Whether God's discipline is in response to our blemishes or a way of perfecting and maturing us further, his discipline is intent on refining us so that the imperfections and weaknesses can be removed, with our lives purer and stronger as a result. The fire may need to be hot indeed to complete the process of refinement. [24] Experiencing God's discipline, then, may be prolonged and painful but it arises from the privilege of being loved by him, and his motives are always good. He does not put more on us than we can bear, which is why the greatest of saints sometimes experience his heavier hand and hotter fire than those who are young or weak in faith.

5. The response to discipline (12:9–10)

There is a strand of evangelical spirituality that displays the traits of masochism. For all evangelicalism's emphasis on grace, there are some Christians and congregations that are never happier than when they are being 'challenged', rebuked, told what failures they are, and commanded to pull their socks up. It often makes little difference to their behaviour and simply means they return the following week for a further dose of discipline. Hebrews gives no quarter to such attitudes.

Nonetheless, it encourages us to *submit* to God's discipline, just as we submitted to parental discipline, not only because the one who disciplines has rights but because it is *for our good* (10). The writer recognizes that parental discipline was not perfect. He as good as says, in verse 10, that parents did their best. Sometimes they were too strict, sometimes too lenient, sometimes inconsistent, sometimes they lacked understanding. Yet, for the most part, they did a reasonable job and the fact that they cared enough to discipline us called forth respect from us, rather than resentment or rebellion. That being so, the writer argues, *How much more should we submit* to God's perfect discipline, however unpleasant it may seem at the time. It makes more sense to submit to God's discipline than it did to parental discipline, and that was sensible enough.

He backs up his point by a series of contrasts. Human and divine discipline differ in character: human parents are contrasted with *the Father of spirits*. This unique phrase highlights God's transcendent authority as the one 'to whom the heavenly world is subject'.[25] If the

---

[24] Mal. 3:3.
[25] Lane, *Hebrews 9 – 13*, p. 424.

heavenly beings submit to him, how much more should we? They differ in time: human parents exercise a temporary discipline, *for a little while*, but God has an eternal interest in our lives. They differ in expertise: human parents *disciplined us . . . as they thought best* but God knows for sure what is *good*. His 'rules and demands, words of advice and acts of discipline are not arbitrary but, rather, are the guidewires on a sapling designed to help the young tree grow strong and tall'.[26] The point parental and divine discipline have in common is that receiving discipline is never easy. But the rewards of divine discipline outweigh those of parental discipline by far. All this being so, we should willingly accept the discipline our heavenly Father chooses to impose on us. We should never allow *a bitter root* to grow up and cause us trouble as Esau did (12:15–17), leading to his forfeiting God's grace, but welcome his discipline with good grace.

6. The rewards of discipline (12:9–11)

Understanding our natural discomfort when receiving discipline, the writer draws attention to the rich rewards that discipline brings. They are threefold. In verse 9, they lead to life. In verse 10, they enable us to *share in his holiness*. And, in verse 11, *it produces a harvest of righteousness and peace.*

His discipline leads to life. True discipline enables life to be enjoyed more fully and prevents us from adopting actions or habits that, however attractive at the time, lead to harm. Good discipline does not stunt growth or inhibit freedom: it facilitates them. One only has to think of the discipline our laws impose on our driving to see the point. Those laws prevent accidents and, whatever we may occasionally think, enable swifter progress on the roads than if anarchy prevailed. How much more does the discipline of our divine Creator lead to a full and rich life?

His discipline, secondly, results in 'the supreme good'[27] that we *share in his holiness*. Using a unique term in the New Testament, *hagiotēs,* to describe the character of God as holy, Hebrews tells us that the purpose of discipline is to school us to partake in his godly character. 'The clear implication is that it is impossible to share in God's holiness apart from the correction' he administers.[28] God is a skilled artist chipping away at the sculpture of our lives until,

[26] T. Long, *Hebrews*, Int (Louisville: John Knox Press, 1997), p. 134.
[27] F. F. Bruce, *The Epistle to the Hebrews*, NICNT (London and Edinburgh: Marshall, Morgan and Scott, 1964), p. 359.
[28] Lane, *Hebrews 9 – 13*, p. 425.

having removed the flaws and smoothed the roughness, his master-piece is recreated in us. Even the most mature of Christian men and women need God to continue to sculpt them with his hammer and chisel until perfect Christ-likeness is reached which will not be until Christ himself appears.[29]

The third reward of God's discipline is that *it produces a harvest of righteousness and peace for those who have been trained by it.* All the New Testament writers agree that suffering, though painful, is profit-able. For Paul it produced perseverance, character and hope.[30] For James, it produced perseverance, maturity and completeness.[31] For Peter, it proved the genuineness of faith and resulted in Christ being honoured.[32] In Hebrews the reward is a basket of godly fruits, chief among which is *peace,* that is, freedom from resentment, restlessness and rebellion, and the acquisition of a quiet and accepting spirit.[33] Such peace primarily comes to mark one's life with God but cannot help but have an effect on one's relations with others, as verse 14 shows when it turns the promise of verse 11 into an exhortation and encourages them to *Make every effort to live in peace with everyone . . .*

7. The application of discipline (12:12–13)

Having explained the value of God's discipline, which here takes the form of suffering, and, even more, having explained its necessity if we are to *share in his holiness,* the writer urges his readers to stop flagging, renew their energies and get going again in the spiritual race. Picking up the athletic imagery from earlier in the chapter, and using the language of Isaiah 35:3, he tells them: *strengthen your feeble arms and weak knees!* He presents no soft answer to their complaint of weariness but, like any good athletic coach, responds with tough love. Those with fearful hearts and fainting spirits are instructed not to fear but to be strong.[34]

8. Concluding comment

In 1501 when Michelangelo returned to Florence he was fêted as a great artist. The city council asked him to create a massive sculpture

[29] 1 John 3:2.
[30] Rom. 5:3–5.
[31] Jas 1:2–4.
[32] 1 Pet. 1:6–7.
[33] Bruce links this to Ps. 131. *The Epistle to the Hebrews,* p. 361, n. 87.
[34] Isa. 35:4.

of David and presented him with a nineteen foot block of marble that had lain neglected for twenty-five years in the cathedral yard and was damaged and weather-worn as a result. He wrote in his diary, 'I locked myself away in a workshop behind the cathedral, hammered and chiseled at the towering block for three long years' before the masterpiece was finished and then displayed in the Palazzo Vecchio. It took forty men and five days to move it and required arches to be demolished and streets to be widened. But the result was worth it. Michelangelo's David is one of the greatest pieces of Renaissance art: a testimony to the brilliant skill he displayed as an artist, to his careful eye for detail and to his unflagging effort over a long time. As the author to Hebrews might say, if this is what the human artist does, how much more will the divine artist possess the skill, demonstrate care and show perseverance as he hammers and chisels away at our damaged lives, until his image is renewed in us and his godly character is revealed in us.

So, 'My son, do not despise the LORD's discipline, and do not resent his rebuke, because the LORD disciplines those he loves, as a father the son he delights in.'[35]

---

[35] Prov. 3:11–12.

Romans 6:1–23
17. Union with Christ

Having set out the heart of the gospel in Romans 1 – 4, Paul sets out its benefits in chapters 5 – 8. They are peace with God (chapter 5), freedom from sin (chapter 6), freedom from law (chapter 7), and assurance of eternal life (chapter 8). 'Subduing the power of sin is the topic'[1] of chapter 6, which is central to our theme. The importance of this chapter for our theme is further underlined by its two-fold mention of holiness as Paul tells us that becoming a slave of God *leads to holiness*.

The chapter presents an intricate argument where the statement (indicative) of what we are in Christ is enmeshed with the command (imperative) of what we are to become in Christ. Two images dominate the chapter: crucifixion and resurrection, on the one hand, and slavery, on the other. Douglas Moo suggests verses 1–11 stress the indicative, while verses 12–23 bring the imperative to the fore.[2] But then he recognizes that Paul's question in verse 15 might be a more natural break in the argument, with the verses prior to it speaking of our release from sin and the verses after dealing with our dedication to righteousness. Without making any great claims about the structure, it may be helpful for us to divide the chapter into three. The first section lays the foundation for holiness in our union with Christ (verses 1–10), the second section (verses 11–14) is a bridge section which introduces the consequences that arise from the

---

[1] D. Moo, *The Epistle to the Romans*, NICNT (Grand Rapids: Eerdmans, 1996), p. 350.

[2] Ibid., pp. 350–351. James Dunn, *Romans 1 – 8*, WBC (Dallas: Word, 1988), pp. 302–357, splits the chapter at verse 11 and sees the first half as dealing with our death to sin and the second our living for God. John Stott, *The Message of Romans*, BST (Leicester: IVP, 1994), pp. 168–188, divides the chapter at verse 15, with the first half dealing with being united to Christ and the second with being enslaved to God.

foundation, and the third (verses 15–23) makes for personal application.

1. Union with Christ (6:1–10)

Until this point in the letter, Paul has been writing of the righteousness of God and faith as the basis of our justification. Now the language of justification and faith disappears and the language of union with Christ is introduced. This is not an alternative to what he has been saying before. Rather, being joined to Christ 'is rooted in, . . . and fully dovetails with, the doctrine of justification by faith'.[3] Chapter 6 builds on chapter 5 where the assertions about God's grace was thought to throw up a question.

a. The problem (6:1)

If Paul's radical gospel was as good as it sounds and the problem of sin is overcome by the grace of God, should we not *go on sinning, so that grace may increase?* If God's grace is an 'abundant provision' (5:17), should not God be given the opportunity to bestow it even more liberally on his sinful creatures? If it is true that 'where sin increased, grace increased all the more' (5:20), then why not carry on sinning? Indeed, why not provoke God into overwhelming a rising tide of sin with the tsunami of his grace? Far from being a flippant argument, as it may at first sight seem, there were those in the church, and still are, known as antinomians, who argue quite seriously that this is the logic of the gospel. They therefore wish to deny any place for the law or any other restraint on sin in the Christian life. Paul focuses on the law in chapter 7. In this chapter he focuses on sin in the life of the believer.

b. The answer (6:2–4)

Uttering a strong denial, Paul gives his initial answer. The antinomian logic flounders on the rock of our identity. *We are those who have died to sin; how can we live in it any longer?* His initial response may well have provoked perplexity rather than understanding in his readers. How had they died to sin? And when did this death occur? He may have been referring to a teaching which was commonly understood in the early church but his question, *Or*

---

[3] T. Wright, *Justification: God's Plan and Paul's Vision* (London: SPCK, 2009), p. 201.

don't you know. . . suggests that the Roman Christians were ignorant of it or, more probably, had forgotten it.

Consequently he goes on to explain that dying to sin occurred at baptism when believers are incorporated into the death of Christ.[4] His death on the cross became our death, and just as surely, his resurrection became the start of our new lives. The old pre-Christ way of living has ended and the new way of living in which we are conjoined with Christ has begun. Christians have a new status, as did the Israelites when they left Egypt and were 'baptized' in the Red Sea and started on their road to the Promised Land.[5] They had no need to live any longer as slaves in Egypt, though once or twice they tried to go back there. Their status had changed. They were now free and they had to learn to live as a free people. So, for you, a new exodus has happened through the cross and 'living in accordance with a change of status requires that you recognize it and take steps to bring your actual life into line with the person you have become'.[6]

c. The first fuller explanation (6:5–7)

Paul explains the situation more fully, first of all by talking about the 'fusion' that has taken place in our dying with Christ. Using the word which would have been used of a broken bone being knit together again or torn flesh being joined together,[7] Paul speaks of believers' having been integrated into Christ's death. He is self-evidently not referring to their physical death, since they are still alive, but to their death to the way of life they once lived when they took their cue from Adam, rather than Christ (5:12–21). Their death was a dying to a sin-governed way of life and to a lifestyle dictated by the values and morals of this age, rather than the one to come.

Having spoken of a past fusion with Christ's death, Paul now mentions the future union that will take place with his resurrection. We currently live in-between times and it is clear that we have not yet fully entered into all that God has for us in the age to come. But if we have died with him, we can be confident that *we will* (future tense) *also be united with him in a resurrection like his.*

---

[4] By baptism Paul undoubtedly means water baptism, the initiation rite that admitted people to the body of believers.

[5] The case for this as the background to the image, in addition to baptism itself, is found in N. T. Wright, 'The Letter to the Romans', in *The New Interpreters Bible*, *X* (Nashville: Abingdon, 2002), pp. 534, 546 and more popularly in T. Wright, *Paul for Everyone, Romans, Part 1: Chapters 1 – 8* (London: SPCK, 2004), pp. 100–101.

[6] Wright, *Paul for Everyone*, ibid., p. 102.

[7] Dunn, *Romans 1 – 8*, pp. 316, 330.

The means of Christ's death was, of course, crucifixion and Paul develops the thought of what happens in such a death. Once dead, people are usually buried or cremated. The body, with rare exceptions where it is preserved for scientific or historic interest, is *done away with*. But even if the body is preserved, it is no longer responsive. Jeremy Bentham may be preserved in University College, London, and Vladimir Lenin embalmed in Red Square, Moscow, but the former no longer philosophizes and the latter no longer tyrannizes, and it is impossible to have a conversation with either of them. Having died with Christ, the *body ruled by sin,* that is 'old person' who was in Adam rather than Christ, is rendered lifeless and impotent.

The terminology seems abrupt, the action swift. Does this imply we should no longer be responsive to any temptation or sin and that if we are, we have not died with Christ? Does he really mean we are set free from sin, constitutionally unable to respond to it and never to be troubled by it again? That may be an over-hasty conclusion that reads more into Paul than he intended, even if the big picture is right. James Dunn explains,

> To nail someone to the cross was not to kill him there and then but to subject him to a suffering which inevitably resulted in death after some hours or even days; the verb translated 'might be done away with' could be rendered 'might be made ineffective, powerless,' or be taken to describe the end result of crucifixion, in the believer's case at the end of this earthly life.[8]

Crucifixion was both an event and a process and whatever the time-scale, it certainly meant that the victim died. So, by analogy, believers are no longer alive to sin and its seductive power. Throughout this chapter it should be noted that Paul uses the single word *sin,* rather than sins, to indicate sin is not a collection of misdemeanours so much as a potent, unified force. Sin does not die; it remains active. It is the believer who dies. In Wesley's words, sin remains but it no longer reigns.[9]

Believers have new allegiances, are under new management and have come out of the realm of sin and taken up residence in the realm where Christ rules.[10] Persecuted believers may live in fear of their lives while still living in countries which are governed by tyrannical anti-God regimes but once they escape and take up citizenship in a

---

[8] Ibid., p. 332.

[9] Cited by Moo, *The Epistle to the Romans,* p. 358.

[10] Ibid., p. 354. Moo says, Paul uses the language of 'realm transfer' to show how inconceivable is the suggestion that the believer should 'remain in sin'. . .

free country, or one with a Christian heritage, they need no longer be in fear of those old authorities. The displaced authorities may send hate messages from time to time, or seek to entice the person back to the place where they once lived, but they no longer have any power of command. Sin may seek to influence us from time to time but we are no longer *slaves to sin* and have been *set free from sin*. Its power has been broken, its grip loosened and its rights abolished. To pretend otherwise is a deception.

d. The second fuller explanation (6:8–10)

Paul explains further the matter of the past-death and future-resurrection aspect of being joined to Christ. His argument has four steps in it.

Step 1: On the cross Christ gained complete victory over death. Sin had no right to kill the author of life, and death was incapable of keeping its prey. Satan played his trump card, death, but Jesus trumped him. So, there is no possibility that Christ will face death again. Death is no longer a threat to him and will never trouble him further. It is done away with.

Step 2: That *once for all* event of Christ's crucifixion was a death to sin. Although not a sinner himself, he identified with sinners and, on the cross, paid *the wages of sin*, which is death (6:23), to the full. Having met the debt fully, no more demands can be made of him either with regard to the costs of the penalty incurred by sin, or with regard to the power and continuing demands of sin. He is freed from it. If we are 'in him', then we benefit from his work and find ourselves in the same position, dead to the demands of sin.

Step 3: Death was followed by resurrection. He is no longer in the grave but lives. His resurrection life has a particular complexion to it. In saying, *the life he lives, he lives to God*, Paul is highlighting the fact that Jesus now lives to please God and carry out his will. It is not that he did not do so before, for no man has ever lived for God as he did, but the resurrection brings about a new phase of that perfect obedience that was to be seen in him.[11]

Step 4: Believers have to wait for this aspect of their union with Christ to be fulfilled. Having died with Christ *we believe that we will also live with him*, but we have not yet reached the point where we do so completely. We too live for God but we also experience a tension: the tension of being dead in Christ and yet still a part of

[11] Hebrews, having stressed the perfection of Christ (4:15), still argues, in 5:8, that 'he learned obedience from what he suffered'. It was not that perfection was lacking but there was a perfection which was appropriate to each stage of his life.

this world, still subject to the assaults of temptation and to 'the old person' rearing its head. The transition between death and life has begun but is not yet complete. We lie *buried with* Christ (6:4) awaiting the fullness of the resurrection. But that does not mean we should lie back and let sin have its way with us. No! The point Paul is making is that although we have not yet risen with Christ, a decisive act has taken place which gives us the confidence that one day we will enter fully, and without qualification, into the benefits of his resurrection. Through the decisive act of our uniting with Christ in baptism 'the crucial transition has begun'[12] and we get some idea in the present life of what this new life will be like. So, while we live in the tension of the 'already . . . but not yet' of the Christian life and the kingdom of God, we do so with our eyes firmly fixed on the future.

2. Breaking with sin (6:11–14)

Paul moves from theory to practice. The implications of what Paul has been teaching are now spelled out in relation to our dealing with the continuing threat of sin. These verses speak of a reckoning, a refusal and a recognition.

a. The reckoning (6:11)

Using the language of accounting, Paul invites his readers to add up (*logizesthe*) what the previous verses amount to. Each month we check our bank accounts to ensure we are not over-spending. We need to know where we stand financially and that determines how we behave, whether we should draw in our belts or whether we can spend that extra on the house or a holiday. So, Paul is asking the Christians to see where they stand and then to act accordingly. The TNIV's *count yourselves dead to sin* picks up some of this. The NRSV's *consider* is a bit vague, even though this is something that takes place in the believer's mind, and perhaps lacks the edge of urgency and active thought that Paul intends.

Tom Wright makes an important point about what it means to 'reckon yourself dead to sin', which corrects a misunderstanding I certainly picked up somewhere along the way. He writes, 'The point is not, as in some schemes of piety, that the "reckoning" *achieves* the result of dying to sin and coming alive to God, any more than adding up a column of figures creates the result out of nothing; it opens the

[12] Dunn, *Romans 1 – 8*, p. 333. See pp. 332–333 for a particularly clear explanation of these verses.

heart and mind to *recognize* what is in fact true.'[13] The 'reckoning' does not alter the facts, but it does have implications for what we do with them. This 'reckoning' is not about trying to believe something that is not true; it is not screwing up the eyes of faith and wanting the situation to be different than it is. This 'reckoning' is a coming to terms with the facts; of opening one's eyes to what has happened to us now we are joined to Christ.

Ironically, as I was writing this we were seeking to transfer our bank account from one bank to another which was more convenient. Our new bank said they would arrange it all for us but then we got a letter telling us they couldn't as we had to close our existing account personally. To speed things up we wrote a cheque, drawn on our old account, and transferred money to our new one. The cheque bounced! The fact was they had closed the old account (and not told us!) and it no longer owed us anything. The cheque came back to us firmly stamped 'Account closed'. So our account with sin is closed and when it seeks to draw from us we should firmly say, 'Account closed'! Our account with Christ has opened and it is in him that all our life-giving riches are deposited. And even though the full benefit we have in the account with Christ still lies in the future, we should begin to make use of it as fully as we can now.

b. The refusal (6:12–13)

In practice this means we do not permit sin to have its way with us. It does not reign, so it should not reign in us. We are no longer, to change the metaphor,[14] tenants of sin but have moved to a new residence, owned by a new landlord. The liabilities we had to our old landlord have been discharged, not by us, but by our new landlord. We owe the old landlord nothing. If he comes knocking on the door of our new address we can tell him to go away. He may bluster but he has no case and should be sent away, with his tail between his legs.

Since, however, we are under a new landlord, we do have obligations to him. These obligations do not feel as if we are fulfilling impersonal duties since they are obligations that arise out of gratitude and friendship. As always, Paul balances the negative *do not let . . . do not offer . . .* with the positive, *but rather offer yourselves to God as those who have been brought from death to life.* This is the equivalent of his 'putting off the old person' and 'putting on the

---

[13] Wright, 'The Letter to the Romans', p. 541.
[14] Used by Tom Wright, *Paul for Everyone, Romans: Part 1*, pp. 105–106, but a common picture, as he admits.

new' elsewhere.[15] Holiness is not about the rejection of sin alone. It is as much about the cultivation of godliness. We are not to remain aloof from sin, but useless. We are to be free from sin so that we can serve God in new ways.

This refusal to sin and the renewal in Christ affect every part of our lives. If we are not *to offer any part of [ourselves] to sin*, we are to *offer every part of [ourselves] to [God] as an instrument of righteousness*. The instruments of our minds and bodies, emotions and actions, work and skills, leisure and cultural gifts, politics and citizenship, homes and car, and our credit cards, are to be at his disposal.

c. The recognition (6:14)

Romans 6:14 is a verse Christians love to quote flippantly, especially when they are breaking the speed limit! We are *not*, they say, *under the law* any longer but *under grace*. That is true but an example of the danger of quoting only half a verse and ignoring its context and real meaning. Paul concludes this bridge section, somewhat surprisingly, with the words *For sin shall no longer be your master, because you are not under the law, but under grace*. The first clause is not surprising, as it is a succinct expression of what he has been arguing. The surprise comes when he introduces the law at this point, which has not been mentioned since the end of chapter 5. We might have expected him to say 'for you are no longer under sentence of death but looking forward to life', but he does not. Whatever his reason for introducing the law at this point, saying that we are not under it cannot possibly be used to justify antinomianism, since the whole thrust of his argument is quite the reverse.

In fact, Paul is not wishing to lose sight of what he said in 5:20 and is pointing forward to the fuller exposition of the place of the law he will give in 7:1–25, where he will explain the ambiguous nature of the law. It is both 'holy, righteous and good', and yet it frequently serves the negative purpose of pointing out sin to us and even provoking sin in us. Like sin itself, Paul now says that we should recognize the law no longer has a hold over us. Because we live in the realm of grace, it does not have any right to entice us into breaking it.[16] We need again to reckon with the facts. When we were joined with Christ and participated in his death, we were set free from the power of sin and the power of the law, so that we live for God and aim for holiness.

In Wesley's memorable words,

---

[15] Eph 4:20 – 5:2; Col 3:5–17.
[16] See, Wright, 'The Letter to the Romans,' p. 543.

He breaks the power of cancelled sin,
He sets the prisoner free;
His blood can make the foulest clean;
His blood availed for me.[17]

Knowing this, gives us strength and courage in the battle against the old way of living.

3. Living for God (6:15–23)

The question with which the chapter began is repeated, in verse 15, as Paul builds on the foundation he has laid in the earlier part of the chapter and finishes constructing its application for believers. Dying with Christ and being buried with him in baptism is not a nice but abstract theological principle, but a vital principle of daily living.

a. A new slavery (6:15–18)

Being joined to Christ has released us from slavery to sin and the law. Our freedom, however, does not mean we wander anarchically, aimlessly and unaccountably through life, fearful of any other slavery and refusing to bow to the authority of any other master. Unless we come under the authority of a new master, the old powers will soon come and occupy again the rooms they have just vacated. As Jesus pointed out, sweeping a house clean is one thing, but unless it is occupied with something different, the old tenants will happily return in force and squat there.[18] If nature abhors a vacuum, the spiritual world abhors it even more.

In so far as we have a choice, Paul tells us the choice we make is whether we remain under the regime of sin and the law or transfer to become slaves of God. 'There is no third possibility.'[19] In speaking in this way about slavery, it is not that Paul is a pessimist who sees life itself as a drudge. Rather our fallen human condition results in our alienation from God and that means we are inevitably slaves of sin.[20] The only way out is to become a slave of God.

But having become slaves, that is where our choice ends. We have no choice but to obey our master; that is the very essence of

[17] From Charles Wesley's, 'O for a thousand tongues to sing'.
[18] Matt. 12:43–45.
[19] C.E.B. Cranfield, *Romans*, Vol. 1, I – VIII, ICC (Edinburgh: T & T Clark, 1975), p. 321.
[20] M. Harris, *Slave of Christ: A New Testament metaphor for total devotion to Christ*, NSBT (Leicester: Apollos, 1999), p. 83.

slavery. A normal slave may try to get away with only partially fulfilling his master's command or may do that which looks good to the eye but which will not bear much close examination. But the Christian slave has voluntarily placed himself or herself under the authority of this master and that, in itself, brings to bear a greater motivation to service. Furthermore, we know that the Master whom we serve has an all-seeing eye.[21] But the greatest difference between being a normal slave, or a slave to sin lies in the nature of the one we serve.

On the basis of his half apology in verse 19, Cranfield thinks Paul may be embarrassed to use the metaphor in his argument and knows it could even be misleading.[22] But, given that Paul widely talks about himself as a slave and freely uses the metaphor elsewhere I am not convinced this is so. It is true, however, that when we talk of being a slave of God we must divest ourselves of notions of human slavery with their overtones of harsh subjection, cruelty and of people being reduced to mere chattels. There is nothing, humanly speaking, which adequately compares to being a slave of God for, as presented in the New Testament, this status has 'a wholly positive image'.[23] In contrast to other forms of slavery, there is no room for cringing servility, no fear of being abused, no threat of punishment. Our master is gentle and gracious, having himself assumed the form of a slave (Philippians 2:7).[24] At the same time as we are slaves, we are also sons and that puts our slavery into an altogether different light.[25] Being enslaved to God is, paradoxically, the way to perfect freedom. It is a liberating slavery.

In spite of this, slavery is slavery and obedience lies at the heart of it. The slave does not choose what to do with his life, how to spend his time and has no freedom to go off when he likes to do what he likes. The slave has to do his master's bidding and be available at all times to respond to his command. Those of us who are no longer slaves of sin but now have become slaves of God have voluntarily renounced our freedom of choice and live to please God. In practice this means obeying *from your heart the pattern of teaching* which is found in the gospel (6:17) and living a righteous life (6:16, 18–20). *Righteousness* here is used as a contrast to sin and means the out-working of the righteous status we have received in Christ and, in turn, results in holiness (6:19, 22).[26]

[21] Prov. 5:21; 15:3.
[22] Cranfield, *Romans,* Vol. 1, p. 321.
[23] Harris, *Slave of Christ,* p. 142.
[24] These sentences are based on ibid., pp. 85, 136–137.
[25] Gal. 4:1–7.
[26] Moo, *The Epistle to the Romans,* p. 403.

b. A new destination (6:19–23)

Having admitted the believer lives in the unfortunate situation of not having yet fully entered into the fullness of Christ's risen life, Paul ends this part of Romans by keeping his eye firmly on the contrasting destination to which the two forms of slavery lead. Slavery to sin, renamed, in verse 19, as *impurity* and *wickedness* (literally, *lawlessness*), was a dead end. Paul asks what benefit it brought, to which the expected answer is, 'None'. Worse than that, its impact was not just neutral but detrimental and ultimately destructive. With hindsight, believers, who thought they were enjoying the epitome of freedom without any interference from God, could see that their behaviour was shameful and would only have led to their eternal death (6:21).[27] Like many a drug addict who rejects the wisdom of advice from others and ploughs ahead on the road to what they think is liberty, slaves of sin subsequently wake up to the fact that their bondage has done them no favours but has, in fact, robbed them of true and lasting life.

On the other hand, those who are slaves of God may, because of the resurrection of Jesus Christ, confidently look forward to reaping the benefits of their slavery in holiness which, in turn, results in eternal life (6:22). It is unclear whether the *holiness* mentioned here is the final status of wholeness and total consecration we achieve when the image of God is perfectly restored in us, as some think,[28] or whether it is a reference to a work still in progress that will one day end in the destination of eternal life, as others think.[29] The tenses could be read either way. But the point is clear. The path of righteousness leads to a very different destination from the path of wickedness.

Some may believe the way to reach this destination is by obeying the law, but Paul says it is by producing the fruit of a life lived in union with Christ.[30] This end goal is not something we can ever achieve or accomplish ourselves. It is not something we earn, as the distinction in the well-known and final verse in the chapter, verse 23, makes clear. Slavery to sin pays its slaves the wage they deserve: death. But God's slaves do not earn wages. Instead, they receive a gift from God which he generously longs to give them which is life in the age to come. It is 'a gift beyond imagining,

---

[27] All will die physically whether slaves to sin or slaves to God, but it is what happens to life after death that Paul has in mind.

[28] Cranfield, *Romans, Vol. 1*, p. 327. Moo, *The Epistle to the Romans*, p. 405.

[29] Dunn, *Romans 1 – 8*, p. 347.

[30] Ibid. Paradoxically, bearing this fruit leads to becoming all that the law would have ever desired. It is the route, not the objective, which is different.

and the measure of that gift is the death and resurrection of Jesus the Messiah'.[31]

4. Concluding comment

Two major themes dominate this chapter with one single purpose in view. The first theme, which governs the first half of the chapter, is about union with Christ by which, through baptism, we have already died with Christ and are buried with him, and one day will join with him too in fully experiencing his new risen life. The other theme, which controls the second half of the chapter, is that of slavery. It confronts us with the stark choice of being either a slave of sin or a slave of God, but we cannot be both. The one aim is to enable believers to understand their position so that they can overcome the pull of sin while they live here on earth.

The two images complement one another in presenting the case that for believers still to be living a sinful life is incompatible with their status, not only in the sense of being mildly inappropriate but, more strongly, in the sense of being antagonistic and totally at variance with what it means to be a Christian. In dying with Christ we became dead to sin, so that it no longer had any legitimate hold over us. If it does hold sway in our lives it is either because it has tricked us into thinking it still has influence, or because we, knowing the facts, culpably admitted it. This does not mean that sin will no longer trouble us at all. While we are in our present bodies it remains active and will always be seeking ways to make us fall. Occasionally it may be successful. But these should be very much the exceptions.

In being set free by Christ we have been set free *from* slavery to sin and released from its tyrannical nature that ends inevitably in misery and destruction. But we have been set free 'from' being slaves to sin in order that we might become slaves 'for', living a life of righteousness that ends in eternal life.[32]

This slavery leads to holiness, as does our being crucified with Christ. It is impossible, as well as unnecessary, to be too specific about the definition of holiness Paul had in mind. It is about our status and our practice. It is both a process (whose path we are on), and an end-point (in terms of the end we will reach). The context of the argument gives *holiness* a rich and varied meaning. Seen from one perspective, given the discussion of law, it is about being separate for God. From another perspective, given the discussion

[31] Wright, 'The Letter to the Romans,' p. 546.
[32] Slavery 'from' and slavery 'for' is found in Harris, *Slave of Christ,* pp. 71–84.

about slavery to God, it is about our total dedication to him. From yet another perspective, given the emphasis on right living, it is about living a moral and ethical life. Overall, though, it is about our freedom not to sin, and the new ability we have in Christ to overcome it, if only we daily *count [ourselves] dead to sin* and never seek freedom from being a *slave of God,* to whom *we offer every part of [ourselves]. . . as an instrument of righteousness.*

A cartoon in a Christian magazine once pictured a cell group discussing this passage and had one of its members saying, 'I don't think I can remember dying to sin, but I do remember feeling faint once.' But that falls far short of what it means to have been joined with Christ. Union with Christ does not mean feeling queasy about sin, fainting, having the occasional blackout or even being near death but constantly being resuscitated. Union with Christ means being dead to sin.

Ephesians 6:10–18
18. Conflict with the enemy

What is the normal Christian life? Is it one where we enjoy the unclouded presence of God continuously, where we are no longer troubled by sin and can easily defeat any temptation that comes our way? Or, is it one of struggle and conflict, where temptation still dogs us and the 'old self' rears its head? To put it in terms that an earlier generation did: are we to live like the 'wretched man' of Romans 7, desiring to do good, but unable to carry it out, or should we have left that behind and live the life of the continuously Spirit-filled man of Romans 8?

I remember feeling condemned and defeated in my student days because I did not live perpetually on the higher plain, free from sin and the attraction of temptation, that some taught was the normal Christian life. Then I read J. C. Ryle's classic book on *Holiness* which taught that 'he that would understand the nature of true holiness must know that the Christian is "a man of war." If we would be holy we must fight.'[1] 'The true Christian', wrote Ryle,

> is called to be a soldier, and must behave as such from the day of his conversion to the day of his death. He is not meant to live the life of religious ease, indolence, and security. He must never imagine for a moment that he can sleep and doze along the way to heaven, like one travelling in an easy carriage . . . He must 'fight'.[2]

Ryle's honest realism was a relief. This teaching did not make false promises that could easily end in despair, but taught me that death and resurrection, setback and victory, inward conflict and inner peace were simultaneously to be the Christian's experience.

[1] J. C. Ryle, *Holiness* (Cambridge and London: James Clarke, 1956), p. 51–52.
[2] Ibid. p. 52.

1. The reality of conflict

The pursuit of holiness involves us in a life-long battle. Our union with Christ, expounded in the last chapter, puts us in an entirely different situation than we were in before we came to be 'in Christ'. We are no longer 'slaves to sin', doomed to do its every bidding. But that does not stop us from being tempted into the old ways and 'sin' has, as we shall see, plenty of allies to help it in its illegitimate, yet alluring, schemes. To use an old illustration: in Christ, sin no longer occupies the keep at the centre of the castle of our lives. It has been thrown out of the castle. But that does not prevent it from seeking to batter on the door or storm the ramparts in order to gain re-entry.

The truth is that, 'even after conversion [the Christian] carries within him a nature prone to evil, and a heart weak and unstable as water'.[3] Giving in to sin is no longer part of our core identity, but, sadly, it remains our peripheral and real experience. Until the perfect is reached and we are completely transformed to be like Christ,[4] we will find ourselves in a perpetual battle situation. The weapons raged against us may vary, the enemies' strategies may change over time, but the conflict will continue. As Jim Packer admits with disarming honesty, 'The most that happens is that with advancing age, ups and downs of health, and shifting personal circumstances, indwelling sin finds different modes of expression.'[5] Forty years after I sought to be lifted to the higher plain so I could be free from all this, I can confirm the truth of Packer's judgment from my own experience. To do anything else is to deny reality and live an illusory dream, and false expectations are certain, at some stage, to disappoint and cause bewilderment or disillusion.[6]

The New Testament frequently speaks of conflict as part of the normal Christian life. Paul speaks of our sinful natures and the Holy Spirit as 'in conflict with each other', preventing us from doing what we want (Galatians 5:17). James acknowledged the battle within (James 4:1). Peter spoke with some feeling about 'sinful desires, which war against your soul' (1 Peter 2:11). John knew of the 'cravings' and the 'lust' that lead us to love the world when we really want to love God (1 John 2:15–17).

Traditionally, Romans 7 is seen as the place where this conflict

---

[3] Ibid., p. 53.
[4] 1 John 3:2.
[5] J. I. Packer, *A Passion for Holiness* (Cambridge: Crossway Books, 1992), p. 108.
[6] J. I. Packer, *Keep in Step with the Spirit* (Leicester: IVP, 2nd ed., 2005), p. 111.

is discussed most fully in the New Testament.[7] The debates have focused on the identity of the 'I' in this chapter: is it Israel personified, Paul in his pre-Christian way of life or is Paul speaking of his present experience as a Christian? How we answer that question has implications for our understanding of holiness. And yet, whatever conclusion is reached, it has not stopped Christians identifying themselves with verse 15, 'I do not understand what I do. For what I want to do I do not do, but what I hate I do.' This epitomizes what so many feel; the frustration of longing to be holy, of knowing that they are in Christ, and yet still behaving and speaking, thinking and reacting in ways they know are wrong. With Paul we often want to cry, 'What a wretched man I am! Who will rescue me from this body of death?'

In spite of this, recent biblical scholars have (controversially) questioned the use of this chapter in this way. Indeed, they have called into question the interpretation of Romans that we have inherited from the Reformation altogether, with its focus on the individual's struggle to be righteous before God. In what is called 'the new perspective on Paul' (which is, in fact, not a single 'new perspective' but a variety of related views that differ from each other in detail), Romans is seen not as dealing with the individual's quest for righteousness but the righteousness of God in relation to his covenant with Israel and his incorporation of the Gentiles into that covenant.[8] It is primarily about God's grand salvation plan, rather than about the salvation of individuals. Whatever one's verdict on the particular arguments, it has to be said it makes sense of the way in which Paul develops his argument in Romans, with chapters 9–11 being central to the argument rather than an embarrassing detour, which most preachers conveniently miss out when preaching through the letter! At its simplest, the position of 'the new perspective' in regard to Romans 7 has been expressed by Tom Wright as follows:

---

[7] See for example, Packer, *Keep in Step with the Spirit,* esp. pp. 127–129. A variation of the argument may be found in J. R. W. Stott, *The Message of Romans,* BST (Leicester; IVP, 1994), pp. 189–215.

[8] The 'new perspective' has been controversial and generated a huge literature. M. B. Thompson's *The New Perspective on Paul,* Biblical Series, 26 (Cambridge: Grove, 2002) is a good entry point for the uninitiated. Key advocates of the 'new perspective' are: J. Dunn, *The New Perspective on Paul* (Grand Rapids: Eerdmans, rev. edn, 2008), and N. T. Wright, *What St Paul Really Said* (Grand Rapids: Eerdmans and Oxford: Lion, 1997), *Paul: Fresh Perspectives* (London: SPCK, 2005) and *Justification: God's Plan and Paul's Vision* (London: SPCK, 2009). Criticisms of the view may be found in D. A. Carson (ed.), *Right with God: Justification in the Bible and the World* (Grand Rapids: Baker and Carlisle: Paternoster, 1992) and J. Piper: *The Future of Justification: A Response to N. T. Wright* (Wheaton: Crossway and Nottingham: IVP, 2007).

Some people simply read Romans 5–8 as a description of the Christian life. That leads them to suppose that the picture of moral wrestling in 7:14–15 is a picture of what it's like to lead a Christian life, halfway (as it were) between the bracing commands of chapter 6 and the final goal set out in chapter 8. That gives the chapter a role within an overall reading of the section of the letter,[9] but seems to ignore the fact that the main subject of the chapter is not the Christian life, but the law itself – and that Paul says again and again that the Christian is not 'under the law'.

I think Paul's main reason for writing Romans 7 is that he wants to do two things in particular. He wants to explain what the law was given for, and how, in a strange sense it actually did the work God set it up to do, and that it is now, in a new sense fulfilled in the work of the Messiah and the spirit[10] (he comes to in chapter 8)...[11]

For our purposes, the truth that the believer is involved in a battle for holiness is not dependent on the interpretation of this single chapter. It is evident in a number of the New Testament writings, as we have seen, and it is to these we now turn.

2. The enemies we fight

Conversion to Christ not only involves a restored friendship with God and adoption into his family, but the stirring up of hostility on the part of those who are opposed to God. Until we lined up with Christ and were to be found 'in him' the enemies could afford to be complacent about us, keeping, as it were, only a watching brief. The bottom line meant we were on their side. But once we became Christ's, the situation changed and we provoke active opposition.

The New Testament identifies three major enemies as on the offensive against believers in their fight to be Christ-like. All three of these opponents are mentioned in Ephesians 2:1–3 where Paul speaks there of 'the ways of this world', 'the ruler of the kingdom of the air', and, 'the cravings of our sinful nature' as having governed our lives before we came alive in Christ.[12] This trio of evil

---

[9] But, he explains later, not in the overall strategy of the whole letter of Romans.

[10] In his writings Tom Wright uses 'spirit' for the Holy Spirit.

[11] T. Wright, *Paul for Everyone, Romans, Part 1: Chapters 1 – 8* (London: SPCK, 2004), pp. 119–120.

[12] C. E. Arnold, *3 Crucial Questions about Spiritual Warfare* (Grand Rapids: Baker Books, 1997), p. 32. See also Jas 3:15.

influences, however, still seek to exercise an influence over believers, even though they have no authority over them.

a. The world

In typically black-and-white terms, John says, 'Do not love the world or anything in the world. If you love the world, love for the Father is not in you' (1 John 2:15). In saying this, John has a particular definition of the world in mind. He does not mean the natural world of planet Earth, which God created good, or the people whom God loved so much 'that he gave his one and only Son' for them (John 3:16). He means the world as an organized system of values that are opposed to God, which are adopted and supported by people who are under the influence of the evil one. It is 'the unhealthy social environment in which we live'.[13]

Sensitive to the need to define things further, John uses 'world' in a variety of different ways;[14] he speaks of 'cravings', 'lust' and 'boasting' as characteristic of the attitudes he has in mind. 'Cravings' may, of course, be legitimate, as when someone is genuinely hungry and craves to eat. But the 'craving' mentioned here is qualified as 'the cravings of sinful people', indicating that the craving is for objects or experiences which are contrary to God's will for us. The mention of 'the lust of their eyes' takes us back to the teaching of Jesus in Matthew 5:27, who also mentioned the eyes as significant. Boasting, a typically human activity, is perpetually manifest in the media, not least in the worship of celebrities. It prevents a person from giving gratitude to God, from whom we receive all things, and stands in opposition to the humility which is truly Christ-like. The popular culture in which we live promotes these anti-God values daily and in doing so whets our own appetite for that which is sinful. And behind the strong allure of popular culture there lie the philosophies, assumptions, arguments and worldviews that undergird it. It's tough being a nonconformist, but that is what we are called to be.

We sometimes find ourselves dabbling in the shallows of 'the world' only to discover, too late, that there is a strong under-tow to its current and we are sucked away to spiritual disaster and in need of rescuing by God. It would be better for us to heed the warning flags rather than ignore them and think that we can beat the currents of the world that have defeated so many others.

---

[13] Arnold, 3 Crucial Questions about Spiritual Warfare, p. 34.
[14] See the summary note in C. Kruse, The Letters of John, Pillar (Grand Rapids: Eerdmans and Apollos: Leicester, 2000), p. 74, n. 36.

b. The 'flesh'

Throughout Paul's teaching there is a recognition that 'the flesh' (his usual word is *sarx*), that is, our 'old nature', may be dead but it won't lie down! Christians live in the realm of the Holy Spirit. He resides within them and gives them new attitudes, ambitions and abilities in serving Christ. They seek to keep in step with him.[15] But while the battle against sin may have been decisively won, the skirmishes still go on and the conflict remains. It is not only the Holy Spirit who resides within but the remnants of our old sinful natures as well. This 'sinful nature', as Paul explains, 'desires what is contrary to the spirit, and the Spirit what is contrary to the sinful nature. They are in conflict with each other . . .' (Galatians 5:17).

The battle between the flesh and the Spirit is not a conflict between the physical and the spiritual, between the material and mystical. It means neither that we have somehow to escape life in our bodies, perhaps through the practices of extreme asceticism, nor to withdraw from the physical world, perhaps by retreating into 'a holy space' of some sort. Both the flesh and the Spirit manifest themselves in our whole beings, including the physical aspects of our lives, and are manifest in the environment of the world. They are two principles by which we might live, rather than two different forms of material existence. Hijacking one of Tom Wright's insightful metaphors, 'It is the difference between asking on the one hand "is this a wooden ship or an iron ship?" (the material from which it is made) and asking on the other "is this a steam ship or a sailing ship?" (the energy which empowers it).'[16] The difference between the flesh and Spirit is not a difference between the materials from which we are made but a difference between one of two principles that energizes the life we live in our physical bodies and in the flesh and blood reality of our every day world.

The New Testament writers recognize that 'desire' is the theatre in which this war is frequently engaged. Desire, in itself, can be neutral. There are good desires as well as bad, which is why James adds the adjective 'evil' to 'desire' when he first introduces the idea in his letter. 'Each of you is tempted', he writes, 'when you are dragged away by your own evil desire and enticed. Then, after desire has conceived, it gives birth to sin; and sin, when it is fully grown, gives birth to death' (James 1:14–15). The flesh is not eradicated and the pull of sinful desires remains. As mentioned, these desires, James

[15] Gal. 5:16–25. See chapter 14.
[16] T. Wright, *Surprised by Hope* (London: SPCK, 2007), p. 168. Wright uses this in reference to 1 Cor. 15:44.

says, 'battle within you' (James 4:1) and Peter concurs, saying, in even more vivid language, that these sinful desires 'war against your soul' (1 Peter 2:11).

Clinton Arnold summarizes it like this, 'The flesh is the inner propensity or inclination to do evil. It is that part of our creatureliness tainted by the fall that remains with us until the day we die. It is our continuing connection to this present evil age, which is destined to perish but against which we must struggle now.'[17]

The fact that the struggle remains throughout this life is no excuse for moral defeatism. Since the decisive power of the flesh has been broken by our union with Christ's death and resurrection, we need to remain in him and realize that 'Those who belong to Christ Jesus have crucified the sinful nature with its passions and desires' (Galatians 5:24). Once more, then, the key is to understand who we are in Christ and, by conscious, daily consecration, seek to live up to our true identity in the power of the Holy Spirit. And when the flesh wins a temporary skirmish, we must realize that whatever Satan, the accuser, says, we are not defeated. In repentance and faith our unbroken union with Christ is renewed.

c. The devil

The third enemy who conspires to throw us off the path of holiness is the devil. We must neither over-estimate his influence, as some do, nor under-estimate his impact, as others do. Those who over-estimate his influence tend to blame him for every failing in their lives and discount the influence of the world and their own flesh. In doing so, they often abdicate their own moral responsibility and displace the real battles they face on earth into the heavenlies. They often seek the answer in exorcism rather than in moral reformation, aided by the Spirit. Those who under-estimate the devil's influence tend to consign him to some mythical past or remote sphere where he is thought to have little impact on the believer's life. Some believe him to be 'the strong man' of Mark's Gospel,[18] whom Jesus has bound and they therefore conclude he has no power over them. But to ignore him or to underrate him is to play into his hands and give him a freedom to cause havoc which confronting him would deny.

To quote Clinton Arnold's succinct description once more, 'The devil is an intelligent, powerful spirit-being that is thoroughly evil and is directly involved in perpetrating evil in the lives of individuals

---

[17] Arnold, *3 Crucial Questions about Spiritual Warfare*, p. 34.
[18] Mark 3:27.

as well as on a much larger scale.'[19] Ephesians 6:11 tells us he adopts a number of evil schemes in dealing with us, knowing that we will not all be vulnerable in the same way.[20] In some minds he works subtly, sowing the seed of doubt or anxiety; in others, discouragement; in others, pride; in others, it is enough to distract them from the main thing. In most he works through the ordinary, using the foothold we give him if we do not maintain our guard, through our lying, anger, dishonesty, filthy talk and such like.[21] In some lives he works through a more direct offensive, through strong and seemingly irresistible temptation; or through deviation into heresy, cultic activity and spiritual deception. In still other lives, he engages in a full frontal assault through demonic activity. As 'an intelligent being' he knows what strategy will be effective in the lives of those he wishes to bring down.

He has a whole battery of assistants to help him achieve his aims including, *rulers, . . . authorities, . . . powers of this dark world,* and *spiritual forces of evil in the heavenly realms* (6:12). Some get fascinated by such a list and have sought to map the differences between the terms and the organisation of the spiritual armies which are ranged against Christ's people. But this is not Paul's intention and 'there is no special meaning to each of the terms that would give us further insight into the demonic realm'.[22] He simply wants to make the point that the devil has support and is not easily avoided or defeated.

Peter is conscious that the devil is on the prowl, seeking to devour believers, but offers no elaborate strategy as to how he is to be defeated. He simply advises, 'Resist him, standing firm in the faith . . .' (1 Peter 5:8–9). No esoteric strategies are recommended. There is no mention of challenging territorial spirits in cosmic spiritual warfare, no mention of special prayer walks, or particular acts of

---

[19] Arnold, *3 Crucial Questions about Spiritual Warfare,* p. 35.

[20] The fullest and most brilliant exposition of his schemes is found in D. M. Lloyd-Jones, *The Christian Warfare: An exposition of Ephesians 6:10–13* (Edinburgh: Banner of Truth, 1976).

[21] Eph. 4:24–32, see esp. v. 27. P. T. O'Brien, *The Letter to the Ephesians,* Pillar (Grand Rapids: Eerdmans and Apollos: Leicester, 1999), pp. 463–464.

[22] Arnold, *3 Crucial Questions about Spiritual Warfare,* p. 39. It has been fashionable in recent scholarship to demythologize these 'beings' and interpret them as the powerful political and economic forces in our world which often enslave people and appear demonic in their effect. There can be little doubt that originally the title referred to 'intelligent beings' rather than impersonal structures. But there can equally be no doubt that the devil and his minions work through such impersonal structures. On the debate see, C. Arnold, *Powers of Darkness* (Leicester: IVP, 1992), pp. 194–209 and J. R. W. Stott, *The Message of Ephesians,* BST (Leicester: IVP, 1979), pp. 263–275.

deliverance. It is simply by 'standing firm in the faith' that we discover the real secret of victory over Satan. We are not to, indeed cannot, resist him in our own strength, but if we take refuge in the gospel and take our stand, unflinchingly, on what Christ accomplished on the cross and in his resurrection, then we will have the power to overcome. For, as Paul eloquently explains in Colossians 2:15, 'He stripped all the spiritual tyrants in the universe of their sham authority at the Cross and marched them naked through the streets.'[23] The devil does not want to be reminded of the humiliating and decisive defeat that he experienced on that first Good Friday.

The world, the flesh and the devil combine to form a strong three-stranded opposition to Christian believers, aimed at preventing their progress in holiness. But the conflict, though real and sometimes intense, is not loaded against us. God knows our predicament and has provided us with resources to ensure that we need not suffer defeat, even if we may experience the occasional setback.

3. The resources we have (Ephesians 6:10–18)

a. The power of God (6:10)

Friends used to have a cartoon of a tug-of-war in their lounge which pictured several powerful demons at one end of the rope, pitted against a solitary feeble saint on the other. The contest looked uneven until your eye traced the rope on the believer's side to its end and discovered that it was anchored by a powerful divine thumb! Paul is convinced that the spiritual battle is not an open contest whose outcome is yet to be determined but one where the Christian can stand up to the enemy with confidence. We are to *be strong in the Lord and in his mighty power* (6:10). The power that brought the world into being out of nothing, that wrought salvation for Israel (Isa. 59:17), and that caused the tomb of Jesus to be emptied (Eph. 1:20), is the power which is at work on our behalf.

Language associated with power is common in Ephesians[24] and reflects the ethos of Ephesus, where the conflict of spiritual powers was palpable, as we see in Acts 19.[25] Paul is acutely conscious that a greater power is at work in the believers than any kind of power that would oppose them. In concluding Ephesians with the topic

---

[23] *The Message.*
[24] The word itself is used in 1:19 (x 2), 21; 3:7, 16, 18, 20 and 6:10.
[25] For the background see C. Arnold, *Ephesians: Power and Magic* (Cambridge: CUP, 1989).

of spiritual warfare, then, Paul is not introducing a new topic but drawing the threads and themes of the earlier letter together.[26] So we must not isolate spiritual warfare as a specialist activity or of interest only to some. It is an integral element of the gospel Paul has been expounding and of our being made new in Christ.

b. The armour of God

The source of Paul's teaching is to be found in Isaiah 11:4–5 and 59:15–19, where God puts on the armour of a warrior so that in the absence of anyone else intervening, he himself executes judgment and vindicates his people in salvation. The prophet's use of the armour explains where Paul derived most of the imagery from, even if it was modified a trifle by his own ever-present experience of Roman soldiers and their weapons. So the armour we are invited to wear is the tried and tested armour of God himself.

The purpose of the armour is so that *when the day of evil comes, you may be able to stand your ground, and after you have done everything, to stand.* The objective appears limited and the armour suited to its purpose. The armour is not given so that we might advance into enemy territory, but so that we can *stand* our ground without capitulating or retreating, resisting the devil's incursions into our lives. The point is made not only by the fourfold repetition of *stand* (verses 11, 13 [x 2] and 14) but also by there being no mention of protection for the back, or of a spear, or, even, of protection for the shins. All the armour seems calculated to maintain a defensive posture.[27] In what sense, then, can this be described as *the full armour of God*? John Stott explains, quoting an older commentator Armitage Robinson, that 'the divineness rather than the completeness of the outfit is emphasised'.[28] The armour is God's armour made available to us and is fully sufficient for the task he intends. The emphasis is on who is equipping us rather than the amount of the equipment. We stand, rather than advance, because he is the warrior who has already won the victory on our behalf.

---

[26] I owe this insight originally to Max Turner who points out the mention of many other words in Eph. 6 which are found earlier in Eph. 1–3, such as 'truth', 'peace', 'faith', 'salvation', 'word' and 'Spirit'. See further, A. Lincoln, *Ephesians*, WBC (Dallas: Word, 1990), p. 432 and B. Witherington III, *The Letters to Philemon, the Colossians and the Ephesians* (Grand Rapids: Eerdmans, 2007), pp. 344–347.

[27] The word for armour, *panoplia*, usually refers to all the armour of a foot soldier, which was used both for defensive and offensive purposes. Here only some of the armour is listed.

[28] Stott, *The Message of Ephesians*, p. 275.

Six pieces of armour are mentioned. First is *the belt[29] of truth, buckled around your waist* (6:14). Truth, a major theme in the letter, refers to the truth of God, which is seen both in his character as a God of integrity, and in the gospel revealed by Christ.[30] Our first means of protection, then, is this God and his gospel. But, as with the other weapons, it has an inevitable follow-through into our own lives, for we stand against the devil not only because of the truth of the gospel, but because we ourselves speak the truth and do not lie, thereby preventing him from getting his foot in the door of our lives (4:25).

Secondly, we put *the breastplate of righteousness in place* (6:14). God himself is righteous and it is because of this that he steps into the world to judge those who oppress the poor and to mete out justice. This righteousness of God has also been revealed in the gospel,[31] through which Jesus makes us unrighteous people righteous in God's sight.[32] When Satan hurls his accusations against us, we shelter behind God's verdict which has declared us to be 'not guilty'. Satan has no authority to appeal against that sentence. Having been declared in the right through the grace of God, we too now need to manifest a righteous way of living, again, so that we give the devil no entry into our lives.

The third piece of the uniform is our shoes. Our feet need to be *fitted with the readiness that comes from the gospel of peace* (6:15). Having a firm footing is vital if the soldier is going to withstand the enemy and the right footwear contributes to that significantly. The most appropriate footwear is again *the gospel of peace*. Other teaching may look more fashionable than the old-fashioned gospel and it is tempting to discard the boots in favour of something more attractive. But we have all seen women who have found it difficult to walk, or even stand upright, in the interests of wearing the latest fashionable shoe. Fashion is not the issue! It very quickly passes and then seems foolish. Usefulness, which goes hand in hand with truthfulness, is! Paul's focus, however, is not essentially on the type of footwear to be worn as the purpose to which it is put. Echoing Isaiah 52:7, his concern is not so much on the gospel as protection but the gospel as an announcement to be made. Rather than sitting at home with our feet up and our slippers on, Paul urges us to be ready to share the good news, which is about peace and

---

[29] 'Belt' is probably more akin to the breeches a soldier would wear than the belt that would buckle around the waist and carry the sword. But it is wise not to be too precise in interpreting the imagery. Lincoln, *Ephesians*, p. 447.

[30] Eph 1:13; 4:21, 24; 5:9. See also Isa. 11:5.

[31] Rom. 1:17.

[32] 1 Cor. 1:30.

reconciliation and therefore the best weapon to repel those who delight in conflict and destruction.

Fourthly, Paul commands his readers to *take up the shield of faith, with which you can extinguish all the flaming arrows of the evil one* (6:16). Without wishing to be too dogmatic, the use of *flaming arrows* may suggest the sudden attacks that the devil mounts against us, such as blasphemous thoughts entering uninvited into our minds, sudden doubt or the onset of depression without warning. The shield that will protect us is to exercise faith, which quickly needs to be manoeuvred into position. Faith always has to have an object; it is always faith in someone or something. So, here, it is not the mere exercise of faith that matters but who that faith is in. Faith as a mere looking to our own inner resources, or a summoning up of our own strength to get us through, will be inadequate to protect us from the devil's flaming arrows. Faith in Christ alone will afford us all the protection we need, as Paul suggests by using the word *thyreos* for the shield. The *thyreos* was not a small shield but a shield that measured 125 by 75 centimetres and covered the whole body and so offered complete protection.

The penultimate piece of equipment is *the helmet of salvation* (6:17).[33] Salvation had been the subject of 2:5–9. That passage rings with the certainty that the one who exercises faith has been 'made alive with Christ', 'raised . . . up with Christ' and is 'seated . . . with him in the heavenly realms'. These people 'have been saved'. So when the enemy attacks there is no need for fear or anxiety. Believers have been united with the risen Christ and find their security in him. The devil's threats have no authority over them.

The final piece of equipment is that of the *sword of the Spirit, which is the word of God* (6:17). If any element of the armour is offensive it is this one.[34] The message of God, which is what Paul meant by *the word of God*, and the whole of Scripture in which that gospel is enshrined, is a powerful weapon against the enemy, as Jesus himself found when tempted by Satan.[35] But unlike the experience of Jesus, as James Philip perceptively warned, 'The enemy is not always defeated with one slash of the sword.'[36] A great deal of sword practice is required to defeat the enemy and therefore the believer needs to know the Scripture thoroughly and confidently to be able to use it effectively.

[33] Isa. 59:17.
[34] The *machaira* was the short sword which was standard issue to the Roman infantry. But the verse also alludes to Isa. 11:4, where the divine warrior strikes 'the earth with the rod of his mouth'.
[35] Luke 4:1–13.
[36] J. Philip, *Christian Warfare and Armour* (Eastbourne: Victory Books, 1972), p. 105.

Although not strictly part of the armour, Paul concludes by speaking of the importance of prayer. Clinton Arnold has suggested Paul deliberately chose not to make this just another piece of the armour so that it might stand out and receive emphasis. Its four-fold use of *all* – *all occasions,* . . . *all kinds of prayer,* . . . *always,* and *for all the Lord's people* – equally adds emphasis. Prayer 'is at the heart of spiritual warfare'[37] and gives voice to our inability to fight the enemy on our own and our need for divine help in doing so. It also expresses our confidence in God and his gospel, or else, why pray? But prayer does not remove the need for us to remain *alert.* The devil's landmines are strewn all over the place, subtly disguised, and waiting for that moment of inattention when they can blow up and cause us harm. Watchfulness is crucial.

Armour is of no value if it is left behind in the guardroom. It can only be effective if we put it on, piece by piece (6:11). Equipping ourselves with his armour in not meant to be reserved for the special occasion when we feel the spiritual battle intensely, but is to be our ordinary everyday wear. And that requires a 'habitual lively faith'.[38]

4. Concluding comment

The pathway to holiness is strewn with traps and conflict. The world, the flesh and the devil jointly conspire to make it so. Spiritual warfare is as much about advancing in holiness as it is about advancing in mission or miraculous engagement with supernatural powers. While we are in this physical body we remain subject to its frailties, we have not left the old age completely behind, and we are only ever in process towards completeness in Christ. God's restoration of his image will always be a work in progress.

The acceptance of this truth should not lead us to accept defeat or be content with moral mediocrity.[39] Our objectives are to resist our enemies, prevent their advances, and remain faithful, standing secure in the gospel. To do this, we must be alert to his strategies in our lives, whether they are subtle, devious or forthright. Complacency is dangerous when people are at war. We must also make use of the ample resources God has given us to repulse the enemies within and without. As a regular spiritual discipline we should *put on the full armour of God* and *pray in the Spirit on all occasions.*

---

[37] Arnold, *3 Crucial Questions about Spiritual Warfare,* p. 43.
[38] Ryle, *Holiness,* p. 58.
[39] D. Bloesch, *The Holy Spirit: Works and Gifts* (Downers Grove: IVP, 2000), p. 333.

We will never know when one or other member of the evil trinity may strike. They will choose their moments to attack carefully. But we must be ready at any moment, during our average and routine days, to counter their attack knowing that it will never be an even fight, for the mighty power of God is on our side. The victory is already determined. So, in spite of occasional setbacks, we continue on our path to holiness with confidence, humility and joy.

2 Corinthians 6:14 – 7:1
19. Separation from the world

In earlier generations the call to *be separate* (6:17) was a fundamental tenet of teaching on holiness. Popular preaching identified a few places, like pubs, dance halls, theatres, casinos and brothels, and labelled them as dens of iniquity to be avoided at all costs so as to prevent contamination. Implicit in the call was a negative view of the world which meant some avoided any involvement with politics and artistic culture. Providing one kept one's distance one could be judged to be holy. Having rediscovered, in the 1960s, the biblical call to engage with the world, today most largely ignore the call to separation as an embarrassment.[1] If it is mentioned at all it is used as a rallying call by a minority in a way that Paul did not intend.[2] Given this, it is time to revisit Paul's teaching so that we might *purify ourselves from everything that contaminates body and spirit, perfecting holiness out of reverence for God* (7:1).

Paul appears to change tack sharply in 2 Corinthians 6:14 and to use a number of unusual words, as well as using familiar words in an unusual way, in the paragraph that follows. Consequently some argue that this paragraph was not written by Paul but penned by someone else and inserted later into the letter. This conclusion is unnecessary and the themes he introduces are consistent with the rest of the letter.[3] The words cannot be dismissed as inauthentic and

---

[1] J. D. Hunter has charted the changes in America in *Evangelicalism: The Coming Generation* (Chicago: University of Chicago, 1987), although his research has been criticized by J. M. Penning and C. E. Smidt, *Evangelicalism: The Next Generation* (Grand Rapids: Baker, 2002).

[2] See further pp. 140–141.

[3] For a discussion of the arguments and a rebuttal see P. Barnett, *The Second Epistle to the Corinthians* (Grand Rapids: Eerdmans, 1997), pp. 338–341; M. J. Harris, *The Second Epistle to the Corinthians* (Grand Rapids: Eerdmans, 2005), pp. 15–25 and R. Martin, *2 Corinthians*, WBC (Waco: Word, 1986), pp. 191–195.

therefore of no concern to us today.

The argument is intricate, switching back and forth between directives and explanations, command and promise. At the centre of the paragraph is the instruction to *come out from them and be separate.* But this blunt command needs setting in its context if it to be understood properly and not simply paraded as a miserable slogan for killjoy puritans. For our purposes, we may understand the passage under three headings. There is a command to obey (6:14–16a), an identity to grasp (16b–18), and some action to take (7:1).

1. A command to obey (6:14–16a)

a. The content of the command

Do not be yoked together with unbelievers is a general prohibition using the imagery of Deuteronomy 22:10, which forbade ploughing with an ox and donkey 'yoked together' because it was an uneven match that would inevitably harm one of the partners. The command is similar to James's call for Christians to keep themselves from being polluted by the world (James 1:27).

It is clear that the command applies to separation from unbelievers. The statement seems so obvious that it is hardly worth saying, except that some in the contemporary church have taken it as a command to separate from fellow believers who hold different views from them on particular issues, especially in regard to the ecumenical movement and some ethical issues.[4] But to use this passage in this way is to misuse it. 'Nothing in the passage suggests that "unbelievers" are false believers.'[5] The only possible way in which such an interpretation can be justified is if the separatists consider that those from whom they differ are not in fact believers at all.

So much is clear. What it means to be *yoked together with unbelievers,* however, is less obvious. It cannot be a blanket condemnation on all social contact with unbelievers since Paul had previously written, in 1 Corinthians 5:9–10, that trying to live in complete isolation from non-Christians was absurd and would necessitate in us departing from the world altogether.[6] The teaching that Christians should live in segregated communities, secluded from the world and quarantined against sinful defilement, plays no part in the biblical

---

[4] Mark 9:38–40 seems to be relevant to such a stance.

[5] Barnett, *The Second Epistle to the Corinthians,* p. 344.

[6] See also 1 Cor. 10:27 (regarding dining out); 7:12–15 (regarding marriage to an unbeliever); and 14:23 (regarding unbelievers attending worship).

teaching on holiness. So what does it mean that we should avoid being yoked with unbelievers?

The clue lies in Paul's stress on believers as *the temple of the living God* which occurs in verse 16. In doing so the identity of believers is implicitly contrasted with those unbelievers who worship the dead gods of idolatry in other temples. Picking up the concern about eating meat which had been dedicated to idols, spoken of in 1 Corinthians 8:1–13, his call is for separation from the idol cults that were prevalent in Corinth. Given this, Paul Barnett argues that his plea is for cultic separation, not social separation.[7] As others explain, the converts in Corinth would have come 'from backgrounds where no deity demanded exclusive worship from his or her devotees'.[8] Consequently, some of the early Christians would not have thought there was any need to choose between the worship of the living God and the continuing worship of idols.

If this is the correct interpretation, the contemporary relevance is that those of us who live in multi-faith societies are called to abstain from multi-faith worship. In cultures where tolerance is valued above all other values, and where political correctness shuns dogmatism about faith issues, this is a tough call; but no more so than it would have been to our predecessors in Corinth.

However, interpreting the passage in this way may be right but too narrow. Religion permeated every aspect of life. It would have crept into social life, business life, and certainly into agricultural life, as well as being evident in civic ceremonies. As Ernest Best points out, a bad harvest would have resulted in the community desiring to placate the local deities with sacrifices. What were the Christians to do? Were they really expected to exempt themselves from community involvement at such a time?[9] The answer would seem to be 'yes'. Wherever the relationship with unbelievers was such that believers had close and on-going ties with unbelievers which implied that the living God was not supreme, unique, and worthy of exclusive worship, the yoke needed to be broken.

Reducing the interpretation, then, to one of avoiding idolatrous worship, unless that worship is interpreted widely, may give the wrong impression. Paul Barnett, who stresses the cultic connection of these verses, rightly says that even if its immediate application is to worship practices in our multicultural world 'there are also implications for cases, for example, in which through entering a marriage or a business partnership a Christian would be involved in an overly

---

[7] Barnett, *The Second Epistle to the Corinthians*, p. 349.
[8] E. Best, *Second Corinthians*, Int (Atlanta: John Knox Press, 1987), p. 65.
[9] Ibid., pp. 65–66.

close association with those who engage in the cultic practices of other religions'.[10]

The application today, however, is subtler than this. It is rare for people in the modern Western world to encounter visible idols but it would be a mistake thereby to conclude that they do not exist. The invisible idolatry of the Western world is, if anything, even more pernicious because of its invisibility than its tangible counterpart. The next step in Paul's argument will help us understand why, so we will postpone further consideration of the application of this command until we have reviewed that.

b. The reason for the command

Paul sets up a series of five contrasting pairs that are in strong opposition to each other, just like the opposite poles of a magnet which repel each other. Using five synonyms ('*common*', '*fellowship*', '*harmony*', '*common*' and '*agreement*', in TNIV), he asks rhetorically what possible partnership there can be between these conflicting couples. The answer expected is clearly, 'None'.

The two lists of irreconcilable principles at work are:

- righteousness *versus* wickedness,[11]
- light *versus* darkness,[12]
- Christ *versus* Belial,[13]
- believer *versus* unbeliever,
- God *versus* idols.

To us such strong contrasts might seem unreasonable, but Paul was doing no more than updating the contrast between the way of life and the way of death that was presented by Moses in Deuteronomy 30:11–20 or by the psalmist in Psalm 1. There are two ways of living and we face the choice of being harnessed to one or to the other mindset and one or the other lifestyle. Between them there can be no compromise.

The invisible idolatry of our world pervades every aspect of our lives, as surely as idolatry permeated every dimension of life in

[10] Barnett, *The Second Epistle to the Corinthians*, p. 358.

[11] Literally, 'lawlessness', demonstrating the attitude of the Jews to those without the law.

[12] See 2 Cor. 4:3–6.

[13] Belial is an unusual title for Satan and means, variously, anything from 'worthlessness' to 'an opponent of God'. Paul may have been drawing on his Rabbinic training in using this title. See Barnett, *The Second Epistle to the Corinthians*, p. 347 and Martin, *2 Corinthians*, pp. 199–201.

ancient Corinth. Writing a few years ago, Scott Hafemann stated, 'Most often, the idolatry we face is our culture's smothering covetousness, in which happiness is derived from more possessions and security comes from increasing financial stability'.[14] As I write, the unexpected financial insecurities of the capitalist world means the idol of materialism is wobbling on its stand and may soon come crashing down and be smashed to pieces.

But there are other idols we serve.[15] Chief among them is our demand for an increasingly comfortable way of life and the satisfaction of our desires, whether those desires were worthy or not. Hand-in-hand with this is the addiction to entertainment and the fascination with celebrities. There are also idols of scientism which excludes God, or sexual licence which rides roughshod over God's wisdom, or an ethnocentrism that is xenophobic, or unbridled self-expression which takes no account of our fallen natures, or, for some, a sport that demands unquestioning devotion. The idols confronting the church today are subtle and often so thoroughly mixed with values and goals of contemporary culture that we find it hard to identify them. Nonetheless, to be the authentic church of God, we need to live holy lives that display a richer, alternative lifestyle. We are never to be 'resident citizens' in the world who feel so much at home that we belong without any discomfort. Nor are we to be 'resident absentees' in the world, withdrawing from it into our holy ghettos, for our calling is to influence the world for God. We are called to be 'resident aliens' in the world, who engage with the wider community but never quite fit, living alternative lives that are fully in harmony with the living God.[16]

What began as a healthy involvement in the world for the sake of mission has too often in recent days paid the price of compromise. The sharp dichotomy which Paul presents sits ill-at-ease with the blurring of the boundaries which we find more comfortable in our culture. But the call to holiness necessarily involves a call to separation.

[14] S. Hafemann, 2 Corinthians, The NIV Application Commentary (Grand Rapids: Zondervan, 2000), p. 298.
[15] Hafemann, ibid., p. 302 writes, 'The heart of sin is to bring an idol into the Most Holy Place (i.e., into our lives) through adopting the values and goals of the godless culture in which we live.'
[16] One of the most insightful books on this topic in recent years has been S. Hauerwas and W. H. Willimon, Resident Aliens: Life in the Christian Colony (Nashville: Abingdon, 1989) which Hafemann, ibid., p. 296, describes as 'a wake-up call to the cultural accommodation that has crept into evangelicalism. . .'

2. An identity to grasp (16b–18)

a. The identity they had (6:16b)

Central to Paul's argument is the identity of the Christians to whom he writes. Remarkably, he claims that the Christian community in Corinth are *the temple of the living God*. They are, as it were, the address where God could be found to be at home on earth. They were his dwelling place. He was not limited to them, nor constricted by them and yet, as Murray Harris puts it, they were 'the place where the living God most fully expressed his presence'.[17] Paul chose his words with care. The temple he refers to is not the total complex of the temple buildings and their environs, but the inner sanctuary (*naos*), the place where God was believed to reside in the physical temple of old. He also, as we have noted, speaks of it as the sanctuary of *the living God* in contrast to being the dwelling of a lifeless idol. God lived among them by his Holy Spirit,[18] in fulfilment of the promises made in the old covenant.[19] The Spirit's express role among them was to enable them to focus on the glory of the Lord and so be transformed, one degree after another, 'into his image' (2 Corinthians 3:18).

b. The privileges they enjoyed (6:16c, 18)

Since God lived among them a number of privileges followed. Mixing up his Old Testament texts, as so often, Paul quotes, in verse 16c, from Leviticus 26:12, Jeremiah 32:38 and Ezekiel 37:27. What were merely promises for the future when originally spoken have now, he says, become a reality. The first quotation gave the assurance of God's presence among them. Eden was restored as God again lived with his people and walked among them. God's presence transformed everything. The latter quotations speak of God's protection as they come under his patronage and swear loyalty to him as their God. As their covenant God he would provide guidance for them when they were lost, protection for them when they were attacked, sustenance for them when they were hungry, life for them in the face of barrenness, and miracles in the face of despair.

Even the harshest expression of the command to be separate is accompanied by the promise that God would *receive* his people. While at first sight that does not seem much of a promise, based on

---

[17] Harris, *The Second Epistle to the Corinthians*, p. 505.
[18] 1 Cor. 3:16–17; 6:19.
[19] Ezek. 36:27; 2 Cor. 3:7–18.

Ezekiel 20:41 it speaks of God's acceptance of his people. Separation from the common practices of their communities would inevitably lead to them being alienated from their neighbours and, no doubt, subject to gossip, suspicion and misunderstanding by the authorities. In those circumstances, it makes a great difference to know that there is one who will not turn them away but will welcome them with open arms, especially when that one is the living God.

The final promise complements and expands the promise of their acceptance. They will be welcomed not as guests in God's dwelling but as family members. Quoting now from God's promise to David about his offspring, in 2 Samuel 7:14, Paul assures his people that they will not only be accepted but accepted as family, as blood relatives. The closest of unbreakable bonds would be forged with God by their separation from the world.

It is the privileges that believers enjoy which form the basis of the call to separation and holiness. Holiness is neither rule-bound nor driven by a slavish adherence to the law;[20] rather, it is focused on our relationship with God, and dependent on his very great and precious promises. The balance of holiness then weighs in on the side of the positive and not the negative.

c. The consequences that follow (6:17)

Immersed in this abundance of promise, Paul commands them, in the words of Isaiah 52:11 – which refer to Israel's departure from exile in Babylon – to *Come out from them and be separate. . . . Touch no unclean thing. . .*[21] He introduces the command with *Therefore*. The call to separation is an inevitable consequence of our identity and the promises that are attached to it.[22] It would be obvious to all that a soldier who had enlisted in one army and received its training, pay and privileges, should not fight in an enemy army and receive any benefits from them. A clear choice has to be made. The soldier belongs to one or the other, but cannot belong to both without

[20] Rom. 6:14.

[21] This is in contrast to the exodus from Egypt when the Israelites took silver, gold and clothing from their Egyptian neighbours (Exod. 12:35) for their journey. Now the people were to rely totally on God's provision and not compromise by also trusting in some of the material wealth of Babylon.

[22] Again, we should be careful to note separation does not mean total isolation. Donald Bloesch helpfully remarks in a comment that could relate to Isa. 52:11, 'God does not call us into the desert in order to escape the follies of the world. Instead, he creates a highway in the wilderness to lead us to a new city that will arise out of the ashes of the old. By means of this highway the holiness and truth of God will find access to all areas of human life.' *The Holy Spirit: Works and Gifts* (Downers Grove: IVP, 2000), p. 319.

committing treason. Nor can believers identify themselves with the opposition party of unbelievers and benefit from their idolatrous way of living. Where close relationships involve compromise and accommodating to the beliefs and practices which are in opposition to the living God, a distance has to be kept and a separation observed. For us, this will especially mean rejecting the secular mindset of our culture and the ethical consequences that flow from it. And we should not fool ourselves into thinking that we can be separate from the godless mindset and still be accepted by the people who advocate it. Separating ourselves from the idolatrous philosophies of our time will mean we face rejection as people. But, no matter, for God welcomes us into his family.

3. An activity to pursue (7:1)

Paul's argument reaches a climax in 7:1, where he writes pastorally to his *dear friends*, encouraging them to bring to completion the holiness they have begun to experience. His desire for them is that they be the very best they can be for Christ, and so he urges them forward to the highest of standards, refusing to accept that they should be content with going only so far in holiness but not go all the way.

a. The basis for the activity

Paul goes out of his way to ensure that no one misses the point. *Therefore* points back to the promises he has just enumerated; *since we have these promises* draws added attention to them. The task of *purify[ing] ourselves* and *perfecting holiness* does not arise from command so much as promise; from grace not law. An understanding of God's desire to restore Eden (6:16a), of the faithfulness of our covenant God (6:16b), and of his accepting fatherly grace (6:17c, 18) will mean that we will work at being the very best we can be for him, even if we do not always achieve it.

b. The nature of the activity

As our part in this process we will *purify ourselves from everything that contaminates body and spirit*. Paul's readers were familiar with people undergoing ritual purification so that they might take part in the worship of their idols, but the purification he calls for is much more thorough. We see in the many arguments Jesus had with the religious leaders of his day how concerned they were with washing their hands before they ate and keeping themselves outwardly clean.[23] But the purification for which Paul calls is that of *body and spirit*,[24] of the outward and physical, and the inward and spiritual. Viewing human nature as a unity, Paul calls for comprehensive purification because one aspect of our lives affects the other: 'to defile one's body in immorality is also to defile one's spirit'.[25] They cannot be compartmentalized.

The purification he envisages smacks of the decontamination process sometimes pictured in a modern drama or sci-fi film, where chemical warfare has infected people or a virus has been unleashed which is fatal unless people are immediately cleansed from it. So, the victims strip off everything, subject themselves to be thoroughly hosed down and take the antidote either orally or intravenously in order to prevent the poison from doing its deadly work. Equal care needs to be taken in our commitment to holiness. No sin is small in the eyes of God. Toying with sin leads to disaster. Hence Paul's insistence that we should remove *everything*, not just some of the things, contaminating *body and spirit*.

To do this we need to:

1. carefully and honestly review our lives, both our outward behaviour and our inner desires and attitudes;[26]
2. confess and repent of those things that defile us, renouncing them and turning to replace them with the positive graces of the new life;[27]
3. seek the Spirit's help in overcoming them through regular prayer;[28]
4. put in place the practical steps of discipline that will remove, or

---

[23] Matt. 15:1–20; 23:25–26; Mark 7:1–8; John 2:6.

[24] Paul usually contrasts *sarx*, the word he uses here for 'body', with *pneuma*, the word he uses for 'spirit'. Here he uses them as complementary. More usually he calls for the *sarx* to be crucified rather than cleansed (Gal. 5:24). But Paul also uses *sarx* in a neutral sense, as an alternative to the more usual word *sōma* for 'body' (2 Cor. 4:11; 7:5; 10:3; Gal. 2:20). There is no need to question the authenticity of the passage because of this, as some do. See Barnett, *The Second Epistle to the Corinthians*, p. 356, n. 71 and Harris, *The Second Epistle to the Corinthians*, p. 512.

[25] Harris, ibid.

[26] Ps. 139:23; 1 Cor. 11:28; 2 Cor. 13:5; Gal. 6:4.

[27] Eph 4:17 – 5:2; Col. 3:5–17. Donald Bloesch reminds us, 'Confession of sin does not lie simply at the beginning of the Christian life; it is the hallmark of the entire Christian life. In Luther's words, "the whole life of the Christian is to be one of repentance" (*Ninety-five Thesis*, no. 1).' (Bloesch, *The Holy Spirit*, p. 327.) For a thorough exposition of the life of repentance see J. I. Packer, *A Passion for Holiness* (Cambridge: Crossway Books, 1992), pp. 119–156.

[28] Rom. 8:14–27.

minimize, the source of our temptation,[29] centre our thoughts on godliness,[30] and fill our time in constructive service of the Lord;[31] and,

5. ask one or two to be soul-mates who can encourage us in the battle.[32]

c. The consequence of the activity

The consequence as we *purify ourselves* is that we might bring to completion the work of holiness in our lives, or, perhaps better still, 'put into operation'[33] the holiness which is ours in Christ. Paul's use of the present tense of *perfecting* (*epitelountes*) indicates that he has a process in mind; that a progressive advance towards holiness is the result.[34] Earlier in his letter, Paul had written of the way in which Christians who focus on the Lord's glory 'are being transformed into his image with ever increasing glory, which comes from the Lord, who is the Spirit' (3:18). Here, using different words, he urges the Corinthians to work towards the progressive removal of sin from their lives so that the full image of God might eventually be restored within them.

A significant stream of Christians (or rather several significant streams of Christians, since they are not all identical) mostly tracing their roots back to John Wesley,[35] have taught that perfect holiness or entire sanctification is possible now.[36] This perfection is reached, according to this teaching, through a crisis experience, whether it be that of a second blessing or baptism of the spirit, as in the Holiness

---

[29] Matt. 5:29–30; 2 Tim. 2:22.

[30] Phil. 4:8–9.

[31] 1 Cor. 15:58; Gal. 6:9.

[32] 1 Thess 5:11; 2 Tim. 4:2; Heb 3:13; 10:25.

[33] D. Peterson, *Possessed by God: A New Testament Theology of Sanctification and Holiness*, NSBT (Leicester: Apollos, 1995), p. 88.

[34] Harris, *Second Corinthians*, p. 513; Martin, *2 Corinthians*, p. 198; contra Barnett, *Second Corinthians*, p. 357, who, recognising the present participle, says it 'probably does not imply a process of perfection in moral holiness' but is about covenantal holiness and the church's separation from idolatry.

[35] J. Wesley, *Plain Account of Christian Perfection* (Definitive edition 1777). For Wesley holiness was not to be judged in terms of moral perfection but an unbroken relationship with the Lord. Wesley wrote in a letter (21 February 1871), 'Entire sanctification is neither more nor less than pure love, love expelling sin, and governing both heart and life of a child of God. The Refiner's fire purges out all that is contrary to love.' Cited in P. M. Bassett and W. Greathouse, *Exploring Christian Holiness* (Kansas City: Beacon Hill Press, 1985), p. 231.

[36] The literature about perfectionism is immense. For an accessible entry point see M. Dieter *et al. Five Views on Sanctification* (Grand Rapids: Zondervan, 1987).

stream and in some of the Charismatic movement[37], or through an experience of total surrender, as in classic Keswick teaching.[38] One admires the ambitious appetite this builds up in believers. Those who believe that we will not be perfect until the day of Christ can become complacent in their battle against sin, while those who seek perfection now can put them to shame in their pursuit of the goal. It is also true, however, that it can build frustration into the lives of believers who seek a particular experience of God to give them constant victory over sin, only to discover that they do not, in reality, live a life of moment-by-moment victory.

Whatever may be said, however, in favour of holiness teaching the idea of perfection in the here and now has no real foundation in the Bible.[39] Paul is clear that he himself has not achieved perfection; 'Not that I have already obtained all this, or have already arrived at my goal, but I press on to take hold of that for which Christ Jesus took hold of me' (Phil. 3:12). And his use of the present participle, in 2 Corinthians 7:1, confirms that he has a process in view which is not yet completed. Similarly, John, who could write strongly about the Christian life being incompatible with sin, still acknowledged that Christians would sin and then need forgiveness and renewed purification (1 John 1:9). He even went so far as to say, 'If we claim to be without sin, we deceive ourselves and the truth is not in us' (1 John 1:8).

Here, as elsewhere, Paul talks of perfection being attained as a process not through a crisis, however significant special moments of God's presence and his Spirit's work in our lives may be. It is a goal to which we still advance, though rarely, as David Peterson delightfully puts it 'in a straight line'.[40]

d. The motive of the activity

All this is done *out of reverence for* [literally, *fear of*] *God.* Our great incentive is to please and honour him. How much time we spend preparing to please our fellow humans, whether it be our wife, boyfriend, boss or examiner. Careful preparation is undertaken so that we might respect their wishes and act to bring them pleasure. How much more should our respect for God ensure that we give careful

---

[37] The baptism of the Spirit, as understood by many in the Charismatic movement, has often been more closely associated with the power to exercise spiritual gifts or to be effective in witness than with holiness.

[38] On the Keswick movement, see C. Price and I. Randall, *Transforming Keswick* (Carlisle: OM Publishing, 2000).

[39] For a theological critique see, J. I. Packer, *Keep in Step with the Spirit* (Leicester: IVP, 2nd ed., 2005).

[40] Peterson, *Possessed by God*, p. 125.

attention to the daily perfecting of holiness in our lives so that we avoid his displeasure. If ever a man knew what it was to be separate and yet engaged in society it was William Wilberforce. He lamented that the church of his day no longer recognized 'the promotion of the glory of God and the possession of his favour as the objects of our highest regard and most strenuous endeavours'.[41] He warned, 'if the affections of the soul are not supremely fixed on God, and if our dominant desire and primary goal is not to possess God's favour and to promote his glory – then we are traitors in revolt against our lawful Sovereign'.[42] His comments could have been written about the church of our own day.

4. Concluding comment

The lines between separation, engagement and isolation are finely drawn and Christians find it hard not to stray from the lane marked out for them into one of the other lanes. On the one hand, holiness requires separation from the idolatry of the world. Although these idols may be embodied in certain practices or places, the idolatry of our world is largely invisible and involves mindsets that are ego-centric, hubristic and given to the pursuit of vacuous pleasure. By definition worshipping at the shrine of these lifeless idols cannot lead to life, but only to death. Christians, being the temple of the living God, need to sweep out all the dirt and dust of idolatry in their lives, whether it finds expression in behaviour or remains within the mind, in the form of guiding values or principles.

On the other hand, this separation does not require a retreat from the world. Even if we were to do so, the idols of the world would invade our minds, as many a monk has found. We are called to be God's servants in the world and therefore engagement, rather than isolation, is called for. But it is an engagement that aims to be involved without compromise. It may be an old cliché, but it is one that has substance: Christians are called to be in the world and not of it, whereas too often they are of the world and not in it.

Conscious of failure, of how much progress there is to make, and of how far short from perfection we are, we need alert minds and consecrated determination to persevere. There are no quick fixes to

---

[41] W. Wilberforce, *Real Christianity* (Colorado Springs: Victor Books, 2005), p. 94. Original title: *A Practical View of the Prevailing System of Professed Christians in the Higher and Middle Classes in This Country, Contrasted with Real Christianity*, originally published in 1797.
[42] Ibid., pp. 97–98.

make us instantly holy. Our life-time's vocation is to bring holiness to completion and increasingly to manifest to the world our true identity as we become what we are, the place where the living God can be found on earth.

Part 6
The destination of holiness

1 John 2:28 – 3:10
20. To be like him

There are some passages of Scripture that are like a finely-crafted poem or a beautiful symphony. Their appeal is transparent and if anyone ventures words to explain them further they are in danger of diminishing rather than enhancing their enchanting power. Speaking of 1 John 3:2, the text at the heart of our consideration here, Martyn Lloyd-Jones said,

> I suppose we must agree that nothing more sublime than this has ever been written, and any man who has to preach upon such a text or upon such a word must be unusually conscious of his own smallness and inadequacy and unworthiness. One's tendency with a statement like this always is just to stand in wonder and amazement at it.[1]

Even so, the risk must be taken in the desire of hearing more than we might otherwise hear with our uninstructed ear. The symphony of these verses may be understood as being composed of a prelude, a main movement and a postlude.

1. The prelude (2:28–29)

If this passage were a musical score, the last two verses of chapter 2 would be the overture. Those verses are integral to the main movement that follows in chapter 3 and introduce its theme. The chapter division is badly placed. As always, even when saying the harshest of things, John writes with gentle compassion to his *dear children.*

[1] M. Lloyd-Jones, *Life in Christ: Children of God,* Studies in 1 John, Vol. 3 (Wheaton and Nottingham: Crossway, 1993), p. 21.

Having just explained that they live 'in the last hour' (2:18) and that antichrists are active who deny the truth and preach a false gospel, he encourages them to prepare for the time when the last hour will come to an end and the clock strikes a new time as Jesus Christ reappears in history. How are they to prepare for such a coming? Three things need to be in place to make them ready for that day.

a. They are to continue in him: the What (2:28)

His instruction that they should *continue in him* is not a sharp command but rather a natural conclusion to what John has been teaching. It is a reminder to stay with the truth they have heard through the apostles (2:24) rather than being distracted by new, erroneous teaching. The teaching of the apostles was built on the solid foundation of what they had heard, seen and examined (1:1). It was about Jesus, fully God and fully man, who lived a flesh and blood life, died a real death and rose as a transphysical[2] person.[3] The temptation to novelty, bred into us today by the education system which prizes originality above all else, is to be resisted. Continuing on the same path, however, should not be mistaken for complacent inactivity, nor mere intellectual allegiance. To continue *in him* implies a very close personal, even intimate, relationship that involves perseverance and which implies progress that comes from active obedience and increasing love of God (2:15).[4]

b. They are to be confident before him: the Why (2:28)

As often happens, their present behaviour was to be determined by their future destination. They were, and we with them are, to *continue in him, so that when he appears we may be confident and unashamed before him at his coming.* John Stott comments that 'the two words [*appear* and *coming*] together imply that our Lord's return will involve the personal presence of one now absent, the visible appearing of one now unseen'.[5]

---

[2] 'Transphysical' is the description N. T. Wright gives to the resurrection body of Jesus. He defines it as meaning 'a body which is still robustly physical but is significantly different from the present one'. *The Resurrection of the Son of God* (London: SPCK, 2003), p. 478.

[3] 'John does not refer in so many words to the resurrection of Jesus, but he clearly presupposes it.' I. H. Marshall, *The Epistles of John*, NINTC (Grand Rapids: Eerdmans, 1978), p. 52.

[4] *Menete* (continuing, remaining or abiding) is used seven times in 1 John and speaks of 'a deep and permanent relationship'; Stephen Smalley, *1, 2, 3 John*, WBC (Waco: Word, 1984), p. 129.

[5] J. R. W. Stott, *The Letters of John*, TNTC (Leicester: IVP, 2nd edn., 1988), p. 121.

But how should we greet him? We greet the arrival of people in very different ways, depending on the circumstances. The sudden arrival in a classroom of an old-fashioned headmaster where pupils were conducting mayhem provoked fear, and caused the boisterous pupils suddenly to duck behind their desks and pretend it was nothing to do with them! On the other hand, the small child who has been told that the grandparents are coming to stay at lunchtime will be eagerly badgering her mother from breakfast time onwards asking, 'Is it time yet?' Mum (and Dad?) will have been busily preparing for their arrival by cooking, cleaning up and getting their room ready. This, rather than the appearance of the headmaster, captures how the early Christians, and many generations since, looked forward to the coming of Christ. Their vibrant hope kept them on their toes and motivated them to live a life of such holiness that whenever he came they would not be ashamed of how they had lived.[6]

His *coming*[7] is the coming of a king, and no royal person, especially in the ancient world, would have been met casually and without great care having been exercised in the preparation. If that was so, how much more should we exercise great care so that we are ready for the arrival of the King of kings.[8] The last thing any believer would want is for the King to arrive and to earn his rebuke because the preparations are incomplete. Confidence rather than nervous timidity, joy rather than shame, should mark our greeting of the king.

John's voice blends with those of Paul and Peter in urging believers to prepare themselves for his coming by their commitment to holiness. Paul says of the church that 'Christ loved the church and gave himself up for her to make her holy, cleansing her by the washing of water through the word, and to present her to himself as a radiant church, without stain or wrinkle or any other blemish, but holy and blameless' (Ephesians 5:25–7).[9] Unlike the bride on her wedding day, the preparations in which we must engage are more than cosmetic. Peter similarly urged, 'make every effort to be found spotless, blameless and at peace with him' (2 Peter 3:14) because the day would come when 'the Lord will come like a thief'[10] – suddenly and unannounced.

The loss of this hope of Christ's return has had a debilitating effect on modern Christianity. Some greet the news with indifference, for

---

[6] 2 Pet. 3:11–14.
[7] The word *parousia* was used of the visit of royalty.
[8] 1 Tim. 6:14–16.
[9] Eph. 1:4; and, similarly, 1 Tim. 6:14.
[10] 2 Pet. 3:10.

they are so sucked into the here and now that they would regard his coming as an interruption to their plans and dreams. Others regard preparing for his coming rather as some young people view the dire warnings about smoking. They have little impact because any lung cancer seems such a long way off that it's not to be taken seriously yet. Still others are ignorant of this truth, even though it was so central to the early Christian faith, and much the poorer for it. What a difference it makes to know, and believe, the Lord will come at any time, so we need to be prepared, at all times.

c. They are to be secure in him: the How (2:29)

John's idealism could easily have the unintended effect of causing anxiety. The insecure person would soon find something in their lives of which they were ashamed or some lapse of holiness that might undermine their courage. But pastor John is sensitive to this and therefore offers reassurance. Children are like their parents and the children *born of* God display his family's likeness. *He is righteous,* and consequently they are righteous as well. They are not perfect, and John never suggests that they should be, for he knows that we do occasionally sin (see 1:8–9), but they essentially behave in a righteous way. Righteous living, as it were, characterizes the climate of their lives, even if they know the occasional day of inclement or even stormy weather. And it is the climate, rather than the weather on a particular day, that John is primarily concerned about. Consequently, they can be secure in him and have no need to lack confidence.

John returns to this theme more fully in the postlude (3:4–10), as we too will do.

2. The main movement (3:1–3)

The golden nugget of 3:1–3 is seen by some as a parenthesis, interrupting the main flow of argument at 2:28 until it is picked up again in 3:5.[11] There may be good logical reason for seeing it in this way but from another perspective, far from being a parenthesis, these verses may be seen to be the climax of John's teaching in this passage. What precedes leads up to them and what follows leads away from them. Shaped like an arrowhead, these verses are the

---

[11] Colin Kruse, for example, regards them as parenthetical to the main argument about sin, in *The Letters of John*, Pillar (Grand Rapids: Eerdmans and Leicester: Apollos, 2000), p. 114.

sharp tip, the effective point of impact, that enables the rest of the arrow to do its work.

a. Our position: who we are (3:1)

In the opening verse of chapter 3 we find 'the assurance which the Apostle gives his readers (in 2:29) is carried to its height, and their fears receive a full reproof'.[12] God's love has not been given to us in a measured way. He did not calculate the return he would receive and give us 'just enough' to provoke the right response. No, he *lavished* his love on us. That he should shower us with love is characteristic of his generous nature. Like the father in the story of the prodigal son he goes well beyond what would have been 'admirable generosity' in taking the boy back home, and instead is excessive in his welcome and his gifts, 'even more prodigal than the boy!'[13] Throughout the Gospels 'the Father is presented as a God of overflowing goodness, whose one desire is to share whatever he has with as many as possible'.[14] The same portrait of a generous God is found here.

This love, John says literally, is given to us and secures for us a place in God's family. Through it we become his children, as opposed to others who display that they belong to other families (3:8). Some say this love is an 'inalienable possession' that cannot be taken away from us.[15] While that may be reading a little too much into it, it is true that, having become children of God, no one can ever alter that fact. We are his, we belong! We enjoy the benefits of having him as our Father, take pleasure from the intimacy it brings and express trust in his wise direction, as well as accepting the responsibilities that go along with being a member of the family. Our status has changed for sure.

All this describes our present position in relation to God. But it also raises a question. If we are currently God's children (note the *now* in verse 2), why don't people recognize that? Why is our experience a troubled one, and why don't people accept and respect us in the way we might expect, rather than persecute and ridicule us? John's reply (3:1), in effect, is to say that such a reaction on the part of those who are not in the family confirms, rather than undermines, his claim that we are. In suffering hostility or misunderstanding now

---

[12] G. C. Findlay, *Studies in John's Epistles: Fellowship in Life Eternal* (1909, Grand Rapids: Kregal, 1989), pp. 259–260.

[13] G. W. Hughes, *God of Surprises* (London: Darton, Longman and Todd, 1985), p. 115.

[14] Ibid.

[15] Smalley, *1, 2, 3 John*, p. 141.

we are only experiencing what Jesus himself experienced. Jesus had explained to his disciples that 'In this world you will have trouble' (John 16:33). Since people had failed to recognize who Jesus truly was and had not received him warmly, why should they recognize who his disciple are and be expected to receive them more positively? The negative reaction they encounter simply goes to bear out that they belong to the same family. It does not undermine their position as children of God who can enjoy utter security in their relationship with their Father.

b. Our prospect: what we will be (3:2)

Children of God is what they, and we, are *now*! But that is only part of the story. Any parent longs to see not only what their children are but what they will become and that, says John, is fairly unimaginable because it *has not yet been made known*. Human beings frequently find it hard genuinely to envisage the future. It is a gift given only to a few. To explain a television to a person in the nineteenth century would have made no sense. To explain the computer and the internet would have made even less sense, and was beyond most people's imagination until very recently. It is as if John is saying we live now in the days of the black and white TV, with its tiny, snowy screen. But one day we will enjoy the full-colour LCD flat screen with full-surround sound. Or, it is as if he was saying to the person who used a manual typewriter that one day they would enjoy the benefit of word processing on a laptop. What we have now is good, but nothing in comparison to what is to come.

We may not be able to say much about our future prospect but what we can say is significant: *when Christ appears, we shall be like him, for we shall see him as he is.* That simple wonderful sentence speaks of our completion in, our transformation by, and our imitation of Christ.

God's work of restoring his image in us will be completed *when Christ appears*, but not until then. John echoes Paul when he wrote 'that he who began a good work in you will carry it on to completion until the day of Christ Jesus' (Philippians 1:6). Unlike many a human craftsman, God's work will be finished on time, without delay or postponement and without any need of an excuse. But the work of restoration will take that amount of time to be completed. In the meantime, we change 'from one degree of glory to another' (2 Corinthians 3:18, NRSV).

By the time we die, or Christ returns, most of us will still only be works in progress with a great deal still to be accomplished in holiness. But his appearance will take care of whatever remains to be done and then our final transformation into his likeness will occur. Then, *we shall be like him.* Paul says the same. Writing of the resurrection he says, 'we will all be changed – in a flash, in the twinkling of an eye, at the last trumpet' (1 Corinthians 15:51–52).[16] But whereas Paul's concern was with the nature of our bodies in the resurrection and the way in which our corruptible, mortal bodies would be transformed into imperishable, immortal bodies, John's concern is with the transformation of our characters. It has to do with our purity, as the following verse makes clear.

The way this transformation comes about is through our imitation of Christ: *for we shall see him as he is.* The apostles had already seen Jesus when he was incarnate on earth (1:1) but this sighting will be different. No longer in the form of a humble Galilean, his second appearance on earth would disclose his true identity, majesty and glory. The vision of his full persona would not merely make a deep and lasting impact, as Isaiah's vision in the temple had done, but would lead believers to a complete and eternal change into his likeness.[17] The imitation of Christ is an important theme for John.[18] It starts now as we 'live as Jesus did' (2:6) and love as Jesus loved (3:16). But when he returns our imitation will be perfect and unblemished in any way.

Again, Paul had talked about fixing our eyes on Jesus as the secret of our 'being transformed into his image' (2 Corinthians 3:18), but what Paul saw as a work in process and with an inevitably limited vision, John sees as a completed process. We will be perfectly like him when we encounter him face to face. Our destination will have been reached. Holiness will at last mean sinless perfection. God's image will be finally restored and the work of reconstruction completed.

c. Our progress: what we should do (3:3)

What are we to do in the meantime? Since God will bring this transformation about on Christ's return, does it mean we can sit back and indolently wait for that appearance to take place? After all, if God is going to make up any shortfall in our lives, why should we bother to invest effort in reducing the holiness deficit now?

The question is misguided and John takes the implication of his teaching in the totally opposite direction. Our future destination frequently determines our present behaviour. If we are moving

---

[16] Cf. Phil 3:21.

[17] R. Law summed it up as 'Vision becomes assimilation', cited by Smalley, *1, 2, 3 John*, p. 146 and Stott, *The Letters of John*, p. 124.

[18] Smalley, *1, 2, 3 John*, pp. 53, 146.

house in some months' time we measure up for the curtains and the fittings and plan the redecoration of the new house, not the old. We save up so the money will be available when we need it and we don't spend any more than is essential on where we currently live. We gather the materials in advance and place the order for the things we have to purchase. Our interest is taken up with preparing for the future. So it should be with Christ's appearing. The fact that we shall be like him when he appears means we should seek to be as much like him now in readiness for that appearance.

The particular aspect of preparation John has in mind is to do with increasing holiness. John tells us that if we have this *hope in him,* we should purify ourselves,[19] just as he is pure. (This is John's version of *Be holy, as I am holy.*) For Jesus to be pure, as he says a few verses later, is to say that *in him is no sin* (3:5). The purpose of his coming was to *take away our sins* (3:4) and to *destroy the devil's work* (3:8), which is to embroil people in sin. Purification, then, must mean getting rid of sin in our lives and cleansing our lives from it. The process of decontamination from sin needs to begin here and not be left until later, as we live in imitation of the one who loves us and in anticipation of our entering fully into his presence.

In this passage John, in common with other New Testament writers, holds the 'now' of the Christian life in tension with the 'not yet'. They never teach us that the chapter of our lives entitled 'Now' needs to be finished before the chapter entitled 'Not yet' can begin. Rather the 'Not yet' chapter has already begun and overlaps with the 'Now'. The new age has arrived even if it has not yet arrived fully. Consequently, while still grappling with the limitations of the 'now', we live as much as it is possible to do in the 'not yet'. Tom Wright puts it beautifully when talking about ethics (in our terms, the same is true of the deeper concept of holiness). He writes, 'It is not about trying to obey dusty-rule books from long ago or far away. It is about practising, in the present, the tunes we shall sing in God's new world.'[20] Holiness, as mentioned earlier, is an invitation to choir practice!

3. The postlude (3:4–10)

In musical terms the postlude is perhaps best understood as chiefly playing the same melody as the main movement but in a minor

---

[19] Purification sometimes has ceremonial overtones rather than moral implications but here it is about moral purity, as in Jas 4:8 and 1 Pet. 1:22. Kruse, *The Letters of John,* pp. 116–117.

[20] T. Wright, *Simply Christian* (London: SPCK, 2006), p. 189.

key and at a slower pace. It firmly links into the main movement and picks up line after line of its music, but comes at it, as it were, from the opposite angle. Howard Marshall has said that in this section John is still talking about 'the importance of continuing in Christ, doing what is right, and purifying oneself in anticipation of his coming. [But] now he deals more closely with the negative side of all this, the need for believers to abstain from sin and the possibility of their doing so.'[21] Look at the transposition of key John develops.

The main movement had spoken of Christ's future appearance (2:28; 3:2); the postlude speaks of his past appearance (3:5,8).

The main theme spoke of what he will accomplish (3:2); the postlude of what he has accomplished. His first appearance on earth dealt with our sins by offering atonement for them (3:5),[22] and broke the power of the devil and condemned him to defeat (3:8).

The main theme spoke of believers as children of God (3:1–2); the postlude of others as children of the devil (7–10). The difference between them, John says, can be seen in how they display their family's likeness. The family of God are characterized by righteous behaviour; the family of the devil by sinful behaviour, for it is inherent in his nature to sin.

The main theme spoke of his purity (3:3), picking up the statement from the prelude that *he is righteous* (2:29). The postlude not only repeats that statement (3:7), and underlines it in saying that *in him is no sin* (3:5), but then develops the implication of this in saying that those *born of God will not continue in sin . . . they cannot go on sinning* (3:9). *No-one who lives in him keeps on sinning* (3:5).[23] It would be foolish of anyone to say that the Christian is incapable of sin because it is obvious to all, including ourselves, unless we are deceiving ourselves, that we can and do sin. John knows that (1:8–9). But, although we may occasionally fall we do not habitually sin. Our lives are not oriented toward sin but towards Christ. They are not mired in sin but moulded by holiness. Doing wrong, as a life stance and prevailing habit, has been replaced by doing right. Sin is no longer normal but an aberration. John is not denying sin in believers, but he is challenging indifference to it and pointing out how incongruous it is. As Robert Law said, 'To believe in Christ and to believe in sin, to love Christ and to love sin, to live in Christ

---

[21] Marshall, *The Epistles of John*, p. 175.

[22] On atonement in 1 John see 1:7; 2:2; 4:10.

[23] The tenses John uses emphasizes that he has sin as a habit or continuous activity in mind, not a one-off or occasional lapse. Stott, *The Letters of John*, p. 140, quotes David Smith saying, 'The believer may fall into sin, but he will not walk in it.'

and to live in sin, as one's element, is as unthinkable as that one should face north and south at the same moment.'[24]

We have become *righteous* both in the sense that Jesus' death has put us in a right relationship with God (justification) and in the sense that we increasingly practise right conduct day by day (sanctification).

The main theme spoke with assurance about our future transformation (3:2); the postlude, with equal clarity, speaks about our present transformation, made possible because *God's seed remains in* us (3:9). The male seed planted in the female womb leads to the birth of a child. So we have been born of God, but John's point is that having been born did not mean the seed had finished its work. The life-giving power of the seed remains inside us after it has given us initial life, giving us power to overcome the drag of sin. John does not tell us more precisely what he has in mind by this seed but it is almost certainly the Holy Spirit, or the Word of God, both of which are seen as dynamic and transforming powers, or possibly a combination of them both.[25]

The main theme spoke about what *has not yet been made known*: the full nature of our resurrection life (3:2). The postlude speaks about what *we know* already: from the lives we currently lead (3:10).

In short, the main theme spoke about what we shall be in the future (3:2); the postlude speaks about what we should be in the present: those who do right and love our brothers and sisters (3:10).

4. Concluding comment

John is as convinced as Paul that living in sin is incompatible with living in Christ. Christ, the sinless one, appeared to break the power of sin and defeat its agent, the devil. Consequently, those born of God can no longer continue in the habit of sinning. As Bishop Gore once said, 'Christians who sin forget themselves.'[26] Christians have no need to sin, since the life of God is within them giving them power to resist sin and live righteously.

John teaches that the antidote to remaining sin in the believer is not law but love. The incentive for overcoming sin is to understand how rich is the love that God has already poured out in our lives, as he has given us the security and the many other privileges of being

---

[24] Cited by R. E. O. White, *An Open Letter to Evangelicals* (Exeter: Paternoster Press, 1964), p. 87.
[25] See chs. 13 and 14, and Marshall, *The Epistles of John*, p.186.
[26] Quoted in White, *An Open Letter to Evangelicals*, p. 86.

his sons and daughters. It is, furthermore, to understand how rich is the love God has yet to pour out on us when Christ appears a second time and we are fully transformed into his likeness. Our destination is to have the image of God fully restored in us, one day. When we are like him, we shall be pure, just as he is pure, and holy, just as he is holy.

Until then, we set out compass towards that future, so that *when he appears we may be confident and unashamed before him.*

1 Thessalonians 5:23–24
21. He will do it

At the end of a book on holiness there is need for perspective. So many ideals have been set out, so many dimensions opened up, so many demands made, so many truths expounded and so many bypaths explored that it is easy to fail to see the wood for the trees. Given all that has been said, can we live up to the ideals and can we keep it up over the long haul? Paul would give an emphatic 'yes' in answer to these questions. Having told the Thessalonians that God's will for them was their sanctification (4:3) and having spoken to them fairly directly about their need to amend their lives to bring them into conformity with God's will, Paul ends his first letter to them on a note of great confidence. But his confidence is not in them but in God. His final prayer for them is: *May God himself, the God of peace, sanctify you through and through. May your whole spirit, soul and body be kept blameless at the coming of our Lord Jesus Christ. The one who calls you is faithful, and he will do it.* Here, in a nutshell, is the most crucial teaching about holiness.

As so often, its profound teaching is best understood by approaching it through a number of simple questions.

1. Who? God's personal involvement

A worship song which is currently popular says, 'It's all about you, Jesus'. But the truth is that the way we speak and act betrays that our Christian lives are really 'all about us'. Paul never falls into that trap. He knows, to quote Tom Wright's recent words, that *'we are not the centre of the universe. God is not circling around us. We are circling around him.'*[1] As a result, Paul's final word to the

[1] T. Wright, *Justification: God's Plan and Paul's Vision* (London: SPCK, 2009), p. 7. Italics his.

Thessalonians about holiness is God-focused. Two things are said of God.

a. Holiness is the result of God's personal attention

Paul prays that these insignificant Thessalonians, who represent all those who seek to be holy, might receive the personal attention of God as their lives are prepared for the coming of Christ. *God himself* is emphatic, not incidental. It used to be a mark of pride, and maybe still is, that no Rolls Royce radiator grill was mass-produced. Each was individually crafted and had the craftsman's initials engraved on its back. So God handcrafts us, lovingly restoring us into his image, shaping and moulding us to reflect him and etching, as it were, his own character into ours. He does not delegate his responsibility to others and will never abdicate it either. Unlike the CEO of a business, the Vice-Chancellor of a University, a member of the Government, or the Chief Constable of a police force, he does not shelter behind layers of bureaucracy or shield himself behind ramparts of underlings. Though Overlord of all and King of the universe, God personally knows our name, takes an interest in us and is on our case, restoring his image within us. What amazing grace!

b. Holiness is a result of God's peaceful intention

Paul describes God at this point as *the God of peace*. Although he uses this description of God elsewhere,[2] why does Paul specifically highlight this characteristic of God in this context? He may be using it to highlight the way in which sanctification will bring an end to the discord he had hinted at in the Thessalonian church in the preceding verses. Verse 13 had instructed them to 'Live in peace with each other'. So to remind them that their God was *the God of peace* would be particularly appropriate. But most commentators agree that the title is not used as a reaction to their discord but rather as a positive expression of salvation.[3]

Peace, says F. F. Bruce, is 'the sum total of the Gospel blessings'.[4] The title picks up the idea of *šālôm*, so prevalent in the Old Testament, which is a rich and wide expression of the heart of God, far wider than the inner, emotional equanimity to which we often

---

[2] Rom. 15:33; 16:20; 2 Cor. 13:11; Phil. 4:9.
[3] G. L. Green, *The Letters to the Thessalonians*, Pillar Commentary (Grand Rapids, MI and Leicester: Apollos, 2002), p. 267 and I. H. Marshall, *1 and 2 Thessalonians* NCB (Grand Rapids: Eerdmans and London: Marshall, Morgan and Scott, 1983), p. 161.
[4] F. F. Bruce, *1 & 2 Thessalonians* WBC 45 (Waco, TX: Word, 182), p. 129.

reduce the concept today. *Šālôm*, far from being the mere absence of conflict, refers to experiencing the blessing of well-being in every area of life, and therefore being in a right relationship with God himself, with the creation, with one's fellow humans in community, and even knowing peace within oneself.[5] As such, 'it approximates closely to the idea of salvation'.[6] God desires us to partake in his *šālôm*, to enjoy his positive well-being in our lives, but we can only fully do this if we are holy.

2. What? God's purposive activity

Some forms of Christian preaching verge on the sentimental as they stress that God enjoys friendship with us, and ignore the fact that sin mars our friendship. God's friendship with us, here and elsewhere, is shown to be a purposeful friendship. His friendship grows stronger as sin is increasingly conquered. He walks with us so that we might walk in a particular direction, as Enoch did in ancient times (Gen. 5:24). His purpose in relating to us is that he might *sanctify [us] through and through.*

David Wells distinguishes between 'Agape spirituality' and 'Eros spirituality'. In 'Agape spirituality' God reaches down to find the sinner and gives the gift of salvation. In 'Eros spirituality' human beings reach up to God and 'build on the presumption that they can forge their own salvation'.[7] They are, he writes, 'not variations upon a common theme but stark alternatives'.[8] In these terms, Paul is definitely an advocate of Agape sanctification. It is God who makes us holy.

a. His aim is holiness

To be holy is to be separate from sin. It is to refuse loyalty to any other god, power or idol and to serve *the God of peace* alone. It is to be exclusively dedicated to him and his service. It necessarily involves standing out from our environment and adopting a different lifestyle, oriented around the living God. It is to imitate God's character and display it to an unbelieving world. It is, using J. C. Ryle's words, to cultivate 'the habit of being of one mind with

[5] H. Beck, C. Brown, '*eirēnē*', in *NIDNTT*, 2, pp. 776–783 and W. Foerster, '*eirēnē*', in *TDNT*, 2, pp. 400–420.

[6] *DNTT*, p. 777.

[7] D. Wells, *Above All Earthly Pow'rs* (Grand Rapids: Eerdmans and Leicester: IVP, 2005), p. 159.

[8] Ibid., p. 175.

God'.[9] That involves death to self but, far from that leading to a miserable negativity, we die to self in order that we might live the fuller life of the risen Christ.

Inherent in God's commitment to our salvation is his commitment to enable us to become holy. It is his priority for us. Unlike much contemporary Christianity, God is more interested in our purity than our popularity, our faithfulness than our fashionableness, our innocence than our relevance.

b. His approach is thorough

God's work within us is thorough. He works *through and through*. The word *holoteleis* is only used here in the New Testament and is rare elsewhere. It means 'entirely', 'in every part of each of you', '"reaching the full end or goal" for which you were saved'.[10] God is not slap-dash in his work, or content when he has partially completed his work of transformation in us. He is thorough and perseveres to the end.[11]

We frequently admire, and demand, thoroughness in others. We complain about shoddy workmanship that betrays a careless or a make-do attitude. In our family we are thankful for the thoroughness of a skilled medical consultant who showed daily concern for every detail of my wife's treatment over several months that led to the birth of our son. Without such thoroughness we would not have known the enjoyment of having a child. Half-measures and carelessness would have resulted in a failed pregnancy – in death, not in life. At one unpleasant stage of the treatment my wife, understandably enough, asked the consultant if he could relieve her discomfort. He gently but firmly replied, 'Your discomfort is not my concern; the healthy delivery of your baby is.' His focused thoroughness led to life, and we are grateful. God is just as focused, caring more for our sanctification than our comfort, and just as thorough as he works to restore his image in us.

3. Where? God's comprehensive work

Paul's emphasis on God's thoroughness is expanded as he prays further, *May your whole spirit, soul and body be kept blameless at the coming of our Lord Jesus Christ.* This is the only time Paul uses

[9] J. C. Ryle, *Holiness* (Cambridge and London: James Clarke, 1956), p. 35.
[10] Green, *The Letters to the Thessalonians*, p. 267.
[11] Phil. 1:6.

this particular trichotomy of spirit, soul and body and, although we shall examine each in turn, we must understand that his point is not to give us an analytical essay in anthropology[12] but rather to stress that no part of our beings, however we analyse them, is exempt from God's attention. His interest is in us as united, integrated beings, through and through.

The *spirit* may well be what we are in relation to God. It draws our attention to the need to be holy in our personal devotion, in our corporate worship, in our daily obedience and practical piety. We know we are making progress in this dimension of our lives when there is a smooth, trusting and open relationship between ourselves and God, such as we see in couples who've been married for years and know each other intimately.

The *soul* is a person's vital life force and might well approximate to what we today would call personality. In sanctifying his people God has no intention of making everyone a dull, monochrome copy of everyone else. The God who created the world in all its wonderful diversity has created each person to be an individual, and the work of holiness brings that individuality to full flavour in our lives, whilst straining out the sinful tangs of self-centred individualism. God knows that each of those wonderfully diverse individual personalities he has made needs refining: the negative characteristics of those personalities need removing and the positive aspects of them need strengthening. Holiness does just that, creating lives which others long to savour.

New Testament teaching constantly gave attention to the body's role in the pursuit of holiness. Its spirituality was never abstract, nor ethereal, but always thoroughly physical and earthed.[13] Unlike some Greek philosophical teaching one never became virtuous by escaping the body into a different realm of the spirit, an error which is still to be found among some who are super-spiritual today. Biblical Christianity is an incarnational faith, grounded in the real world, lived out in specific cultures and operative in the realm of the material and physical. Holiness is always embodied holiness. This has an obvious implication for our sexual lives, as Paul had already explained to his readers in 4:1–12.[14] But it is not limited to that. Holiness has implications for all that we do with our bodies, including what we eat, whether we keep fit, how we express ourselves both with our tongues and in non-verbal communication, physical

---

[12] For such a discussion see J. D. G. Dunn, *The Theology of Paul the Apostle* (Edinburgh: T & T Clark, 1998), pp. 51–78.

[13] See, for example, Rom. 12:1–2.

[14] See also 1 Cor. 6:12–20.

contact, and what we 'let in' to our minds through our eyes. Our bodies not only witness to our mortality but to our spiritual vulnerability as they are often the cause, or at least the vehicle, of our failures. However disciplined we might naturally be, or however much training we may undertake, most of us are weak and helpless in this area of our lives and we know why Paul prays for God to sanctify our bodies for without his doing so we have little hope.

In speaking of the sanctification of our soul, spirit and body, Paul is wonderfully comprehensive. These comprise the thinking, wilful and emotional aspects of our lives. They are about what we think, what we decide and what we do. The external and internal dimensions of our lives are embraced and the depth and the surface of our beings included.

4. When? God's planned future

The prayer relates to the present, but, true to the heartbeat of New Testament Christianity, as he prays Paul's eye is on the future. Paul's prayer is that our spirits, souls and bodies may *be kept blameless at the coming of our Lord Jesus Christ.* In praying this Paul is virtually repeating the prayer he already voiced in 3:13. There it was very evident that being *blameless* was something which still lay in the future. And here it is evident that Paul's focus is on the final result of God's action in our lives, even though the idea of being *kept blameless* implies we already are. The aorist tense which Paul uses to express his wish for them is one that embraces the whole process of the Christian life. Starting with their conversion (1:9), through their present experience (3:11–13) and onto the coming of Christ (5:23), he longs that they may be blameless. Hence his prayer embraces our past (we were made holy at conversion), present (we should live holy lives now), and future (we will be made completely holy when Christ returns).

What does it mean to be *blameless*? It means to be like the sacrificial animals that Israel used to offer, which were required to be without blemish and physically sound and whole. The perfection of the sacrificial animal was a symbol of the need for someone's moral conduct to be blameless, especially as their life was evaluated at the end. Paul's hope, then, is that when the final verdict on our lives is pronounced we will be found not guilty in any way.[15] This would be impossible but for the saving and keeping power of God. Although not exempt from responsibility, which is addressed elsewhere,

[15] Green, *Thessalonians*, p. 180.

Paul's emphasis here, possibly with the intent of reassuring his readers, is that we are mainly passive in this process. We do not keep ourselves but are *kept* by God for the day of Christ's return. God takes responsibility for us.

The forward thrust of Paul's teaching encourages us to keep our eye on the future. There is no reason for discouragement in the battle for holiness and no room for giving in to the temptation to give up. Like any job of restoration, whether it is restoring an old building, repairing a damaged work of art, or renewing a worn out part of our bodies, we may often feel we're making little progress. The rubble remains which we long to get rid of, the cleaning and repair of the picture seems a slow process, and the body is perhaps still in pain for some time after the operation, as it begins to heal. But the process has started and will one day be completed. We're called to persevere because God perseveres with us. Therefore we must keep our eye on the goal, the day when the final assessment deadline is reached, and not stop short. Until then the verdict is not in. But then, by God's grace, we hope to be judged to be 'blameless and holy in the presence of our God and Father' (3:13).

5. How? God's perfect character

If we were to aim for blamelessness in our own strength we would be condemning ourselves to failure. To pursue holiness unaided is a futile exercise. It leads either to a slavish drudgery to rules, instead of living the life of freedom and fullness that God intends, or to despair and giving up. We have our part to play, but our hope lies in God, not ourselves, therefore the goal is reachable.

What Paul says to the young converts at Thessalonica is something he later repeats in very similar words to the morally chaotic church at Corinth (1 Cor. 1:8), and later still, in different words but the same meaning, to the church in Rome (Rom. 8:30). Paul's language in Thessalonians is, once again, emphatic: *The one who calls you is faithful*! When God calls he remains faithful to those whom he has called, as Israel had good cause to know if they cared to review their history, even though their faithfulness to him was often questionable. Unlike us fickle human beings, he doesn't get weary or bored; he does not change his mind after he has spoken; he does not regret his decisions and plot to see how he can wriggle out of his commitments.

What is more, he is not only *faithful* but also able. We may often intend well, or promise much, but at times we do not deliver on our promises, sometimes because we have promised more than we are able to deliver and sometimes due to circumstances beyond our control, or even because of plain forgetfulness. But God suffers from none of these limitations. He 'is completely dependable. If he said it, he'll do it!'[16] His power is always sufficient to accomplish his plans. Nothing can stop what God has determined to do.

The source of our confidence lies in the character of God. His integrity, trustworthiness and power are aspects of his holiness, channelled to good effect in restoring his fallen image in our lives. The restoration will be completed on time, that is, on the return of Christ. Then at last, we shall be holy, in the fullest sense of the word, as he is holy.[17] His image will be perfectly restored and reflected in us.

[16] *The Message.*
[17] Lev. 11:44, 45; 19:2; 1 Pet. 1:15-16.

Study guide

HOW TO USE THIS STUDY GUIDE

The aim of this study guide is to help you get to the heart of what Derek has written and challenge you to apply what you learn to your own life. The questions have been designed for use by individuals or by small groups of Christians meeting, perhaps for an hour or two each week, to study, discuss and pray together. When used by a group with limited time, the leader should decide beforehand which questions are most appropriate for the group to discuss during the meeting and which should perhaps be left for group members to work through by themselves or in smaller groups during the week.

PREVIEW. Use the guide and the contents pages as a map to become familiar with what you are about to read, your 'journey' through the book.

READ. Look up the Bible passages as well as the text.

ANSWER. As you read, look for the answers to the questions in the guide.

DISCUSS. Even if you are studying on your own try to find another person to share your thoughts with.

REVIEW. Use the guide as a tool to remind you what you have learned. The concluding comment sections at the end of each chapter will also be useful. The best way of retaining what you learn is to write it down in a notebook or journal.

APPLY. Translate what you have learned into your attitudes and actions, considering your relationship with God, your personal life, your family life, your working life, your church life, your role as a citizen and your world-view.

PART 1. THE FOUNDATION OF HOLINESS

Exodus 19:1–25

1. God of the smoking mountain (pp. 31–41)

1. How far do you agree with David Wells' assessment of the problem in the evangelical world today (p. 31)?
2. Can you give specific examples of the ways contemporary Christianity has turned inwards (p. 32)?
3. How had God's grace to Israel been demonstrated in the past (p. 33)?
4. In what way would God's future relationship with his people be different from his initial rescue (p. 33)?
5. Under the covenant Israel would be 'distinguished from other nations'. In what ways (pp. 33–34)?
6. What distinguishes covenants from carefully-negotiated contracts (p. 34)? Why is the difference important?
7. In Exodus 19:9–15 Moses' words to God are not recorded. Why is this significant (p. 35)?
8. What were the chief lessons, (a) for Moses and (b) for the people, in the way God revealed himself? What are the wider implications for us (pp. 35–36)?
9. What three preparations were the people required to make before God descended to the mountain and what should we learn from them (pp. 36–37)?
10. What phenomena accompanied God's self-revelation and how do they contribute to our picture of God's holiness (pp. 38–39)?
11. Why was a specific warning given to the priests (p. 40)?
12. 'Most of our worship takes place well short of the mountain' (Walter Brueggemann). Are there ways in which this verdict is reflected in your own circle of worship (pp. 40–41)?

'Holiness starts with God, not with us. Our concern with holiness arises because the God we serve is holy. Ever since God appeared to Moses at the burning bush he had made himself known as one who is holy. It is his essential nature, the essence of his being' (p. 42).

Isaiah 6:1–13
2. God in glory (pp. 42–54)

1. Why is God's holiness distinctive and different from other ways of describing God in human language (pp. 42–43)?
2. In what way does the historical setting of Isaiah 6 contribute to the central message of God's holiness (pp. 43–44)?
3. How do the visual aspects of Isaiah's vision enhance its meaning (pp. 44–45)?
4. Turning to the aural aspect of the vision, 'the song is something of a surprise'(p. 46). Why?
5. Outline the implications of the seraphs' song in your own words (pp. 46–47).
6. 'Little is made of his emotions.' What aspects of Isaiah's response are highlighted (pp. 47–48)?
7. How do the explanations of Rudolf Otto and John N. Oswalt differ (pp. 48–49)?
8. In what three ways is the costly grace of God manifest in Isaiah 6 (p. 50)?
9. What is the connection between fire and holiness (pp. 50–51)?
10. How does Isaiah 6 elucidate the true nature of forgiveness (pp. 51–52)?
11. What do you understand by God's 'severe mercy' (pp. 52–53)?
12. How should verse 13 be interpreted (p.53)?

1 Peter 1:1–2, 13–21
3. God in Trinity (pp. 55–66)

1. How do J. H. Elliott and J. B. Green differ in their understanding of the terms 'exiles' and 'foreigners' in 1 Peter (p. 55)?
2. How does the *Epistle to Diognetus* describe the Christian community – negatively and positively (p. 56)?
3. What distinctive aspects of holiness does Peter associate with God the Father and how do they impact upon us (pp. 57–58)?
4. What distinctive aspects of holiness does Peter associate with God the Spirit and how do they impact upon us (pp. 58–59)?
5. What distinctive aspects of holiness does Peter associate with God the Son and how do they impact upon us (pp. 59–61)?
6. What illustration does Peter use in verse 13 and how would you express it in today's culture (p. 62)?
7. What negative factors influence us as fallen human beings and how can they be counteracted (pp. 63–64)?

8. 'The essence of holiness lies in the imitation of God.' How does Peter develop this truth and what two observations do we need to note (pp. 64–65)?
9. What incentives do we have for persevering in a holy life (pp. 65–66)?
10. How can the analogy of natural human development help us to understand the development of holiness (p. 66)?

'Joel Green explains that imitation calls for "a creative perform-ance" of the script that Christ has provided, not a wooden repeti-tion of it, so that we bring his holiness alive in our day and apply it to the form of 'ignorant' culture in which we live' (p. 65).

PART 2. VISIONS OF HOLINESS

Leviticus 11:1–47
4. Holiness as purity (pp. 69–80)

1. Whose particular vision of holiness is presented in Leviticus and how far does that affect their perspective (pp. 69–70)?
2. What questions were thrown up by the world-view of Leviticus (pp. 70–71)?
3. How would you defend the relevance of the food laws in Leviticus 11 (pp. 71–72)?
4. Why is the concept of being owned positive rather than nega-tive (pp. 72–73)?
5. How had the grace of God been shown in Israel's history (p. 73)?
6. What conclusion should we draw from the fact that to be holy is a repeated command (pp. 73–74)?
7. What provision was made for breaches of holiness? Where do we see this reflected in our Christian life (pp. 74–75)?
8. What are the major divisions and themes of the book of Leviticus (pp. 75–76)?
9. How would you counter the criticism that Leviticus is only concerned with external rituals (pp. 76–77)?
10. What examples do we find of God's holy concern for the physi-cal conditions and functions of life (pp. 77–78)?
11. What is the thread that unifies the various themes of Leviticus 19 (pp. 78–79)?
12. 'The focus of Leviticus 19 might be said to be on personal ethics.' How would we need to qualify that statement (pp. 79–80)?

Proverbs 2:1–22
5. Holiness as wisdom (pp. 81–93)

'At first sight, it is foolish to turn to Proverbs for an understanding of holiness ... Yet the book dances to the tune of holiness. Here, Israel's commitment is made over into another key. Here, holiness is transposed into wisdom' (p. 81).

---

1. Why might the book of Proverbs seem a strange choice for inclusion in a study on holiness? How would you justify it (p. 81)?
2. What features of the father's teaching demonstrate the principles of good educational practice (pp. 82–83)?
3. How does wisdom differ from knowledge? Can you think of some examples from contemporary life (p. 84)?
4. 'Wisdom is elusive.' Why is this a good thing (pp. 84–85)?
5. What shift takes place between verses 4 and 5 and what lesson should we learn from it (p. 85)?
6. What do verses 5–8 teach concerning the basis, the goal and the rewards of wisdom (pp. 86–88)?
7. What is the new theme introduced in verse 9? How is wisdom to be measured, and how not (pp. 88–89)?
8. Which themes recur in verses 10–11 and what new elements are introduced (pp. 89–90)?
9. How are the wicked described in verses 12–15? How can their seductive attraction be resisted (pp. 90–91)?
10. Why is sexual sin so common and why is it so serious (p. 91)?
11. What two pictures are used in verses 20–22 and what does each contribute to our understanding of holy wisdom (pp. 91–92)?

Isaiah 58:1–14
6. Holiness as justice (pp. 94–105)

1. What evidence is there that justice is a key element in the prophetic understanding of holiness (p. 94)?
2. What tone do we detect in God's voice in these verses (pp. 95–96)?
3. What were the characteristics of the people's worship in Isaiah's day and why was it falling short (pp. 96–97)?
4. In what three ways should we seek to please God according to verses 6–7 (pp. 98–99)?
5. What is significant about verses 8–9b in terms of their place in the chiastic structure (pp. 99–100)?

6. Where do verses 9c–10b reflect the themes of verses 6–7 and in what way do they develop them? What features of contemporary society underline the relevance of Isaiah's teaching (pp. 100–101)?
7. Which images in verses 8–9 are repeated in verses 10c–12 and how are they developed (pp. 101–102)?
8. In what way might the instructions of verses 13–14c be misunderstood and what is their true connection with verses 2–5 (pp. 102–103)?
9. How would you interpret 'pharisaic legalism' and 'social justice' in the context of contemporary society (pp. 103–105)?

PART 3. THE TRANSFORMATION OF HOLINESS

Luke 1:35; 4:1, 34; 23:41
7. Holiness personified (pp. 109–119)

1. In the Gospels 'the word "holy" and associated words are rarely used'. Why, then, are the Gospels so important for our understanding of holiness (p. 109)? In what ways was Christ's holiness different from that of the Israelite priests (p. 110)?
2. Why do some argue that Luke 1:35 does not present Christ as unique and how would you counter that argument (pp. 110–111)?
3. Were the temptations which Jesus faced different from those that we face (pp. 112–113)?
4. What was the secret of Christ's ability to resist temptation (p. 113)?
5. Which aspect of the Holy Spirit's power in Jesus is highlighted in Peter's address to Cornelius in Acts 10 (pp. 113–114)?
6. How is Christ's goodness interpreted in the letter to the Hebrews (p. 114)?
7. What three features of holiness evident in the exorcism in Luke 4 reflect those of the vision in Isaiah 6? What three words summarize them (pp. 114–116)?
8. In what ways do the Gospels present the sinlessness of Christ (pp. 116–118)?
9. What is the correct starting point for holiness teaching (pp. 118–119)?

Matthew 5:20, 48; Mark 5:1–43; 7:1–23; Luke 14:1–14
8. Holiness redefined (pp. 120–134)

1. How was the quest for holiness in Jesus' time handled by (a) the Essenes, (b) the Zealots, and (c) the Pharisees (p. 120)?
2. What were the three primary institutions of Jesus' day and what two things emerge when we read the Gospels against this background (pp. 120–121)?
3. What is Matthew's word for holiness and what is its essential nature (pp. 121–122)?
4. What did Jesus mean by 'surpassing righteousness' and what features make it distinctive (pp. 122–124)?
5. 'Be perfect … as your heavenly Father is perfect.' How can such a command be possible (pp. 124–125)?

'Through the prism of righteousness, holiness refracts into the colours of a new inner purity, a new depth of character, a new quality of serving, a new way of relating, and, above all, a new kind of loving' (p. 125).

---

6. How do the three miracles recorded in Mark 5:1–43 elucidate Jesus' redefined concepts of purity and impurity (pp. 125–128)?
7. What radical reversal of conventional thinking did Jesus promote? What specific practice did he challenge in Mark 7:1–23 and why (pp. 128–130)?
8. What is the 'different voice' we find in Luke's perspective on purity (pp. 130–131)?
9. In what situation does Luke frequently place the focus in his record of Jesus' challenge to the conventional views of his time (p. 131)?
10. What features of the situation in Luke 14:1–5 suggest that a trap had been laid for Jesus (pp. 131–132)?
11. How might Jesus' teaching on taking the lowest place be misconstrued and how can that be avoided (pp. 132–133)?
12. What further lesson was taught by Jesus in Luke 14:12–14 (p. 133)?

John 17:6–19
9. Holiness orchestrated (pp. 135–144)

1. How does John differ from the other Gospel writers in his portrayal of Jesus (p. 135)?

2. What elements in John 14:15–21 undergird his understanding of holiness (pp. 135–136)?
3. 'Holy Father' (17:11). What does this title tell us about God and in what two ways is our holiness derived from him (pp. 136–137)?
4. What are the four petitions in Jesus' prayer (17:12–17) and why does he identify these as their needs (pp. 137–140)?
5. Why has the image of a dance appealed to theologians as a way of illustrating the unity for which Christ prayed (pp. 138–139)?
6. In what way does the climax of Jesus' prayer echo the Old Testament perspective on holiness (p. 140)?
7. Where does Jesus envisage the consecrated service of his disciples taking place (pp. 140–141)?
8. How should disciples of Jesus be different from the world, and how not (pp. 141–142)?
9. The climax of Jesus' self-consecration is the cross. What two reasons did Jesus give for going to the cross (p. 143)?
10. How would you sum up the distinctive 'music' of John's presentation of holiness (pp. 143–144)?

'Disciples do not serve God by withdrawal from the world into a sacred and protected community but by engagement with the world and involvement in its life. That is the sphere in which they discover the protection of God. The protection, unity, joy and consecration for which Jesus prays is with a view to mission' (p. 140).

PART 4. THE DIMENSIONS OF HOLINESS

Psalm 51
10. Inner purity (pp. 147–158)

1. Which of the aspects of holiness quoted from J. I. Packer speak most powerfully to you (p. 147)?
2. 'A template for those who wish to give in to temptation.' What were the steps in David's downfall (pp. 148–151)?
3. What two things are noteworthy about the beginning of Psalm 51 (pp. 151–152)?
4. David shows 'a rare honesty'. How is this expressed (pp. 152–154)?
5. Compare the strategies for minimizing the horror of sin. Which

can you identify with most strongly (pp. 152–153)?

6. What three metaphors does David return to in verses 7–9 and what added insights can we detect (p. 154)?
7. What kind of change was David seeking and what texts elsewhere in Scripture reflect the same desire (pp. 155–156)?
8. What were the outcomes of David's prayer (pp. 156–157)?
9. Why does holiness demand more than just a determination of the will (pp. 157–158)?

1 Thessalonians 4:1–12
11. Personal holiness (pp. 159–171)

1. What do we know about the circumstances of Paul's first letter to the Thessalonians (p. 159)?
2. In what ways is Paul's letter a model of pastoral wisdom (pp. 159–160)?
3. In what two ways does Paul understand sanctification? Which does he develop here (p. 161)?
4. Which of J. C. Ryle's characteristics of holiness speak most directly to your situation (pp. 161–162)?
5. What seven reasons does Paul give for pursuing holiness (pp. 162–166)?
6. Is there any significance in the order in which he places them (pp. 165–166)?
7. Which of Paul's reasons do you find most motivating (pp. 162–166)?
8. Why does Paul focus on sexual purity in particular (pp. 166–168)?
9. What are the negative and positive aspects of Paul's teaching on sexual morality (pp. 168–169)?
10. What does Paul imply by leading 'a quiet life' (pp. 169–170)?

1 Peter 2:4–10; Ephesians 4:17 – 5:20
12. Corporate holiness (pp. 172–186)

1. How do you respond to the different concepts of 'flying solo' and 'flying in formation' (pp. 172–173)?
2. In what ways did Israel fail to be a 'holy nation' (pp. 173–174)?
3. What is the Old Testament background to the description 'a chosen people' (pp. 174–175)?
4. What does Peter mean, and not mean, by 'a royal priesthood' (p. 175)?
5. Does 'holy nation' indicate a new status or a new life-style (pp. 175–176)?

6. Does 'God's special possession' primarily refer to the present or the future (pp. 176–177)?
7. How does Peter envisage the outworking of corporate holiness (pp. 177–178)?
8. In what two ways does Paul explore the implications of new life in Christ in Ephesians 4:17–24 (pp. 178–180)?
9. Why are the mind and the emotions important in developing a holy life (pp. 179–180)?
10. What imagery does Paul use in Ephesians 4:25 – 5:20 and how is it developed (pp. 180–182)?
11. Which of the six categories identifiable in Ephesians 4:25 – 5:20 speak to your situation (pp. 182–185)?
12. 'Just a collection of odd individuals.' Why is that the wrong way to think about the church (pp. 185–186)?

'Whereas an older generation sought to foster holiness by withdrawing from the world, the contemporary generation passionately believes in the need to be a transforming presence in the world. Holiness consists not in insulating themselves against corruption but in being salt and light in the world, and viewing "the church as the 'embodied presence' of Jesus Christ" among the people he loved' (p. 187).

Micah 6:1–8
13. Social holiness (pp. 187–199)

1. Which of the evangelical emphases described here do you identify with most and why (pp. 187–188)?
2. What was the background to Micah's prophetic mission and what 'device' does he use to present his message (pp. 188)?
3. In what ways had Israel 'chosen to fundamentally misinterpret their God' (pp. 189–190)?
4. What defence did the people make and why was it inadequate (pp. 190–191)?
5. What was 'the great principle around which the case revolved' and how is it summarized (pp. 191–195)?
6. Why and in what ways do the responses of Micah 6:8 go beyond personal responsibility (pp. 192–195)?
7. Where is the mandate for social holiness implicit in the Gospels (pp. 195–196)?
8. Why did the early church not espouse a more explicit policy of social transformation (pp. 196–197)?

9. Where is the mandate for social holiness hinted at explicitly in the New Testament letters (pp. 197–198)?
10. Where in the New Testament is the 'ultimate vision' of a transformed society (p. 198)?
11. How can we balance the concepts of 'holiness' and 'worldliness' (pp. 198–199)?

PART 5. PATHWAYS TO HOLINESS

Galatians 5:13 – 6:10
14. The Spirit of God (pp. 203–215)

1. With which do you associate the letter of Galatians more: justification or the Holy Spirit (p. 203)?
2. What three aspects of the Christian life does Paul link with the work of the Spirit and what do you imply from that (pp. 203–205)?
3. Which three phrases shape Paul's teaching in Galatians 5 (p. 205)?
4. 'The indicative outweighs the imperative.' What does this mean and why is it significant (p. 205)?
5. What aspects of the Christian life are indicated by the imagery of walking (p. 206)?
6. What promise follows the command in Galatians 5:16–17 and what does Paul mean by 'the sinful nature' (pp. 206–207)?
7. In what way does the new life of the Spirit affect our thinking about (a) Jewish law, and (b) Gentile vice (pp. 207–208)?
8. Why is fruit such an appropriate metaphor for the life of holiness (pp. 208–209)?
9. Expand on the meaning of the qualities contained in the fruit of the Spirit. What is different about the final one (pp. 209–212)?
10. What further imagery is used in 5:25 – 6:6 and in what ways does Paul develop it (pp. 212–213)?
11. What cautions should be observed and what commitments should be made in the light of Paul's teaching (pp. 213–215)?

2 Timothy 3:14–17
15. The Word of God (pp. 216–225)

1. How much weight would you put on the Bible as a means of sanctification (pp. 216–217)?
2. In what six ways does God's Word have a role in helping people to live a blameless life according to Psalm 119 (pp. 217–218)?

3. What do John 17:17, 2 Thessalonians 2:13 and James 1:21 reveal about the place of God's Word in the development of holiness (pp. 218–219)?
4. Against what background(s) should we read Paul's allusions to holiness in 2 Timothy (p. 220)?
5. What are the 'sacred writings' and would we be justified in seeing a wider reference (pp. 220–221)?
6. What is the role of the Scriptures and what misunderstanding should be avoided (pp. 221–222)?
7. What is meant by 'the inspiration of the Bible' (pp. 222–223)?
8. How is the Bible useful – negatively and positively – and how should we assimilate its benefits (pp. 223–224)?
9. Right ways and wrong ways to use the Bible: which of these speak to you in your situation (pp. 224–225)?

Hebrews 12:1–17
16. The discipline of God (pp. 226–236)

1. What two analogies are used in Hebrews to illustrate holiness? Do they remove the need for human effort (pp. 226–227)?
2. In what ways is contemporary society 'ambiguous about discipline' (p. 227)?
3. What is, and is not, implied by the statement that Jesus 'learned obedience' (pp. 227–228)?
4. How is the imagery of verse 1 developed in verse 4 and how is it applied (pp. 228–229)?
5. Why does God allow his people to suffer (pp. 229–230)?
6. What forms does God's discipline take (pp. 230–231)?
7. What can we learn about God's 'training programme' from Joseph's story (pp. 231–233)?
8. How does God's discipline differ from that of human parents (pp. 233–234)?
9. What are the rewards of discipline (pp. 234–235)?
10. Are there lessons from this chapter that apply to you personally and call for a response (pp. 235–236)?

Romans 6:1–23
17. Union with Christ (pp. 237–249)

1. What divisions of Romans 6 have been suggested by scholars and on what grounds (p. 237)?
2. What is the logic behind the position which denies any place for the law or any restraint upon sin, and how does Paul refute it (pp. 238–239)?

3. Why is crucifixion in particular an appropriate description of the change that has taken place in the believer (pp. 239–240)?
4. Is it significant that Paul talks about 'sin' rather than 'sins' here (pp. 240–241)?
5. What are the four steps in Paul's argument in verses 8–10 (pp. 241–242)?
6. 'This "reckoning" is not about trying to believe something that is not true.' What is it about (pp. 242–243)?
7. How are we to respond to our new situation as Christians, negatively and positively (pp. 243–244)?
8. Why does Paul reintroduce the subject of law at this point (pp. 244–245)?
9. Is the representation of service to God as slavery defensible (pp. 245–246)?
10. Where do the two forms of slavery described by Paul lead to (pp. 247–248)?

Ephesians 6:10–18
18. Conflict with the enemy (pp. 250–263)

1. In what terms would you describe your own experience of 'the normal Christian life' (pp. 250)?
2. What is the 'new perspective' on Paul and how does it affect the interpretation of Romans 7 and the 'battle for holiness' (pp. 251–253)?
3. What does 'the world' mean in 1 John 2:15 (p. 254)?
4. What is, and is not, the nature of the battle between the flesh and the Spirit (pp. 255–256)?
5. Are you more in danger of over-estimating or under-estimating the devil's influence (p. 256)?
6. What strategies does the devil adopt in his attacks (pp. 256–258)? Can you identify any particular tactics the devil uses in your life?
7. How is God's power illustrated in Scripture and why was it so relevant in Ephesus (pp. 258–259)?
8. What is the Old Testament background to the armour of God (p. 259)?
9. Which individual items of armour are cited and what is the significance of each (pp. 259–261)?
10. What is the final weapon in our spiritual armoury and why is it not associated with a particular piece of armour (p. 262)?

2 Corinthians 6:14 – 7:1
19. Separation from the world (pp. 264–276)

1. In what way might the call to separation be misunderstood (p. 264)?
2. Who are the 'unbelievers' referred to in verse 14 and what is meant by the command not to be 'yoked together' with them (pp. 265–267)?
3. Does the absence of visible idols in our modern society make the command irrelevant (pp. 267–268)?
4. What is implicit in the description of Christians as 'the temple of the living God' (pp. 269–270)?

'Remarkably, [Paul] claims that the Christian community in Corinth ... are, as it were, the address where God could be found to be at home on earth. They are his dwelling place. He is not limited to them, nor constricted by them' (p. 269).

---

5. How crucial is separation to our identity as God's people (pp. 270–271)?
6. What is the tone of Paul's argument and which words in 7:1 reinforce it (p. 271)?
7. Why is Paul's call for purification 'much more thorough' than that of pagan ritual purification (pp. 271–272)?
8. How important is the word 'everything' in verse 1? Consider prayerfully and honestly the five steps listed (pp. 272–273).
9. How has the concept of complete holiness been understood by Christian thinkers? What is your own conclusion (pp. 273–274)?
10. What is meant by 'the fear of God' in this context (pp. 274–275)?

PART 6. THE DESTINATION OF HOLINESS

1 John 2:28 – 3:10
20. To be like him (pp. 279–289)

1. What aspects of the passage under consideration remind us of a symphony (p. 279)?
2. What three things need to take place in anticipation of Christ's second coming (pp. 280–282)?
3. What is significant about the word *parousia* (see footnote 7) and

what other illustrations does the author use in connection with Christ's coming (p. 281)?

4. How is God's love described in 1 John 3:1 (p. 283)?
5. What can we say, and not say, about our future beyond this earthly life (pp. 284–285)?
6. What impact should our future prospect have on our present way of life (pp. 285–286)?
7. Why is the postlude described as a 'transposition of key' (pp. 286–287)?
8. What are the most significant contrasts between verses 1–3, the 'main theme', and verses 4–10, the 'postlude' (pp. 287–288)?

1 Thessalonians 5:23–24
21. He will do it (pp. 290–297)

1. What two things are said about God's involvement in the pursuit of holiness (pp. 290–291)?
2. What is the scope of the Old Testament word *šālôm* (pp. 291–292)?
3. What is the difference between 'Agape spirituality' and 'Eros spirituality', according to David Wells (p. 292)?
4. Which two aspects of God's purpose determine his commitment to our salvation (pp. 292–293)?
5. How distinct are the meanings of spirit, soul and body and how far should we press the distinction (pp. 293–295)?
6. How does Paul link past and present with the future hope of Christ's return (pp. 295–296)?
7. What does it mean to be blameless (pp. 295–296)?
8. On what grounds can we be confident in the pursuit of holiness (pp. 296–297)?

'In speaking of the sanctification of our soul, spirit and body, Paul is wonderfully comprehensive. These comprise the thinking, wilful and emotional aspects of our lives. They are about what we think, what we decide and what we do. The external and internal dimensions of our lives are embraced and the depth and the surface of our beings included' (p. 295).

The Bible Speaks Today: Old Testament series